Essential Theory for Primary Teachers

Theory for Primary Teachers is a succinct, accessible ıor to the key theories, concepts and policies that have ırimary education as we know it and underpin our practice classroom. Written with the ever-busy training and practising ..d, this straightforward guide offers the foundations understanding of how we teach and learn effectively, we develop as professionals.

..er with key further reading highlights, a glossary of ..s and an at-a-glance timeline of the major events, Acts and ..s in education, it explains core topics:

- a short history of the education system
- what education is for
- inequality and education
- special educational needs and inclusion
- child development
- how children learn
- theories of motivation
- behaviour for learning
- assessment for learning
- understanding and using research evidence
- undertaking your own action research project.

Essential Theory for Primary Teachers brings together, in one volume, theory and knowledge that stand the test of time; it guides you through what others have said about them and will help you relate the [illegible] source of guidance for training and newly qualified teachers, it will support you as you develop the skills you need to teach confidently and help your learners succeed.

Lynne Graham-Matheson is currently Director of Knowledge Exchange in the Faculty of Education, Canterbury Christ Church University, UK.

Essential Theory for Primary Teachers

An introduction for busy trainees

Lynne Graham-Matheson

LONDON AND NEW YORK

First published 2015
by Routledge
2 Park Square, Milton Park, Abingdon, Oxon OX14 4RN

and by Routledge
711 Third Avenue, New York, NY 10017

Routledge is an imprint of the Taylor & Francis Group, an informa business

British Library Cataloguing in Publication Data
A catalogue record for this book is available from the British Library

Library of Congress Cataloging in Publication Data
A catalog record for this book has been requested

ISBN: 978-0-415-72281-0 (hbk)
ISBN: 978-0-415-72282-7 (pbk)
ISBN: 978-1-315-75460-4 (ebk)

Typeset in Celeste and Optima
by Florence Production Ltd, Stoodleigh, Devon, UK

Printed and bound in Great Britain by
TJ International Ltd, Padstow, Cornwall

Contents

Acknowledgements

I am grateful to Helen Pritt and Sarah Tuckwell of Routledge for their encouragement and help, and to Janet Tod and Simon Ellis for providing the behaviour-for-learning framework diagram.

As always, I thank my family for their love and support, in this instance particularly my daughters – Laura, an inner-city primary teacher, was the inspiration for the book, and Helen provided unfailing support and enthusiasm, with very helpful comments on the first draft.

This book is dedicated to teachers everywhere.

Introduction

Theories allow us to organise our ideas and therefore to be clearer about our practices. They empower us.

(Louise Porter)

This book is intended for beginning primary teachers, whether trainees or newly qualified teachers (NQTs), although it may also be useful for trainee secondary teachers. I hope it will also be of interest to mentors in schools and class teachers, in their work with trainee teachers.

This is not a practical 'how to' or 'tips for teachers' book. Although the title is *Essential Theory*, it could have been *Essential Theory, Important Debates and Concepts and Some Other Really Useful Information You Need to Know*, except that that is not a very punchy title. The point of this book is to introduce you to some of the theories, ideas, debates and concepts that have led us to where we are now and that will underpin your practice. It is deliberately a fairly slim volume and it is meant as an introduction for busy people – I have had to carefully choose what to include and what to leave out, so please do not assume that it will tell you all you need to know about a particular theory or topic. There are other books on the market that will do that, and there are suggestions for further reading.

Why theory?

Sometimes, trainee teachers are heard to say that they are not really very interested in theory; they just want to know how to teach. But the two cannot be separated – it is theory that guides practice. It can be difficult to see how theory is relevant when you begin as a trainee teacher, when you are worried about planning lessons and standing up in front of a class of children, and then, when you can see how important it is, you are busy with all the things a teacher has to do. So I hope that this book will give you an overview, a starting point.

When you first go into school as a trainee teacher, it may be just a short time since your own schooldays or since you worked in a school, perhaps as a teaching assistant, or it may be a number of years. Whichever it is, you will bring with you your own thoughts and experiences. When these are added to all the information you will pick up in school and all the things you have to think about, such as organising your work and planning lessons, theories will help you to explain and connect up all that information.

You may think that you can learn what you need to know from observing or talking to more experienced teachers. You can and will learn a lot this way, but what you learn from observation is the 'what' or the 'how' – the 'why' comes from theories.

Perhaps without realising it, you are probably already using theory in your work. If you reflect, for example, about why a particular lesson worked very well (or not), or why children managed to grasp a complicated idea quickly, then you are probably already drawing on theories for explanations – without theory, we have nothing to 'hang' a reflection on.

One of the things you will soon come to realise about education, if you have not already done so, is that there are very few 'right' answers. There are a number of theories, for example, about child development and how children learn. This book will not tell you which are the 'right' theories, or even the 'best' ones. There is no analysis, and I have tried to be objective. The theories I have selected are the well-known ones that have stood the test of time, and I have given some pointers on how you might relate them to your practice, and what others have said about them. As a teacher, you will need to work out which of the theories and ideas make sense to you – it may be bits of theories, rather than a whole theory – and support you in your teaching.

How to use this book

The book is designed to be read from beginning to end, and, if you are training, or just about to begin your training, it will give you an introduction to some of the theories and other information you need to know. Each chapter stands alone, so that later you can just dip into the chapters you need.

How the book is organised

The first nine chapters contain the theories and debates; the last two chapters are to support you in taking your own learning forward. You will need to be able to assess research and evidence, so that you can keep up to date and make sure your practice is evidence-based.

> While underpinning research and theories may not be used explicitly by teachers to make decisions about strategy use (Clandini and Connelly 1995), reference to an evidence-base can, and should, lead to enhanced understanding and improved practice.
>
> (Ellis and Tod 2009, p. 92)

The first chapter looks at the education system in England since 1944. The date is important because the 1944 Education Act provided free secondary education for all for the first time. The chapter picks out some key events and debates, rather than giving a definitive detailed history: it will help to explain how we got to where we are now, particularly if you have no experience of education before the National Curriculum.

Chapter 2 considers the debates around education – what is its purpose, who decides what is taught in schools, the different types of education, etc. It also looks at issues around curriculum.

Chapter 3 is concerned with inequality in education – this is still an important issue in the twenty-first century, and we know that growing up in social disadvantage can affect educational outcomes and future life chances.

Chapter 4 looks at the debates and policy around special educational needs and inclusion, particularly the issues around whether children with special educational needs should attend mainstream schools.

Chapters 5 and 6 give an overview of the main theories of child development – Freud, Piaget, Erikson, Bronfenbrenner, as well as attachment theory and moral development – and the main theories of learning, from early thinkers such as Dewey and Montessori, and including learning through play. The chapters go together because, for thinkers such as Piaget, development and learning are interlinked.

Chapter 7 considers motivation in the context of children and their learning.

Chapters 8 and 9 look at behaviour and assessment, and specifically how teachers can relate managing behaviour and assessing children's work to their learning.

Chapters 10 and 11 are the skills chapters and look at using and undertaking research, and critical reading and writing.

Following Chapter 11, there are appendices containing some reference information, including useful acronyms and a timeline of key events and legislation.

Update

While this book was in press, a new primary curriculum was implemented, as well as a new code of practice for children with special educational needs. You can find details of the new curriculum here:

www.gov.uk/government/collections/national-curriculum

and the code of practice here:

www.gov.uk/government/publications/send-code-of-practice-0-to-25.

A note

In my view, anyone who says, 'those who can't, teach', as if it were somehow an easy way out, should perhaps try spending the day with thirty 5-year-olds! Teaching is not easy, but it is one of the most rewarding things you can do. I hope you find this book useful, and wish you well in your teaching career.

Lynne Graham-Matheson

References

Clandini, D. J. and Connelly, F. M. (1995) *Teachers' 'Professional Knowledge'*, New York: Teachers College Press.

Ellis, S. and Tod, J. (2009) *Behaviour for Learning: Proactive approaches to behaviour management*, Oxford, UK: David Fulton.

1 The English education system since 1944

The further back you look, the further forward you are likely to see.

(Winston Churchill)

The 1944 Education Act and selection

The 1944 Education Act was very significant because it provided free secondary education for all, for the first time. In 1940, Prime Minister Winston Churchill wanted to establish 'a state of society where the advantages and privileges which hitherto have been enjoyed only by the few, shall be far more widely shared by the men and youth of the nation as a whole' (Taylor 1977, p. 158; note the emphasis on men and youth, rather than boys and girls). The First World War had made clear the wide divisions in society, and, between the wars, there was a full debate about education, at a time of high unemployment and with a quarter of the country living on a subsistence diet. There was much consideration of the nature of primary education and growing interest in the work of people such as Dewey and Montessori. The 1944 Act was described as 'a drastic recasting of our educational system' (Giles 1943, p. 21, in Jones 2003, p. 15). Reformers were delighted, because it promised a free, common and universal system of education for students up to the age of 18, underpinned by the principle that, 'the nature of a child's education should be based on his capacity and promise and not by the circumstances of his parent' (Board of Education 1943, p. 7).

The five Hadow Reports (1923–33) and the Spens Report (1938) were produced by the Consultative Committee, and these in turn shaped the Education Act 1944 (the Butler Act), which set out the structure for state education in England following the Second World War. The 1944 Act gave governors and head teachers control of the curriculum and resources. It did not anticipate politicians being in control of the curriculum – in 1960, Sir David Eccles, Conservative Minister of Education, said he was not expected to enter 'the secret garden of the curriculum'. Head teachers were very much in control in schools, and education was rarely the subject of debate at Cabinet level until the 1980s.

Apart from free secondary education for all, the Butler Act's most important provision was a proposal for three types of education – primary, secondary and further. The Act also introduced the controversial 11 plus examination – a set of tests in arithmetic, English, problem-solving and sometimes verbal and non-verbal reasoning – at age 11. These tests sorted children into three categories – academic, practical and technical – and determined whether they went to a grammar, secondary modern or technical school. Some have suggested that this was social policy not educational policy, and debates around selection have continued throughout the recent history of education.

All schools were supposed to have equal status, although catering for different abilities. Three types of secondary school had been recommended by Spens (Board of Education 1943, pp. 2–3):

- *Grammar schools* were for the pupil who was interested in learning for its own sake, who could grasp an argument or follow a piece of connected reasoning.
- *Technical schools* were for pupils whose interests and abilities lay markedly in the field of applied science or applied art.
- *Secondary modern schools* catered for the pupil who dealt more easily with concrete things than with ideas.

As universities wanted a grammar school education for admission, pupils from other schools were excluded. In the 1930s, about 10 per cent of elementary school pupils were selected to go on to secondary schools. There were clear class divides, and secondary schools were failing pupils – twice as many pupils went on to higher education in Germany, even more in France, over three times as many in Switzerland and about ten times as many in the US. Scotland's system, 'based on a widespread respect for learning and a more traditionally egalitarian social outlook' (Benn and Chitty 1996, p. 4), was also doing much better than England's. There were still arguments based on a divided and elitist system, but, whereas before this was about class, now it was based on intelligence and aptitude. As Ball (2013) comments, the history of education is about a complex set of relationships between the state, the economy and social class. Educationists, trade unionists and others wanted a more rational system and an end to plans for differentiated secondary education, but the Ministry of Education was determined on a divided system.

The idea of grouping children according to their ability came from the new technique of psychometrics, or measuring human abilities. In France, Alfred Binet had developed intelligence tests; an American, Lewis Therman, developed Binet's work and, in 1916, came up with the idea of the intelligence quotient, or IQ. These early psychologists believed that intelligence was inherited and you had to make do with what you had, and so it made sense for schools to educate children according to their level of ability. Through a number of studies of twins, Cyril Burt, appointed as the first psychologist for London, became convinced that intelligence was inherited (although with some environmental influence) and fixed, and so the education system should be a segregated system. Promoting testing to categorise children, Burt was one of the most influential members of the Hadow Committee, which was convinced by Burt that:

> by the age of twelve the range has become so wide that a still more radical classification is imperative. Before this age is reached children need to be grouped according to their capacity, not merely in separate classes or standards, but in separate types of schools.
>
> (Cyril Burt evidence to Hadow, in Van der Eyken 1973, p. 320)

Intelligence was believed not to be fixed until children reached the age of 11, hence the 11 plus. It is ironic that the 11 plus came from the idea that intelligence was innate and fixed, and yet parents still expected primary schools to prepare their children to pass it. Rather than being seen as a way of allocating children to an appropriate school, for many it was about gaining entry to a grammar school and a matter of pass or fail. After his death, much of Burt's work was found to be fraudulent and he was largely discredited, but it was the strong conviction that the age of 11 was significant that led to the primary/secondary division we still have today.

Labour's 1964 election manifesto promised to abolish the 11 plus and reorganise secondary education on comprehensive lines, but, although the government expected local education authorities (LEAs) to go comprehensive, it did not compel them to do so. According to Gillard (2011), a fatal mistake was in not looking at how to run comprehensive and grammar schools together, and so comprehensive schools were implemented in an uneven and piecemeal way. Even within comprehensive schools, the General Certificate of Education/Certificate of Secondary Education (GCE/CSE) exam system divided children into academic and non-academic streams.

The 11 plus was abolished in 1976, but 164 grammar schools remain in England. In those counties that still operate the 11 plus, it is optional and used as an entrance test for a specific group of schools. In Northern Ireland, the 11 plus was abolished in 2008, but parents and grammar schools were unhappy about a 'one size fits all' education system, and there are now two 11 plus-type selection tests, run by two school consortia.

Critics claim that it is wrong to label children at 11 years old: 'a system that labelled over two-thirds of children as failures at the age of 11' (Benn and Miller 2006). In the 1950s, the Central Advisory Committee for Education wanted to assess whether the 11 plus was a reliable measure of intelligence and future attainment by tracking children who had passed or failed. It was found that 22 per cent of army and 29 per cent of RAF recruits to national service had been assigned to the wrong type of school, according to their ability or background (Ministry of Education 1959, p. 119). In 1969 Pedley (p. 24) said that, 'Success bred success and failure bred failure'. A child transferred from secondary modern to grammar school increased their score on an IQ test by 23 points (Sumner 2010). Early tests had a class bias, and the 11 plus was redesigned during the 1960s to be more like an IQ test, but research suggests that grammar schools are still more likely to be attended by middle-class children.

Primary schools

In the early 1900s, educationists agreed that the elementary schools did not provide a suitable education for the under-5s, and doctors suggested that attendance at school was prejudicial to health, as it deprived young children of sleep, fresh air, exercise and freedom of movement at a critical stage in their development (Hadow 1933, pp. 30–1). The 1921 Education Act empowered LEAs to provide nursery schools or classes for 2–5-year-olds, whose attendance at such a school was necessary or desirable for their healthy physical and mental development and to attend to the 'health, nourishment and physical welfare' of children attending such schools. By the 1920s, London and some other towns had three-decker schools – the infant department on the ground floor, up to age 7 on one of the other storeys (divided into boys and girls) and up to age 14, the school leaving age. In 1926, Hadow recommended a change of department at age 11 as well as at 7 – the three storeys could have infant, junior and senior, instead of infants, boys and girls (see Plowden 1967, vol. 1, pp. 97–9). This led to the creation of primary or junior schools for 5–11s, which was government policy from 1928 but was formally established in the 1944 Education Act. Local authorities had to provide primary and secondary schools 'sufficient in number, character and equipment to afford for all pupils opportunities for education offering such variety of instruction and training as may be desirable in view of their different ages, abilities and aptitudes' (1944, p. 8, 1c).

The 11 plus and large primary classes in the late 1940s and 1950s meant that the curriculum for younger children was little changed from that of the drill method of elementary schools, with the emphasis on basic literacy and numeracy – 'the tradition derived from 1870 was still dominant' (Galton *et al.* 1980, p. 36) – but a number of factors began to influence this, including the growth of developmental psychology, the kindergarten movement based on Froebel's theory and practice and the work of Dewey, Montessori, Isaacs and others. According to Hadow (1931, p. 93), 'the curriculum of the primary school is to be thought of in terms of activity and experience, rather than knowledge to be acquired and facts to be stored'. Galton *et al.* (1980) argue that although by 1939 this new approach had become the official orthodoxy of teacher training colleges, local authority inspectors and so on, the extent to which it affected actual practice in schools was another matter. Primary schools were in the middle of a number of competing forces, and those who believed in the new ideas about child development clashed with those – who tended to win – who saw the job of primary schools as getting children through the scholarship exams, so that primary schools were seen as 'a sorting, classifying, selective mechanism' (Galton *et al.* 1980, p. 36). When the 11 plus was abolished, teachers, especially in primary schools, suddenly had freedom to experiment with progressive styles of teaching, child-centred learning, open-plan schools, discovery methods and creativity, and there was real optimism about education. 'One of the main educational tasks of the primary school is to build and strengthen children's intrinsic interest in learning and lead them to learn for themselves rather than from fear of disapproval or desire for praise' (Plowden 1967, vol. 1, p. 196).

Before the Plowden Report in 1967, primary schools had mainly fitted in with and fed into secondary schools. The report noted that changes between the wars had been unplanned and unco-ordinated – understandable, perhaps, in the circumstances. The Plowden Committee visited primary schools in many countries and noted that the issues were the same everywhere. With its roots in the Hadow Report, Plowden was probably the single greatest official impetus for progressive education in the twentieth century anywhere – there was a post-war desire for freedom and self-expression, and the report was very much about the new ideas in psychology and sociology and reference to skills and development.

Recurring themes of Plowden were individualised learning, flexibility in the curriculum, the use of the environment, learning by discovery and the importance of the evaluation of children's progress – teachers should 'not assume that only what is measurable is valuable' (Plowden 1967, vol. 1, p. 202). Ideas in the report were firmly grounded in Piagetian theory and ideas about developmental stages (see Chapter 5) and an insistence that discovery learning is best.

Faith schools and religion

For some, the 1944 Act failed, because it did not resolve the problems of church schools and private education. (Now, we refer to faith schools, rather than church schools.) Since the 1870 Education Act, the Church of England had controlled most rural and many urban elementary schools. Almost all were housed in Victorian buildings that the church could not afford to maintain and 'were in many cases the epitome of low-level mass education' (Jones 2003, p. 18). The government could have subsidised them but would have found strong opposition from those who objected to public funds subsidising the church. The solution was to trade influence for cash – public funding in return for majority local authority representation on governing bodies. The Act categorised church schools as either voluntary aided, where the church had greater control and which received 50 per cent of building and maintenance costs from state funds, or as voluntary controlled, where the local authority had greater control and which received 100 per cent of costs. According to Barber (1994), 'The question of the future role of the churches in education proved more complex, more sensitive and more fiercely contested than any other in wartime education reform'.

Church schools provided about a third of school places. The 1944 Act said very little about the curriculum apart from religious education (RE) – state schools were required to provide non-denominational RE and a daily act of worship, but, in aided schools, RE was left to the discretion of churches. The issue of church or faith schools is still controversial:

> The failure to tackle the church school problem in 1944 and the willingness of subsequent governments (especially Blair's) to kowtow to the religious lobby have led to the current scandal of religious extremists being given taxpayers' money to indoctrinate the nation's children.
>
> (Gillard 2011)

In 2001, around 7,000 of 25,000 English state schools were faith schools – 589 primary and 6,384 secondary. The government wanted to create more, but there was widespread concern that faith schools would not help to promote social cohesion. A YouGov/*Observer* poll of nearly 6,000 people found that 80 per cent were against the proposal and only 11 per cent in favour (*The Observer*, 11 November 2001). The issue became even more controversial in the spring of 2002, when it was revealed that at least two state-funded religious schools in England were teaching their students 'creationism' as science. There was widespread criticism of the 2005 White Paper to allow religious organisations to control more schools, and a *Guardian*/ICM poll (23 August 2005) found that two-thirds of the public agreed with the statement that the government should not be funding faith schools of any kind. There was concern about the teaching of creationism as science in academies: organisations representing scientists in sixty-seven countries, including the UK's Royal Society, warned that scientific evidence about the origins of life was being concealed, denied or confused by schools teaching creationism and urged parents and teachers to provide children with facts about the origin and evolution of life on Earth. Concern about faith schools continued, and, in January 2005, Chief Inspector David Bell said that the growth of Islamic schools posed a challenge to the coherence of British society. Senior Muslims called his remarks 'irresponsible' and 'derogatory' (*The Guardian*, 18 January 2005), but Bell was supported by Commission for Racial Equality chair Trevor Phillips: 'We can choose . . . whether we want to bring our diversity together in a single rainbow or whether we allow our differences to fester into separate cultures and separate communities', he said (*The Guardian*, 19 January 2005). Schools Minister Stephen Twigg urged

The *Oxford English Dictionary* definition of **creationism** is 'the belief that the universe and living organisms originate from specific acts of divine creation, as in the biblical account, rather than by natural processes such as evolution'.

faith schools to 'promote understanding' between different religions (*The Guardian,* 18 February 2005).

A controversial proposal of the 2009 Children, Schools and Families Bill was that sex education from the age of 5 would be made a compulsory part of the National Curriculum. Schools would not be allowed to opt out, and faith schools would be given guidance on how to provide sex and relationship education (SRE) – to include contraception, abortion and homosexuality – alongside conflicting religious beliefs. Religious groups objected, and the government amended the regulations, so that sex education lessons would only be compulsory for 15- and 16-year-olds, and parents of children under 15 could withdraw them from the lessons. Further lobbying led the government to make more changes, so that SRE could now 'reflect a school's religious character'. Campaigners said the change would allow faith schools to discourage the use of contraception and teach that homosexuality was wrong. A Department for Children, Schools and Families (DCSF) spokesman dismissed the complaints:

> All maintained schools will be required to teach full programmes of study in line with the principles outlined in the bill, including promoting equality and encouraging acceptance of diversity. Schools with a religious character will be free to express their faith and reflect the ethos of their school, but what they cannot do is suggest that their views are the only ones.
>
> (*The Guardian,* 18 February 2010)

So, a Catholic school would be required to teach children the facts about contraception, but would be allowed to try to persuade them that its use was immoral. An editorial in *The Guardian* commented:

> This looks like a case of the government being led away from the path of righteousness by ecclesiastical lobbying, which has happened several times before. There was, for instance, the climbdown over the plan to force faith schools to take some children from outside their own flock. There was also section 37 of the 2008 Education Act, which undercut Labour's solid record on discrimination at work by allowing schools to handpick staff on the basis of their creed. Many devout people – and

> many believers in faith schools – are represented by the Accord Coalition, which argues that no state-funded institution should be exempted from norms that all other public bodies must follow. Unless all religious schools are required to see the light, the contradictions will become unsustainable. The recurring pattern of church lobbying and Whitehall climbdowns is testing society's faith in church schools as being a force for good.
>
> (*The Guardian*, 24 February 2010)

Inequalities

In the 1950s, it was becoming clear that schools were failing many children, confirmed by the 1963 Newsom Report, *Half Our Future*. In the 1960s, there was a growing public awareness of the unfairness of the selective system and the need for a more child-centred system, especially in primary schools. The election of a Labour government under Harold Wilson, in 1964, meant a move towards more equality in education, but, although between 1964 and 1970 the proportion of children attending comprehensive schools rose to 30 per cent, selection remained. The selective system was perceived as failing for a number of reasons, including research that cast doubt on theories of inherited intelligence. There were inequalities, with the provision of grammar school places per LEA ranging from 10 per cent to over 30 per cent, and many LEAs had single-sex grammar schools, with far more places for boys than girls. Inequality was further emphasised when the Beloe Report, *Secondary School Examinations Other than the GCE*, recommended the introduction of a new exam for pupils considered incapable of coping with the demands of the GCE (O level), leading to the introduction of the CSE in 1965.

Post-war, there had been significant investment in education, including the building of 1,800 new secondary schools in England and Wales, but children of average or lower ability often missed out on this progress. A survey for the Newsom Committee, for example, showed that 40 per cent were still being taught in inadequate and overcrowded facilities, and 70 per cent of schools in slum areas had seriously inadequate buildings – the divisions were becoming sharper.

The 2007 Ofsted annual report warned that social, economic and racial factors still determined how well children performed at school. In the same year, a report for the Sutton Trust showed that, by the age of 7, the ablest children from Britain's poorest homes were outperformed by the least-gifted children from wealthy homes – social class was still the biggest predictor of school achievement, behaviour and the likelihood of getting a degree. It suggested the advantage of being born into a privileged home had not changed over 30 years. Research at the University of Bath from the Cambridge Primary Review showed a child's chances of receiving extra help for special educational needs (SEN) were dictated by geography, class, race and gender, rather than the nature of the learning difficulty. The system of statementing children and allocating resources showed wide variation, middle-class children received better support more quickly, and powerful lobby groups, for example for dyslexia and autism, received disproportionate funding (*The Guardian*, 14 December 2007).

In March 2008, a University of Warwick study showed white working-class teenagers performed more poorly than their black and Asian classmates in GCSE exams. In May, the *Thursday's Child* report from the Institute for Public Policy Research think tank recommended long summer holidays should be shortened – children from the poorest backgrounds suffered most from 'summer learning loss', and youth offending rose during the summer, when children had less access to structured activities.

A study on social mobility funded by the American Carnegie Corporation used data from 10,000 children in the USA and 19,000 in the UK, born in 2000 and 2001. The study found children's vocabulary, cognitive abilities and behaviour were closely linked to family income, and children from the poorest homes were found to be much more poorly equipped to deal with starting school. The effect of being from a low-income home was found to be more pronounced in the UK than in the US, owing to the UK's wider difference in incomes (*The Guardian*, 7 June 2008).

A report by Manchester University School of Education, commissioned by the National Union of Teachers (NUT) and National College for School Leadership (NCSL), considered successful leadership for promoting the achievement of white working-class pupils. The report argued that a cycle of under-achievement has been endemic in this group since mass education was introduced in Victorian times. After more than a century of free, compulsory education and 60 years of the welfare state, family income and status are by far the most important correlates of success in the school system. In 2008, just 16 per cent of white boys on free school meals (FSM) reached the target of five good GCSEs in English and maths, compared with the national average of 48 per cent (*The Guardian*, 12 December 2008).

It is only relatively recently that gender has been seen as an issue in education. Until the 1960s, it was largely accepted that differences in opportunities and achievements reflected the natural, inherent differences between the genders and their future roles – 'in the 1950s middle-class boys were twenty-one times as likely to attend university than working class girls' (Tomlinson 2001, p. 148). Legislation such as the Sex Discrimination Act 1975 and the setting up of the Equal Opportunities Commission promoted change, but much has been the result of work by pressure groups and institutions (Ball 2013).

Today, issues around gender tend to focus on boys – in 2005, 51 per cent of 11-year-old boys reached the expected level 4 in maths, reading and writing, compared with 63 per cent of girls, but boys still outperform girls in science and maths, although girls have caught up. Particularly in the private sector, law and engineering, males with the same level of qualification earn more than females – in November 2006, the Equal Opportunities Commission reported the following:

> Annual statistics from the Office for National Statistics (ONS) were published this month, showing that the full-time pay gap remains at 17.2 per cent. We calculated that this means the average woman working full-time will lose out on around £330,000 over the course of her working life.
>
> (Ball 2013)

Despite this, 'the gender gap is considerably smaller than the inequalities of attainment associated with ethnic origin and social class background' (Gilbourn and Mirza 2000, p. 23). Gender is an independent and significant factor, but the social-class attainment

gap at age 16 is three times as wide as the gender gap (*The Guardian*, 12 December 2008).

The 1970s and 1980s

Times were hard in the 1970s. The need to cut public expenditure led, among other things, to the end of universal free school milk. In 1976, Prime Minister Jim Callaghan gave his famous Ruskin Speech, calling for a debate about the nature and purpose of education. Winter 1978–9 was the 'winter of discontent', with multiple strikes protesting at prolonged pay restraint, and recession led to cuts in education spending in many Western countries. There was the beginning of a 'general disenchantment with education as a palliative of society's ills' (Galton *et al.* 1980, p. 41), which began in the US and led to a call for teachers to become more accountable. This became a priority for both major political parties in the UK following the Ruskin Speech. Circular 10/70 announced that the government would accept no further plans for wholesale comprehensivisation, only proposals for individual schools. As Education Minister, Margaret Thatcher agreed to more comprehensivisation than any other minister before or since, and there were more children in comprehensive schools than selective schools. Many hoped that, when Labour returned to power, there would be full comprehensivisation, but it was not to be – 11 plus selection still existed wholly or partially in half of all LEAs.

The 1964 Education Act permitted transfer at ages other than 11 and gave some experimental status to middle schools. The idea was that schools would be organised for age ranges 5–9, 9–13 and 13–18. The argument was that middle schools would extend the best practice of primary education and give greater support to older children. The Plowden Report suggested transfer at age 12. In 1967, there were no middle schools; by 1980, there were more than 1,400, but there had been no academic research into their effectiveness. Blyth (1980, p. 20, quoted in Crook 2008, p. 122) describes this as 'one of the strangest stories in the history of English education'. The implementation of the National Curriculum, with a split between key stages at age 11, meant that most local authorities returned to a primary/secondary school split, although currently there are still 173 middle schools in England, 13 deemed to be primary schools and 160 secondary (National Middle Schools Forum 2014), and a small number of initial teacher training providers offer programmes aimed at middle school teachers. In line with the Plowden Report, supporters of middle schools argue that they avoid the problems caused by transfer to secondary school at 11, when children can be at their most vulnerable owing to puberty.

Underlying the Ruskin Speech (Callaghan 1976) was a feeling that the education system was out of touch with the need for Britain to survive economically in a highly competitive world. Callaghan praised the enthusiasm and dedication of the teaching profession, but acknowledged criticisms about basic skills and attitudes. The Ruskin Speech was followed by various initiatives regarding the curriculum, the setting up of the Assessment of Performance Unit to 'promote the development of methods of assessing and monitoring the achievement of children at school, and to seek to identify the incidence of under-achievement' and the beginning of mass testing by LEAs. The debate was characterised by increasingly detailed interventions of central government into education. According to Jones (2003, p. 74), 'the education revolution of the 1980s and '90s had its origins in the conflicts, crises and re-alignments of the 1970s'.

The economic climate provided the context for five Black Papers, written by right-wing educationists and politicians between 1969 and 1977. They attacked progressive teaching methods and said comprehensivisation was preventing academic students from achieving good exam results. They called for choice, competition and parental control of schools. In 1976, Neville Bennett produced *Teaching Styles and Pupil Progress*, which concluded that 'formal' methods (whole-class teaching, regular testing and competition) resulted in pupils being 4 months ahead of those taught using 'informal' methods. The study was widely criticised by educationists, but it was represented in the media as 'a full scale scientific study of "progressive" teaching methods which proved they simply did not work' (Chitty 2004, p. 37). Problems with failing schools appeared in newspaper headlines, and there was agreement that the problems seemed to be the fault of 'poor teachers, weak head teachers . . . and modern teaching methods' (Labour Secretary of State for Education Shirley Williams, at the North of England conference in 1977, cited in Ball 2013).

Margaret Thatcher became prime minister in 1979, and neoliberalism became the dominant force in British politics. The twin aims for education in the 1980s were to change the school system from a public service into a market, and to transfer power from local authorities to central government. The Conservatives began work on a series of radical changes, characterised by:

> the absence of any popular demand for them from any section of the education community nationally or locally or even from the populist media. One by one all had to be imposed by means of a parliamentary majority against continuing opposition from all other political parties and from much of the educational establishment.
>
> (Benn and Chitty 1996, p. 13)

There would be action on three fronts:

- the curriculum, previously seen as the 'secret garden' government ministers were not supposed to enter;
- teachers, controlling their training and development and restricting their role in curriculum development;
- LEAs, which Thatcher saw as the enemy, especially Labour-controlled ones.

The government worked to weaken the power of the LEAs, with power going back to the government. The 1986 Education (No. 2) Act further diminished the role of LEAs. Governors had more responsibility, and head teachers had a much greater role, including the power to exclude pupils. The Act introduced the concept of educational law, so that lawyers became involved in education for the first time. In July 1987, the government published the consultation document *The National Curriculum 5–16*.

The 1988 Education Reform Act (sometimes called the Baker Act) was the most important Act since 1944. Although commonly portrayed as giving power to schools, it did the opposite, giving new powers to the Secretary of State. Education became less of a public service and more of a market. Among its provisions, the

The idea of the **market** means the customers are parents and children, and the providers are schools. A good market depends on choice, hence the emergence of academies and free schools. The power of local government is trimmed down, freeing schools from rules and statutory responsibilities such as the need to follow the National Curriculum. More popular schools would thrive; others would just wither away.

This is a supply-side solution – it solves problems by enabling the supply (of schools) to increase.

Economists will say that markets need customers to have as much information as possible to enable them to make choices, and so test results and inspection reports would give parents information about schools.

Act established the National Curriculum, new rules on religious education and collective worship, new curriculum and assessment councils, local management of schools, grant-maintained schools and city technology colleges (CTCs). Grant-maintained schools were independent of local authorities (LAs), funded directly by central government. Local management of schools dramatically changed the role of heads and governors. Heads now became managers and had to know about recruitment and selection, employment law, health and safety and building maintenance. Governors, although unpaid volunteers, now had legal responsibilities in relation to budgets and staff. The freedom offered to schools was largely an illusion – as staff costs amounted to about 85 per cent of the budget, schools had little freedom to change budget priorities. As school budgets were largely based on pupil numbers, schools had to attract pupils to survive. For the government, it was an important part of the creation of an education market, and it took financial control away from LAs.

CTCs, described by Kenneth Baker, then Secretary of State for Education, as a halfway house between the state and independence, were seen by some as just another attempt to reduce the power of LEAs and bring back selection (MacLure 1987). The idea was to involve private enterprise in education, and a hundred CTCs were to be set up across the country, each sponsored by business, with spending per pupil far higher than in LA schools. In the event, businesses were unenthusiastic, and few CTCs were established.

The 1990s

When John Major became prime minister in 1990, he inherited an education system in difficulties. By 1993–4, capital spending on schools was less than half what it had been in the mid 1970s (Jones 2003, p. 112). In 1979, about 10 per cent of children lived in households whose income was less than half the national average – by 1993, this had risen to 33 per cent (ibid.), and, in 1997, Ofsted noted that state schools with large numbers of children from poor homes were by far the worst performers at GCSE. The new government was not, as had been hoped, less harsh than in Thatcher's day – it established a teachers' pay review body, introduced a parents' charter and established Ofsted. Ofsted was to inspect schools, and reports on individual schools would be published. The amount of paperwork and form filling before an inspection was huge, the week of the inspection was stressful, and there were concerns about the accuracy and fairness of some reports. Teachers' morale plummeted.

In 1992, the Education Secretary, Ken Clarke, commissioned Robin Alexander, Jim Rose and Chris Woodhead to produce what became known as the *Three Wise Men Report. Curriculum Organisation and Classroom Practice in Primary Schools: A discussion paper* was, like Plowden, of its time. Where Plowden came from the progressive 1960s, this came from the new age of the National Curriculum and testing. Both have been widely misquoted and misrepresented. Some of the main conclusions of this very controversial report were as follows:

> Piaget's idea of learning readiness as in the Plowden Report was dubious and the progress of primary pupils had been hampered. Teachers should be instructors not facilitators. Teachers should make more use of whole class teaching. More emphasis should be put on the national curriculum subjects.

> There should be more specialist teaching. Pupils should be grouped by ability in subjects (setted) but 'teachers must avoid the pitfall of assuming that pupils' ability is fixed'.
>
> (Department for Education and Science 1992, p. 27)

The 1992 White Paper *Choice and Diversity: A new framework for schools* formed the basis of the 1993 Education Act. It aimed to remove the comprehensive system through promoting specialist schools rather than selection of pupils and to promote grant-maintained schools, further diminishing the role of LEAs. The Act was the largest piece of legislation in education history.

In 1994, it was announced that the government would encourage the setting up of new grammar schools and grant-maintained schools to select more of their intake – this despite a survey that showed that Scotland, which was entirely comprehensive, was achieving significantly better results than England. In Scotland, 52 per cent of pupils achieved the equivalent of five A*–C grades at GCSE, compared with 38.4 per cent in England (Benn and Chitty 1996, p. 164). The government accepted the recommendations of the 1994 *Dearing Review of the National Curriculum* and spent £744 million on changes to the curriculum.

The Tories were defeated in the general election by a landslide victory for Tony Blair's New Labour, but, although the Labour Party called for the end of grammar schools and selection, Tony Blair made headlines by sending his children to the London Oratory School rather than the local comprehensive.

Many had high hopes for the Labour Party, believing that tests, league tables and Ofsted would disappear, grant-maintained schools would come under LA control, and selection for secondary schools would be abolished, but it was not to be, and, in some aspects, such as the belief in market forces, the party was very similar to the Tories.

The 1997 White Paper *Excellence in Schools* proposed, for example, that secondary schools should be encouraged to become specialist schools that could select a small proportion of their pupils on the basis of perceived attributes; class sizes for 5–7-year-olds would be reduced to thirty or fewer; schools would have targets for raising standards, with performance tables showing the rate of progress pupils had made, as well as levels of achievement; and primary pupils would spend at least an hour a day each on English and maths (the National Literacy Strategy was introduced in 1998, the National Numeracy Strategy in 1999). The aim was to have 650 specialist schools opened by 2001. Referring to comprehensive schools, the White Paper said:

> The search for equality of opportunity in some cases became a tendency to uniformity. The idea that all children had the same rights to develop their abilities led too easily to the doctrine that all had the same ability. The pursuit of excellence was too often equated with elitism.
>
> (Department for Education and Employment 1997, p. 11)

Critics argued that the policy of selection by aptitude and specialism would lead to ranking in a hierarchy of status, and assuming that children could be tested for particular attributes went against all the research evidence. The then director of the Institute of Education, Professor Peter Mortimore, argued that, except in music and possibly art, the ability to learn most subjects was often associated with the advantages of coming from a middle-class home, for example, the parents' ability to finance foreign language lessons.

The phrase of the moment from the government was 'standards not structures' – concern with primary pupils' achievement rather than worrying about what type of school they attended, although a number of educationists pointed out that the type of school attended had a significant effect on levels of achievement. Hundreds of comprehensive schools were to be turned into specialist colleges, and David Blunkett said it was time to end the historic campaign against grammar schools. The policy of 'naming and shaming' failing schools began – a vicious circle, as these schools, usually in poorer areas, then found it difficult to keep or attract good staff, so making the situation worse. 'Failing' LA services, such as in Hackney and Islington, were put out to tender. In 2000, the government announced a programme of city academies and private schools funded by the state in public–private partnerships modelled on CTCs.

In May 2003, the House of Commons Education Select Committee criticised the government for spending £400 million on specialist schools without any evidence that the policy was working.

Among the proposals of the government's 5-year plan in 2004 were allowing all schools to become specialist schools, a massive expansion of the academy programme and more independence for schools over budgets, buildings and staff pay. Choice was said to be the key, and there were plans for some very traditional ideas, such as school uniforms and rigorous discipline, designed to stop middle-class parents removing their children from the state sector.

Academies and free schools

The first three academies opened in September 2002. More academies followed, although there had been no research into their cost-effectiveness, and Charles Clarke, then Secretary of State for Education, admitted they were expensive, with no evidence of improving performance. In the US, the charter schools, on which academies were modelled, were having problems. In 2004, it was reported that the performance of charter schools was worse than that of publicly funded schools, and they usually achieved poorer results than other schools serving similarly disadvantaged communities. Teachers called on the government to heed the warning. In March 2005, league tables based on test results for 14-year-olds in English, maths and science showed that nine of the eleven academies were in the bottom 200 schools in England. Head teachers were almost unanimous in their opposition to plans for more academies. The government pushed ahead with the academies programme, despite GCSE results showing half the academies were among the worst-performing schools in England and a 2006 study by Edinburgh University showing that academies had failed to improve exam results compared with the comprehensive schools they replaced.

In 2007, the National Audit Office reported that academies achieved poor results in maths and English, fell well below the national average performance at A level, failed to collaborate with local schools and communities and had cost millions of pounds more than anticipated. The Labour government opened 203

- **Academies** are independent, state-funded schools. They are funded centrally and are outside LA control. They have to offer a broad and balanced curriculum and are inspected by Ofsted. Academies are formed from existing schools.
- **Free schools** are also independent and state funded and are set up by local communities in response to need.
- **Trust schools** have foundation status – they manage their own admissions, own their own assets and establish a charitable foundation or trust to support their improvement. They are part of the local authority, although not governed by it, and the government does not always provide additional funding.

academies and planned to increase this to 400: Gordon Brown praised 'the tremendous success of the academy movement' (*The Guardian*, 20 March 2007).

In his first month as Education Secretary (May 2010), Michael Gove wrote to all primary and secondary schools in England inviting them to become academies and said he had no objection to businesses making profit from academies and free schools. The Academies Bill was rushed through Parliament and:

- removed LAs' powers to veto schools becoming an academy;
- dispensed with parents' and teachers' legal rights to oppose such plans;
- allowed schools regarded by inspectors as outstanding to fast-track the process of becoming academies.

There was widespread concern about the lack of debate in Parliament. Reported in *The Guardian* (6 June 2010), education barrister David Wolfe said:

> It is hard to escape the conclusion that this Bill is undemocratic. What it does is remove the public process. Nobody, apart from the Education Secretary and the governors, will be able to stop the process. It seems to be entirely out of kilter with the idea of a 'Big Society'. You are handing power to the governors to

> steal the school. If they want to change the ethos or make the pupils wear the uniform of Etonians, they will be able to, and parents and teachers will be unable to stop them.

In the same article, John Bangs, head of education at the NUT, said local communities were being 'completely disempowered' from having a say in the establishment of a new school. 'For all that we have heard from the new government about devolving power, this is actually a much more highly centralised system of control.' Former Education Secretary Estelle Morris warned:

> A bill that is intended to fundamentally change our school system is likely to become law with no green or white paper, no formal consultation and having completed all its common stages in eight days. That speed is usually reserved for emergency legislation that has wide support – hardly a description of the Academies Bill.

Gove insisted the plan to transform schools was urgently needed to improve the choices of parents and children, claiming the country was falling behind the rest of the world in science, literacy and maths. He told MPs the programme had lifted standards for all children, the disadvantaged most of all, and change was urgently needed, because more than 1,900 schools had expressed interest in converting to academy status, and more than 1,000 had already applied to do so (*The Guardian*, 19 September 2010). The Academies Act received royal assent on 27 July, when it was revealed that only 153 schools had actually applied for academy status. Of those, only 32 opened as academies in September (*The Independent*, 2 September 2010).

The widespread hostility towards academies showed no signs of abating. There were concerns that academies would not have to take children with SEN, and Toynbee (2010) worried about exclusions, as schools could keep funds for the year for excluded pupils, instead of handing funds over to the child's new school: 'Ministers say it will remove "disincentive to exclude" but how perverse to add a very strong financial incentive to throw out those who risk lowering an academy's standards'. There were also queries over whether there was any evidence that academies raised standards.

> Firstly there is little evidence of real general success by academies and what there is has been hotly contested. Second, the initial tranche of schools that Gove and Cameron are seeking to improve has already been judged as outstanding while under LA control and probably don't really need their standards being driven up a further miniscule amount.
>
> (Beadle 2010)

In January 2014, there were 3,613 academies in England.

Michael Gove was also determined to go ahead with the creation of thousands of free schools. In June 2010, it was claimed 700 schools would be open in 2011 – three months later, he was forced to admit the actual number was 16. Almost half of these were faith schools – three Christian, two Jewish, one Hindu and one Sikh. The free schools policy was based mainly on the Swedish model, but research showed they had not been an unqualified success in Sweden. They had been set up mainly by middle-class parents in affluent urban areas, and so had increased social segregation, and pupils had done no better than others in A level-equivalent exams and were no more likely to participate in higher education. Seventeen years after the reforms were first enacted, there were no decisive changes in the Swedish system. Despite almost 1,000 new independent schools and 150,000 students, researchers found only slightly higher pupil attainment, but higher costs and greater segregation (Wiborg 2010).

The 2000s

Concerns were expressed about the National Literacy Strategy, which had failed to deliver any improvement in reading and writing scores in three consecutive years. In February 2004, chief inspector David Bell said the focus on maths and English in primary schools meant that other subjects were neglected, and a government-commissioned report said exam overload was harming pupils. In 2004, the Children Act established a children's commissioner to champion the views and interests of children and young people and required LAs to promote co-operation with agencies and other organisations to improve children's well-being. Alongside the Act, *Every Child Matters: Change for children* set out radical changes across children's services, including schools.

The 2005 White Paper *Higher Standards, Better Schools for All* made a number of proposals, including that all primary and secondary schools would be encouraged to become independent state schools backed by private sponsors (trust schools and parents). Parenting contracts would be extended, and parents who failed to fulfil their duties could be fined. It was controversial – more than 100 Labour MPs threatened to rebel, and even cabinet ministers were worried. In December, a group of fifty-eight Labour MPs produced an alternative White Paper. They said plans for trust schools were likely to strengthen rather than break the link between being poor and educational under-achievement. By mid January, more than half the Labour backbenchers had signed up to the alternative White Paper. Education Secretary Ruth Kelly told them they did not understand the government's plans and was later found to have suppressed a crucial report warning that her plans would widen the educational divide between rich and poor children.

The government continued its campaign against comprehensive schools, announcing partnerships between grammar and secondary modern or comprehensive schools, with plans for at least 1,500 specialist schools by 2005. The days of the 'one size fits all' comprehensive were over, announced Estelle Morris. The Sutton Trust published research showing that top-performing comprehensives that controlled their own admissions were excluding poorer pupils. Backbenchers argued that the Education and Inspection Bill was the first irreversible step towards the privatisation of the state-schools system, and Tony Blair had to rely on Tory support for the Bill to be passed, the largest ever rebellion suffered by a Labour government at the third reading.

In 2007, parents' leaders called for an end to selection, after exam results showed most of the worst-performing schools were in shires with grammar schools, and Conservative leader David Cameron pledged no return to the 11 plus or grammar schools under a Conservative government. A poll showed three-quarters of party members disapproved of his statement, while Cameron said a pointless debate about grammar schools would not help, promising to raise standards and improve discipline in all 24,000 state schools in England.

Research by David Jesson, at the University of York, showed that children who did not pass the 11 plus were condemned to lower standards of education than if they went to comprehensive schools in non-selective areas (*The Observer*, 19 February 2006). In 2007, Brighton's Labour-controlled council announced it was allocating some places at secondary school by lottery. Middle-class parents fought a battle involving death threats and espionage over whose children had the right to go to the best schools, while critics argued that Brighton's most deprived children were left voiceless and marginalised (*The Guardian*, 1 March 2007).

In November 2005, Education Minister Ruth Kelly announced that primary schools were to be forced to teach reading by synthetic phonics. This had first achieved prominence in 1998, when a study in Clackmannanshire of 4-year-olds showed improved reading ability. The research was universally condemned by experts in teaching reading, as it was a very small, flawed study, but this was ignored by Kelly.

In January 2006, the House of Commons Public Accounts Committee accused the government of wasting £885 million over 7 years in a futile attempt to reduce the number of truants. Despite numerous initiatives to improve attendance and behaviour, the number of children missing lessons each day in England rose by nearly 5,000 a year. Department for Education and Skills (DfES) figures in September 2006 showed nearly 1.4 million children – one in five of all pupils in England – had played truant from school in the previous year (*The Guardian*, 22 September 2006).

In 2007, there was a call for all national tests for 7-, 11- and 14-year-olds to be scrapped – children in England took around seventy different tests before the age of 16, the most tested in the world. This was supported by the Liberal Democrats, but firmly rebuffed by the government and the Conservatives.

Tony Blair stepped down as prime minister in June 2007. Blair and Minister for Schools Lord Adonis were seen by many as a real disappointment – instead of repairing the damage done by the Conservatives, they made the situation worse by extending covert selection under the guise of specialism, expanded privatised provision of schools and services, further diminished the role of LEAs and significantly increased the role of churches and other faith groups in education provision. Although schools had received a 56 per cent increase in budget over 10 years and exam results had improved – the proportion of pupils getting good GCSEs, including English and maths, had risen from 40.7 per cent in 2000 to 47.3 per cent in 2008 – critics saw these as a disappointment (Chitty and Dunford 1999).

In an article entitled 'Missed opportunities and mad ideas: The government's legacy', Peter Mortimore (2009) wrote:

> Much needed to be done when this government came into office in 1997. And many teachers wanted to help improve schools and make our society more equal. But, instead of the formulation of a long term improvement plan based on the two big questions – what sort of education system is suitable for a modern society and how can excellence and equity be made to work together – schools got top-down diktat. Successive ministers and especially their advisers thought they knew 'what works'. They cherry-picked research, suppressed evaluations that gave them answers they did not want and compounded the mess. Trusting teachers – which is what ministers do in the best performing countries – was not on the agenda.
>
> (*The Guardian*, 7 July 2009)

Blair was replaced as prime minister by Gordon Brown. The Department for Education was split into the DCSF and the Department for Innovation, Universities and Skills. The DCSF brought together all policy related to children and schools, sharing youth justice with the Minister of Justice, child poverty with the Treasury and Department of Work and Pensions, children's health with the Department of Health and youth sport with the Department for Culture and the respect agenda from the Home Office.

At a conference at Brighton College in May 2008, Michael Gove, then Shadow Secretary for Education, told teachers a Conservative government would reinstate traditional, fact-based lessons – generations of children had been let down by progressive education policies that taught skills and 'empathy' instead of bodies of knowledge. He condemned pupil-centred learning theories for 'dethroning' the teacher:

> It is an approach to education that has been called progressive but in fact is anything but. It privileges temporary relevance over a permanent body of knowledge which should be passed on from generation to generation . . . We need to tackle this misplaced ideology wherever it occurs.
>
> (Curtis 2008)

In the same article, NUT acting general secretary Christine Blower said, 'Gove's attack on child-centred learning is an absurd caricature of reality. If there has been a dethroning of teachers, it has been because successive politicians have decided that they know better than teachers about how children learn' (Curtis 2008).

In December 2007, the government published *The Children's Plan – Building better futures.* It was an ambitious plan, based on widespread consultations designed to underpin and inform all future government policy relating to children, families and schools. It aimed to eradicate child poverty and reduce illiteracy and antisocial behaviour by 2020. It was an attempt to address very critical reports by UNICEF and others.

In June 2009, the government published the White Paper *Your Child, Your Schools, Your Future,* to form the basis of the 2009 Children, Schools and Families Bill, which was intended to become the 2010 Children, Schools and Families Act, although much was lost in the run-up to the general election. The White Paper saw the end of what many saw as Blair's most significant education reform – the National Literacy and Numeracy Strategies – removed central government's prescription of teaching methods and dramatically cut the use of private consultants to improve schools. Schools would have more freedom and would be enabled to establish networks of school-to-school support to help drive up standards. Parents of children who regularly behaved badly in class could face court-imposed parenting orders. Other points included partnerships of primary schools to share specialist teaching, more academies and trust schools, a new Masters degree in teaching and learning and schools to be given greater flexibility to encourage more innovation.

A House of Lords committee report, *The Cumulative Impact of Statutory Instruments on Schools,* urged the government to stop deluging schools with new regulations. In 2006–7 the DCSF and national agencies produced over 760 documents aimed at schools. Association of School and College Leaders general secretary John Dunford said a 'juggernaut of policies, laws and regulations hurtles at ever increasing speed towards us, seemingly out of control'. Schools in England had been besieged by seventy-nine policy consultations and at least 300 announcements from the DCSF in 2008. Dunford also said the government was promoting the 'Tesco model' of schools, as delivery was the job of postal workers and midwives, not teachers (*The Guardian*, 15 March 2009).

The global recession began in 2008 and forced governments around the world to review spending. In March 2009, Ed Balls urged schools to save £750 million a year by turning off lights, cutting back on heating and sharing cleaners, in order to save front-line staff in the future. At the NCSL conference in February 2010, head teachers were asked to make efficiency savings of £1 billion, without reducing front-line staff. The National Association of Head Teachers general secretary said it would be difficult for heads to find £1 billion without threatening front-line staff – teaching assistants (TAs) were especially vulnerable. The government promised a 0.7 per cent real-terms increase in funding for schools, but, because of the increase in pupil numbers, a further 0.9 per cent would be needed to maintain the status quo (*The Observer*, 7 February 2010).

The general election was held in May 2010. With no overall winner, David Cameron formed a coalition government of the Conservatives and Liberal Democrats. The government's first actions were:

- expansion of the academies programme;
- creation of free schools;
- drastic budget cuts;
- scrapping of the new primary curriculum, school sports partnerships, diplomas, the Qualifications and Curriculum Development Agency and the schools rebuilding programme;
- fewer places in higher education and increased fees;
- the abolition of quangos, including the Qualifications and Curriculum Authority (QCA) and the Training and Development Agency.

Against the background of the global economic recession, the new government published plans with a particular focus on 'the need to reform our school system to tackle educational inequality which has widened in recent years and to give greater powers to parents and pupils to choose a good school' (Cabinet Office 2010, p. 28). Following the Academies Bill, the next piece of legislation was the White Paper *The Importance of Teaching* (Department for Education 2010), with proposals to be included in the Education Act 2011 and suggesting that the government saw teaching as fundamental to the aim of improving the education system. David Cameron and Nick Clegg, prime minister and deputy prime minister, identified three aspects of the education system that needed particular attention:

> The first and most important lesson is that no education system can be better than the quality of its teachers . . . The second lesson of world-class education systems is that they devolve as much power as possible to the front line, while retaining high levels of accountability . . . The third lesson of the best education systems is that no country that wishes to be considered world class can afford to allow children from poorer families to fail as a matter of course.
>
> (Cameron and Clegg 2010, pp. 3–4, in Abbott *et al.* 2013)

There has been rapid reform, but it is too early to say yet how effective the changes have been.

Further reading

Education in England: A brief history
www.educationengland.org.uk/history
Derek Gillard, 2011
An excellent website that covers the history of education in England, with useful links to reports and policy documents.

Education: A very short introduction
Gary Thomas, 2013, Oxford University Press
Exactly what it says – a short, easy-to-read and informative look at key issues.

The Education Debate
Stephen J. Ball, 2013 (2nd edn), Policy Press
A sociological perspective on education policy and debates over the last 20 years or so.

Education Policy
Ian Abbott, Michael Rathbone, Phil Whitehead, 2013, Sage
An in-depth look at education policy since the Second World War, including interviews with Michael Gove, Ed Balls and others.

Fifty Major Thinkers on Education, From Confucius to Dewey
Joy Palmer (ed.), 2001, Routledge
A collection of essays that provide a useful reference guide, giving biographical information, an outline of major achievements and impact and suggestions for further reading.

Fifty Modern Thinkers on Education, From Piaget to the Present
Joy Palmer (ed.), 2001, Routledge
The follow-on volume to the above.

The Learning Game
Michael Barber, 1997, Indigo
A look at how education in Britain has developed and some ideas for solving its problems.

Education, Education, Education: Reforming England's schools
Andrew Adonis, 2012, Biteback
Lord Adonis was an adviser on education to Tony Blair; his book looks at past policies and recommendations for change.

The Routledge Companion to Education
James Arthur and Andrew Peterson (eds), 2012, Routledge

A guide to the key theories, themes and topics in education.

The Dangerous Rise of Therapeutic Education
Kathryn Ecclestone and Dennis Hayes, 2009, Routledge
A controversial book, arguing that therapeutic education is turning children and young people into anxious adults.

Understanding Schools as Organisations
Charles Handy and Robert Aitken, 1986, Penguin
Unfortunately, a bit outdated now, but still has some useful insights into how schools work.

References

Abbott, I., Rathbone, M. and Whitehead, P. (2013) *Education Policy*, London: Sage.

Ball, S. J. (2013) *The Education Debate: Policy and politics in the twenty-first century*, Bristol, UK: Policy Press.

Barber, M. (1994) *The Making of the 1944 Education Act*, London: Cassell.

Beadle, P. (2010) The academy policy is bad news for teachers, *The Guardian*, 15 June.

Benn, C. and Chitty, C. (1996) *Thirty Years On: Is comprehensive education alive and well or struggling to survive?* London: David Fulton.

Benn, M. and Miller, F. (2006) *A Comprehensive Future: Quality and equality for all our children*, London: Compass.

Bennett, N. (1976) *Teaching Styles and Pupil Progress*, London: Open University Press.

Board of Education (1943) White Paper *Educational Reconstruction* (Cm 6458), London: HMSO.

Cabinet Office (2010) *The Coalition: Our programme for government*, London: Cabinet Office.

Callaghan, J. (1976) Ruskin Speech. Available at: www.educationengland.org.uk/documents/speeches/1976ruskin.html (accessed 14 August 2014).

Cameron, D. and Clegg, N. (2010) Foreword by the Prime Minister and the Deputy Prime Minister in *The Importance of Teaching: Schools White Paper*. Available at: www.gov.uk/government/uploads/system/uploads/attachment_data/file/175429/CM-7980.pdf (accessed March 2014).

Chitty, C. (2004) *Education Policy in Britain*, Basingstoke, UK: Palgrave Macmillan.

Chitty, C. and Dunford, J. (eds) (1999) *State Schools: New Labour and the Conservative legacy*, London: Woburn Press.

Crook, D. (2008) 'The middle school cometh' . . . and goeth: Alec Clegg and the rise and fall of the English middle school, *Education 3–13*, 36(2): 117–25.

Curtis, P. (2008) Children being failed by progressive education, say Tories, *The Guardian*, 9 May.

Department for Education (2010) White Paper *The Importance of Teaching* (Cm 7980), London: TSO.

Department for Education and Employment (1997) White Paper *Excellence in Schools* (Cm 3681), London: HMSO.

Department for Education and Science (1992) *Curriculum Organisation and Classroom Practice in Primary Schools: A discussion paper*, London: HMSO.

Galton, M., Simon, B. and Croll, P. (1980) *Inside the Primary Classroom (the ORACLE report)*, London: Routledge Kegan Paul.

Gilbourn, D. and Mirza, H. S. (2000) *Educational Inequality: Mapping race, class and gender: A synthesis of research evidence*, London: Ofsted.

Gillard, D. (2011) *Education in England: A brief history*. Available at: www.educationengland.org.uk/history (accessed March 2014).

Hadow (1926) *The Education of the Adolescent, Report of the Consultative Committee*, London: HMSO. Available at: www.educationengland.org.uk/documents/hadow1926/hadow1926.html (accessed 11 August 2014).

Hadow (1931) *The Primary School, Report of the Consultative Committee*, London: HMSO. Available at: www.educationengland.org.uk/documents/hadow1931/index.html (accessed 11 August 2014).

Hadow (1933) *Infant and Nursery Schools, Report of the Consultative Committee*, London: HMSO. Available at: www.educationengland.org.uk/documents/hadow1933/index.html (accessed 11 August 2014).

Jones, K. (2003) *Education in Britain: 1944 to the present*, Cambridge, UK: Polity Press.

MacLure, S. (1987) Leading from the Centre, *Times Educational Supplement*, 3 April.

Ministry of Education (1959) *15–18 Report of the Central Advisory Committee for England (The Crowther Report)*, London: HMSO. Available at: www.educationengland.org.uk/documents/crowther/index.html

Mortimore, P. (2009) Missed opportunities and mad ideas: The government's legacy, *The Guardian*, 7 July (accessed October 2014).

National Middle Schools Forum (2014) Available at: www.middleschools.org.uk (accessed March 2014).

Pedley, R. (1969) *The Comprehensive School*, Harmondsworth, UK: Penguin.

Plowden (1967) *Children and their Primary Schools: Report of the Central Advisory Council for Education (England)*, London: HMSO.

Spens (1938) *Secondary Education with Special Reference to Grammar Schools and Technical High Schools: Report of the Consultative Committee*, London: HMSO.

Sumner, C. (2010) 1945–1965 The long road to Circular 10/65, *Reflecting Education*, 6(1). Available at: www.reflectingeducation.net (accessed March 2014).

Taylor, T. (1977) *A New Partnership For Our Schools, Report of the Committee of Enquiry (The Taylor Report)*, London: HMSO.

Tomlinson, S. (2001) *Education in a Post Welfare Society*, Buckingham, UK: Open University Press.

Toynbee, P. (2010) Gove's bill spells segregation and tax-funded madrasas, *The Guardian*, 20 July. Available at: www.theguardian.com/commentisfree/2010/jul/20/recipe-state-funded-madrasas-segregation (accessed 14 August 2014).

Van der Eyken, W. (ed.) (1973) *Education, the Child and Society: A documentary history 1900–1973*, London: Penguin.

Wiborg, S. (2010) Learning lessons from the Swedish model, *Forum*, 52(3): 279–84.

2 Education – the great debate

Education is what remains when we have forgotten everything that has been learned at school.

(Albert Einstein)

What is education for?

Some think that 'the great debate' about the purpose of education began with Prime Minister Jim Callaghan's Ruskin Speech in 1976. It was unusual for a prime minister to devote a speech to education. As Callaghan said, 'There is no virtue in producing socially well-adjusted members of society who are unemployed because they do not have the skills': it was clear that one of the main objectives of secondary education was to prepare pupils 'to do a job of work'.

There has long been debate about the purpose of education (education here meaning formal education in schools and other institutions). Is education for education's sake – should children be learning the liberal arts? – or should they be prepared for the world of work?

The debate began long before 1976 – the word education has its roots in the Latin *educare*, meaning *to bring up* or *raise*, although some say it comes from *educatum*, meaning *training*.

The answer to the question 'What is education for?' can depend upon who is asked. Industrialists, for example, will talk about skills for work; others may refer to state control or social engineering. It is only comparatively recently that education was thought to be something that concerned girls – middle- and upper-class girls were educated in the home, to become good home managers and wives, and working-class girls were often not educated at all. In the foreword to *The Importance of Teaching* (Department for Education 2010), Prime Minister David Cameron said that, 'So much of the education debate in this country is backward looking: have standards fallen? Have exams got easier? These debates will continue, but what really matters is how we're doing compared with our international competitors'.

Twentieth-century philosopher Michael Oakeshott (1991) saw education as part of the 'conversation of mankind', where teachers help students to take part in that conversation by teaching them how to participate in the dialogue – how to hear the 'voices' of earlier generations, while cultivating their own unique voice. Referring to universities and their purpose of providing liberal education, Oakeshott said that, whenever other purposes – such as training for employment – appear, 'education (which is concerned with persons, not functions) steals out of the backdoor with noiseless steps' (Fuller 1989, p. 101). It was John Dewey who said, 'Education is not preparation for life; education is life itself'.

According to Ball (2013), Tony Blair's pre-election speech in 1996 was a decisive repositioning of education, placing it at the centre of the policy stage. It became a major political issue, the focus of media attention and recipient of a constant stream of government initiatives and interventions. The same has happened in other countries – education is seen as a crucial factor in ensuring economic productivity and competitiveness. Learning is said to be the key to prosperity, for us as individuals and for society as a whole. In a speech on education at Sedgefield on 18 November 2005, then Prime Minister Tony Blair said:

> Education is our best economic policy . . . This country will succeed or fail on the basis of how it changes itself and gears up to this new economy, based on knowledge. Education therefore is now the centre of economic policy making for the future.

There is an argument, according to Ball (2013) that information and knowledge are replacing capital and energy as the primary wealth-creating assets, just as the latter replaced land and labour 200 years ago. Today, most work is knowledge based not physically based, as it used to be – most people don't produce 'stuff'. There is an element of social justice in education, too:

> It is to modernise our country, so that, in the face of future challenges . . . we are able to provide opportunity and security for all: not for an elite: not for the privileged few: but for all our people, whatever their class, colour or creed.
>
> (Tony Blair's speech to the Labour Party centenary conference, 10 February 2006)

To look at more recent examples, in 2009, Michael Gove MP made a speech to the Royal Society for the Arts (before the coalition government came into power in 2010 and he became Secretary of State for Education). It was then just over 2 years after Gordon Brown became prime minister and since the demise of the Department for Education and the creation of the new Department for Children, Schools and Families. In this speech, Michael Gove argued that the renaming of the department was not 'empty rebranding' but 'reflected a philosophical shift in how Government sees its role':

> Schools have lost their principal purpose [and] are less places of teaching and learning and more community hubs from which a host of children's services can be delivered. In that sense education has indeed been eclipsed . . . We no longer have a single department of state charged with encouraging learning, supporting teaching and valuing education. Instead we have one department which manages schools – and sees them as instruments to advance central government's social agenda . . .
>
> What is education for? I believe that education is a good in itself – one of the central hallmarks of a civilized society – indeed the means by which societies ensure that everything which is best in our society is passed on to succeeding generations.
>
> Education has an emancipatory, liberating, value. I regard education as the means by which individuals can gain access to all the other goods we value – cultural, social and economic

> – on their terms. I believe education allows individuals to become authors of their own life story . . .
>
> And that relates directly to education's second value – as a driver of real social justice. The very best means of helping all realise their potential – of making opportunity more equal – is guaranteeing the best possible education for as many as possible.

The speech continued by discussing what had happened to specific subjects, a comparison between private and comprehensive schools, the importance of teachers and what the Conservatives would do when in power. It concluded by saying that what the British people want is common sense and schools where the principal activity is teaching and learning and the principal goal is academic attainment.

So, according to his speech, education is a good thing in itself. It is for liberation, empowerment, social justice, for passing on the best of human achievement. Not everyone, though, would agree that Mr Gove's policies follow this line. In March 2013, for example, 100 senior education academics wrote a letter to *The Independent* arguing that the proposed new national curriculum would promote rote learning without understanding, would damage education standards by insisting children learn 'endless lists of spellings, facts and rules' and would result in a 'dumbing down' of teaching and learning (Garner 2013). A more recent article (January 2014) by Dr Maggie Atkinson, Children's Commissioner for England, and John Connolly, Principal Policy Adviser (Education), began by saying that it is not *what* but *who* education is for that matters:

> Schools must prepare pupils for the real world. On that, we can all agree. It gets trickier when we try to define what that means. Academic knowledge and qualifications are a vital part of it. They are not the whole story. The large majority of schools do all this very well. I have visited schools all over England where staff bend over backwards to include all students, acting in their best interests. But there are many other pressures on school leaders. There is – inevitably – a temptation to respond to these. Delivering what children and young people need might make it more difficult for an increase in 'EBACC' scores. A school may lose points and places in the league tables, which of course do

not apply to the private sector. And there, surely, is the nub of this Great Debate.

So, the debate – education for education's sake or education for employment – continues. It affects government policy too: in 2010, the government decided to stop funding university arts and humanities programmes, leaving them dependent on income from tuition fees and emphasising the importance of the STEM (science, technology, engineering and maths) subjects.

What should we teach?

The debate about what should be taught in schools, put simply, is really about whether children should be taught 'the facts' or whether they should be encouraged to think and find things out for themselves. Is it about passing on knowledge and skills – and, if so, what knowledge and which skills? – or is it about developing critical thinking and questioning? There are essentially two schools of thought – progressive and formal (also known by other names): see Table 2.1.

Progressive education sees children as keen learners who are open minded and learning from their experience. A child is a blank slate – *tabula rasa,* as Locke put it – ready to learn through discovery. Philosopher John Locke (1632–1704) suggested that parents

Table 2.1 Progressive and formal schools of thought

	Other terms	View of learning
Progressive	Informal Child centred Discovery learning Open education Learning by doing	Learning happens all the time, like the way children learn to talk
Formal	Didactic Teacher directed Chalk and talk Back to basics Traditional	Learning is hard slog, no pain no gain, have to learn the rules

and teachers should not push children into reading too early – it is better to wait than to put children off learning, an idea that is followed in other parts of the world today. In Finland, for example, children do not start school until age 7, and they have the best reading scores. The formal movement says that education is about passing on new information, and the key to this is teaching. Where progressive educators see the development of a child coming from within, for formalists it comes from without (see summary in Table 2.2).

Two schools of education

Most schools (and teachers) will use a mix, rather than one or the other. Primary schools tend to be more progressive than formal. Particularly for the youngest children, the classroom will be arranged so that children sit on the carpet or at tables in small groups, so they can talk, co-operate and share activities and experience. Secondary schools tend to have a more formal arrangement of desks, facing the teacher at the front of the classroom.

Jean-Jacques Rousseau published *Émile* in the mid eighteenth century and paved the way for progressive thinking. He saw children as open minded, keen and ready to learn. They learn from experience and discovery, he said, not from being force-fed facts. Dewey was a supporter of progressive education and, in 1896, founded his Laboratory School in Chicago, with the aim of providing the kind of progressive education not found in schools in the US. His later work, *Experience and Education* (1938, 1963), regretted the way education had split into opposing camps and said we should be concentrating on children and their education. We should think 'in terms of Education itself rather than in terms of some "ism" about education, even such an "ism" as "progressivism"' (p. 6).

Swiss Johann Pestalozzi opened his own schools, building on Rousseau's ideas about the importance of exploration and observation, but had a holistic view of the child that placed tenderness and respect for children at the centre of education. Corporal punishment was not allowed in any of his schools – without care and warmth, neither the physical nor the intellectual powers would develop naturally.

Table 2.2 Two schools of education

Progressive	Formal
Child centred, problem-solving	Teaching
Supporting ability to think critically	Acquiring the skills necessary for success in life
Natural, easy, happens all the time	Can be difficult, just have to learn the hard way
Emphasis on discovery	Cannot expect children to find out things for themselves – ideas, rules and traditions have been handed down through the generations
Discovery means children find out things for themselves and 'own' the knowledge	Need a structure or scaffolding to hold knowledge in place, have to have links and connections
Develops questioning skills – society needs people to be critical and challenging	Agree, but this is for adults – children need security, structure and authority
Children learn best one to one with a teacher or in a small group	How can this work in a class of thirty?
The only meaningful motivation comes from interest in the subject or activity – intrinsic motivation	This is not the real world – some learning is difficult, dull, boring, but it has to be done, part of the real world
	Motivation is extrinsic, comes from praise, rewards, wanting to get good marks
Curriculum is project or topic based, covers all subjects	Curriculum is subject based, subjects are taught separately

Friedrich Froebel, a German student of Pestalozzi, emphasised the education of younger children. From Froebel came the word *kindergarten*, or children's garden. The emphasis was on practical, creative ability and play, with education continuing from pre-school to adulthood, centred on the nurturing and development of the child's own talents. From the ideas of Froebel and Pestalozzi, Maria Montessori developed her method in the early 1900s, putting independence at the centre of the curriculum with tasks such as personal care and care for the environment. For a while, her method was quite widely adapted in Europe and the US, and there are still more than 150 Montessori schools in the UK.

The world-famous Reggio Emilia approach is often seen as the primary example of progressive education. It stresses the discovery approach and the involvement of parents and the community in education. The layout of the school is particularly important, organised so that it encourages work and communication in groups.

This raises an important issue. Often, the work that children do while they are sitting in groups is individual work, not group work. However, the seating arrangement that works for groups does not work for children working on their own – it is too easy to make eye contact or talk to the person next to you and get distracted. So, critics of progressive education say that this shows that, for most teachers, acceptance of progressive ideals is shallow, and this is difficult to achieve in a formal 'chalk and talk' classroom. Therefore, what we often end up with is the worst of both worlds, a hybrid, with individual work being done in groups and done badly. Just as simply taking some work outside on a nice day is not outdoor learning, so just sitting children in groups is not progressive or child-centred learning.

In 1967, a team based at the University of Lancaster conducted a study looking at the outcomes of children in (broadly) formal or progressive classrooms. It concluded that children in open, informal classrooms, where teaching was mainly progressive, learned less in English, maths and reading than those in formal classrooms. Reported by Bennett (1976), it was widely reported and very influential, a serious blow to supporters of progressive education. However, they looked more closely and started to question the design of the study. For example, did all the teachers in the study have the same level of experience? Were the classes of children socially balanced (because formal teaching styles tend to be found in socially advantaged areas, this could have influenced the findings)? And so on. The data were re-analysed, and differences were found to be far smaller. In English, formal teaching seemed more effective, whereas informal classrooms produced better results in reading, and there was no clear difference in maths.

This led to more research. One of the issues was that it was difficult to categorise teachers as either progressive or formal. Project ORACLE involved detailed observation of fifty-eight classrooms. The researchers found that, although teachers tended to have either a mainly formal or a mainly progressive teaching style, they responded to whatever was happening in the classroom, and so sometimes a more formal teacher would have children working in groups and exchanging ideas, and sometimes a progressive teacher would become more didactic and formal. The researchers grouped teachers into categories – group instructors, individual monitors, class enquirers and style changers. Children were categorised as attention seekers, intermittent workers, solitary workers and easy riders. There were more marked differences between progressive or informal teachers than the formal ones – when informal teaching was good, it was really good, but, when it was not, it could be really awful. Formal teaching seemed to be a better option for weaker teachers.

Although the progressive movement has had – still has – its staunch supporters, it has been introduced only patchily and tends to be viewed as experimental or a bit 'hippyish'. There are no strong supporters of formal education in the same way – this is the default position, and the progressives just try to argue against it. So, education is about passing on information, and at the centre of this are teachers. Even within formal education, however, there are different views. Although formal education is about the knowledge, ideas, beliefs and culture of a society, the emphasis can be on telling – the chalk and talk idea – or on the more liberal idea of supporting children's involvement in what they need to learn.

In the 1970s, American researcher Walter Doyle said that teachers develop 'with-it-ness' – good teachers can shift their teaching style as necessary (Doyle 1977, cited in Thomas 2013). They respond to the needs of their class, they adapt. This is why, according to Thomas (2013), top–down initiatives from government do not work – initiatives such as the National Literacy Strategy in the UK and No Child Left Behind in the US, and others. These directives, which tell teachers how they must teach, ignore teachers' experience, instincts and professional skills. There may be short-term gains but, in the longer term, evaluation generally shows that such initiatives do not produce significant improvements. Finland is often held up as a shining example: there, teaching is a highly sought-after career. Teachers are respected, well paid and highly educated, with Masters degrees. There is respect for teachers' knowledge and professionalism, and they are trusted to do a good job. In international comparison tables, other countries lag behind.

What is curriculum?

The Oxford Dictionary defines curriculum as 'the subjects comprising a course of study in a school or college' and the national curriculum as 'a common programme of study in schools that is designed to ensure nationwide uniformity of content and standards in education'.

The history of education in England reveals a number of models of the curriculum, based on very different assumptions about what is educationally worthwhile. Each model has come from what was valued at a particular time, by a particular social class, or promoted by a particular type of school, or a combination. The great public schools were built on the classical humanist tradition and were geared to educating the 'whole man' (not woman) for leadership roles in the church, government and the military. Subjects such as science, modern European languages and geography became important in the academic curricula of the grammar schools with the rise of the merchant and manufacturing middle class. When elementary schooling for all was introduced in the late nineteenth century, teaching was in basic knowledge and skills. When primary education was separated from secondary, after the Education Act of 1944, there was more consideration of what was an appropriate education for younger children and what should be taught in the light of psychological research about developmental needs. More

- **Subject curriculum**: in the National Curriculum, the contents for each subject.
- **Cross-curriculum**: subjects that cut across the curriculum, for example ICT or literacy.
- **Pastoral curriculum**: the care of children, the development of a supportive curriculum and school ethos.
- **Extracurricular**: extracurricular activities are those that happen outside the school day or school premises, such as music, drama and sports clubs, and sports fixtures and outside visits.
- **Hidden curriculum**: tacit messages and lessons learned in school. This could be messages about gender roles or minority groups, attitudes to authority, or understanding of what is acceptable language in the classroom.

recently, the technological age and global economy have led to calls for transferable knowledge and employability skills.

Gillard (1987) notes a shift towards core courses and curricula all having at heart the notion that the child is to be fitted for the service of the state or to fill his/her role in society, evidenced by, 'The school curriculum is at the heart of education' (Department of Education and Science 1981, p. 1). Compare this with, 'At the heart of the educational process lies the child' (Plowden 1967, p. 7).

Who decides the curriculum?

The Expert Panel for the National Curriculum Review (2011) said:

> The first consideration when designing a curriculum is to be clear about the purposes the curriculum is expected to serve. This is essential as the best possible content needs to be selected. This is challenging when pupils have fewer than 10,500 hours of compulsory lessons between the ages of 5 to 16 (5 hours per day × 190 days per year × 11 years) – just about the amount of

time estimated to be necessary to become expert in a single field e.g. playing the piano.

In 1960, Education Minister David Eccles described the curriculum as a secret garden, out of bounds to politicians. This changed with the introduction of the National Curriculum in the 1980s. According to Moon (2002, p. 195):

> The Secretary of State, Kenneth Baker ... closely monitored the direction the working parties were taken [sic]. When the mathematics working party, for example, failed to achieve a model to his liking the chair was sacked and a new appointment made.

A more recent example is that of the Tomlinson Report (Department for Education 2004), which was commissioned to review the 14–19 curriculum. It proposed that GCSEs and A levels should be replaced by a diploma that would include vocational and academic qualifications. Although the proposals had almost universal support, they were not adopted by the government. In 2005, a White Paper confirmed that GCSEs and A levels would remain, and a new diploma would be created for vocational qualifications. According to the BBC (Baker 2005):

> It could be an episode from *Yes Minister*: the government-commissioned inquiry that was enthusiastically set up, its recommendations praised, and then rejected ... Rarely has a government-commissioned inquiry done its job so thoroughly. For two years, Sir Mike's working group sifted the evidence, took advice, cajoled and persuaded. By the end he had achieved the near impossible: a very broad consensus in favour of wholesale reform of the examination system ... [but] While he was beavering away the political landscape was changing.

More recently, two significant reviews of the primary curriculum have been undertaken. The Cambridge Primary Review began work in 2006 and published *Towards a New Primary Curriculum* in February 2009 (Alexander and Flutter 2009a, 2009b) and its final report, *Children, Their World, Their Education,* in 2009 (Alexander 2009b). The government's *Independent Review of the Primary*

Curriculum (IRPC), conducted by Sir Jim Rose, published its interim report in December 2008 and its final report in April 2009 (Department for Children, Schools and Families 2009). Sir Jim Rose was invited to conduct this independent review of the primary curriculum, even though the Cambridge Primary Review was already underway. The justification for this seemed to be that the government had already commissioned a review of the secondary curriculum and had introduced an Early Years Foundation Stage (EYFS). As Rose put it, you could not 'just extend one backwards, the other forwards, tie a knot in the middle and say that's primary education' (Wilby 2008). Another suggestion was that the government wanted an end to headlines such as, 'Poor performance linked to substandard classrooms' and 'Study reveals stressed out 7 to 11 year olds'. There was also concern that the Cambridge Review would condemn SATs tests. So, the IRPC was a diversion, 'with a suspiciously similar email address, a claim that it too is independent, and an identical deadline for its final report of spring 2009' (Wilby 2008). The consideration of SATs tests was not part of Rose's remit. It found overwhelming support for the National Curriculum and much good practice in schools, but said that schools and teachers needed stability so as to be able to plan effectively. The Cambridge Review brought forward publication of its report, to contribute to the IRPC final report. It commented on the politicisation of the curriculum and warned that children's lives were being impoverished by the government's insistence that schools focus on literacy and numeracy, at the expense of creative teaching.

The House of Commons Children, Schools and Families Committee (CSFC) published its report on the National Curriculum in April 2009. It described the Cambridge Review as 'very welcome', but said it contained 'extensive analysis of the problems but has not enough to say about what might be done in practice to address them' (CSFC 2009, p. 23). It continued:

> The Rose Review and the Cambridge Review both recognise that the primary curriculum is overly full, but neither offers a practical basis that appeals to us for reducing the load. As we have indicated, we would see greater merit in stipulating a basic entitlement for literacy and numeracy and offering general

> guidelines on breadth and balance to be interpreted by schools and teachers themselves.
>
> (CSFC 2009, p. 23)

Writing in *The Guardian,* Robin Alexander, Director of the Cambridge Review, described the committee's jibe that the Review offered 'a good analysis of the problems but no solutions' as 'bizarre'. He continued:

> Apart from the detailed proposals on curriculum aims, substance, structure, development and implementation, which the committee appears not to have noticed, other ideas from the Cambridge review appear, almost verbatim, in the committee's own recommendations: abandoning the national strategies in their present form; supporting local ownership; reconfiguring the roles of national agencies, local authorities and schools; making Curriculum Matters central to initial teacher training. More bizarre still, the committee's report includes as an appendix a comparison of the Rose and Cambridge curriculum reports, which says enough to contradict its criticisms of both of them.
>
> (Alexander 2009a)

It should have been possible to implement the new primary curriculum, following consultation on the IRPC's recommendations, in September 2012, as had been planned, but the Labour Party lost the 2010 general election, and the Rose Review was lost too.

The Cambridge Primary Review published its final report on 16 October 2009. The Review involved fourteen authors, sixty-six research consultants and a twenty-strong advisory committee at the University of Cambridge, led by Professor Robin Alexander. Its final report was based on twenty-eight research surveys, 1,052 written submissions and reports from dozens of regional meetings. Its seventy-five recommendations included that formal lessons should not start before the age of 6, SATs and league tables should be replaced with teacher assessments in a wider range of subjects, and the system of generalist primary teaching should be reviewed.

The Review's conclusions were backed by all the teacher unions but not taken up by the government. Ed Balls announced that every

4-year-old in England would be offered a school or nursery place so they could start full-time education a year earlier – the Review had recommended delaying the start of formal education until the age of 6.

Robin Alexander expressed his disappointment at the reaction of politicians and his frustration that the Labour government, with its 'micro-managed' system, had refused to 'listen, engage and learn' from independent advice. He said it was clear from the inaccuracies in their responses that neither government ministers nor their Conservative shadows had actually read it (Alexander 2009c).

Peter Mortimore, former director of the Institute of Education, wrote in *The Guardian*:

> Weep, Cambridge team. Your efforts to produce clear analyses and innovative ideas in the interest of fostering something better than political point-scoring, repetitive myths and ideological rigidity have been strangled at birth. Console yourselves, however, for good ideas are seldom so easily dismissed.
>
> The pity is that politicians, who pollsters tell us are only trusted by 13 per cent of the population, can so easily make such fools of themselves by endeavouring to close down all thinking outside their own. How much wiser to welcome new ideas and give civil society, including teachers – who are trusted by 82 per cent of the population – the chance to debate how best to improve the education of our youngest learners.
>
> (Mortimore 2009)

The National Curriculum

> The national curriculum is a set of subjects and standards used by primary and secondary schools so children learn the same things. It covers what subjects are taught and the standards children should reach in each subject.
>
> (www.gov.uk/national-curriculum/overview; accessed March 2014)

The twelve National Curriculum subjects are divided into core – English, maths and science (and Welsh for some Welsh schools)

– and foundation (see table on page 264). Schools are also required to teach RE to ages 5–18 and SRE for ages 11–18. Maintained schools must publish their curriculum on their websites. Academies do not have to follow the National Curriculum but must provide a 'broad and balanced' curriculum, including English, maths, science and RE. The National Curriculum is an entitlement, and so schools are free to offer other subjects in addition to the core and foundation subjects. The foundation stage (birth to age 5) has its own curriculum, based on areas of learning, rather than traditional subjects: communication and language; physical development; personal, social and emotional development; literacy; mathematics; understanding the world; and expressive arts and design.

The coalition government

After the coalition government came to power in 2010, Education Secretary Michael Gove detailed his plans for wide-ranging education reforms in a White Paper, *The Importance of Teaching*, in November 2010 (Department for Education 2010). He said that, under the Labour government, England's education system had lost its way and slipped down the rankings against its international competitors, but, under the new government, England would become an 'aspiration nation' once again. He called for a return to traditional values, with heads having more power over discipline and backing for schools to introduce blazer and tie uniforms, with traditional prefect and house systems.

The White Paper set out plans to reform and improve the quality of teacher training. Teaching schools, modelled on teaching hospitals, would be set up to showcase good teaching and provide more on-the-job training. Michael Gove said, 'There is no profession more noble, no calling more vital, no vocation more admirable than teaching, and this White Paper gives us the opportunity to become the world's leading education nation.' It also emphasised traditional values in education, with marks for good grammar and spelling in GCSEs and pupils encouraged to study more rigorous subjects, after what Mr Gove described as 'an alarming decline' in the number of pupils studying these subjects in recent years, suggesting too many schools opt for 'softer' subjects to try and boost their league table positions. A new 'English baccalaureate' would encourage pupils to take GCSEs in English, maths, a science, a modern language and a humanities subject. The new benchmark for an underperforming school would be fewer than 35 per cent of eligible pupils achieving five A*–C grades at GCSE. Previously, the benchmark had been 30 per cent, placing 439 schools (using 2009 data) in the category of underperforming. There was a clear tension between Mr Gove's desire to make schools freer, by trimming down the National Curriculum and the inspection process, and his desire to tell schools what to teach. Critics warned of the risk of a two-tier system, where academic subjects are prioritised over students wanting to take vocational courses, and academies and free schools are prioritised over other schools.

The new national curriculum

A new national curriculum will come into force from September 2014, although some aspects will be phased in later – the new National Curriculum for English, mathematics and science will come into force for Years 2 and 6 from September 2015. English, mathematics and science for KS4 will be phased in from September 2015.

The National Curriculum framework document (Department for Education 2013) states that:

> Every state-funded school must offer a curriculum which is balanced and broadly based and which:
>
> - promotes the spiritual, moral, cultural, mental and physical development of pupils at the school and of society; and
> - prepares pupils at the school for the opportunities, responsibilities and experiences of later life.

The school curriculum comprises all learning and other experiences that each school plans for its pupils. The National Curriculum forms one part of the school curriculum. All state schools are also required to make provision for a daily act of collective worship and must teach religious education to pupils at every key stage, and SRE to pupils in secondary education.

Maintained schools in England are legally required to follow the statutory National Curriculum, which sets out in programmes of study, on the basis of key stages, subject content for those subjects

Table 2.3 Complaints after the first draft, and the subsequent changes

Subject/Complaint	Response
Geography	
Failed to mention or allow study of the effects of climate change	Added explicit references to climate change at Key Stage 3, to 'understand how human and physical processes interact to influence, and change landscapes, environments and the climate'
English	
Concentrated exclusively on reading and writing, and ignored speaking skills	Speaking and listening skills restored to the curriculum at primary school level. By age 11, pupils expected to recite poetry from memory, and debate and present a topic
Design and technology	
Business leaders attacked the first draft as 'diluted', with the inclusion of 'life skills' such as bicycle maintenance	The DfE ripped up the first draft, replacing it with technology-based programme that includes 3D printers in secondary classrooms, and primary school pupils will design and test structures and circuits
Computing/ICT	
The ICT course was seen as dated	New computing syllabus to include teaching computer programming and creation and retrieval of digital data. Secondary school pupils to be taught coding. Internet safety to be taught from the age of five
Languages	
Languages that could be taught in primary schools restricted to French, German, Italian, Mandarin, Spanish, Latin or Ancient Greek	Lifted restrictions on languages, giving schools a free choice over which modern or ancient language pupils could study over the 4 years of Key Stage 2
History	
Exaggerated emphasis on British history and linear timescale	Cut back the amount of British history and simplified the early topics. Comparisons of historical figures, including Rosa Parks and Tim Berners-Lee, added

that should be taught to all pupils. All schools must publish their school curriculum by subject and academic year online. All schools should make provision for personal, social, health and economic education (PSHE), drawing on good practice. The National Curriculum sets out the minimum entitlement for every pupil, but schools are free to include other subjects or topics in designing their own programme of education.

The main changes are new proposals for teaching English, history and modern languages.

Schools will have more choice over which languages they teach, the much-criticised British emphasis in history lessons has been pared down, and the teaching of spoken language skills is restored after there was an outcry over its removal. Computing replaces ICT, and children will create and test their own computer programs, instead of learning word-processing. Under the new maths curriculum, 5-year-olds will be taught to read and write numbers up to 100, count in multiples of ones, twos, fives and tens, and learn addition and subtraction. Year 1 pupils will also be expected to do basic fractions, 2 years ahead of the previous curriculum, and algebra will be taught from age 10 (Adams 2013). The Department for Education said there had been unprecedented levels of interest in the consultation documents, with 17,000 responses. Michael Gove said the new curriculum would be more demanding, to help pupils keep pace with their peers overseas, while critics said that not enough effort had been made to design a curriculum for lower-achieving children and children with SEN.

Table 2.3 details some of the comments that were made in the consultation, and the changes made in response.

References

Adams, R. (2013) 'Tough and rigorous' new national curriculum published, *The Guardian,* 8 July. Available at: www.theguardian.com/education/2013/jul/08/new-national-curriculum-published (accessed October 2014).

Alexander, R. J. (2009a) What is the primary curriculum for? *The Guardian,* 7 April. Available at: www.theguardian.com/education/2009/apr/07/crib-sheet-april (accessed October 2014).

Alexander, R. J. (ed.) (2009b) *Children, Their World, Their Education: Final report and recommendations of the Cambridge Primary Review,* London: Routledge.

Alexander, R. J. (2009c) Schools ministers fail to learn lessons, *The Guardian*, 24 October. Available at: www.theguardian.com/commentisfree/2009/oct/24/cambridge-review-primary-education (accessed March 2014).

Alexander, R. J. and Flutter, J. (2009a) *Towards a New Primary Curriculum: A report from the Cambridge Primary Review. Part 1: Past and present*, Cambridge, UK: University of Cambridge Faculty of Education.

Alexander, R. J. and Flutter, J. (2009b) *Towards a New Primary Curriculum: A report from the Cambridge Primary Review. Part 2: The future*, Cambridge, UK: University of Cambridge Faculty of Education.

Atkinson, M. and Connolly, J. (2014) What is education for? Available at: www.greateducationdebate.org.uk/articles.what-is-education-for.html (accessed March 2014).

Baker, M. (2005) Why Tomlinson was turned down, *BBC News*, 26 February. Available at: http://news.bbc.co.uk/1/hi/education/4299151.stm (accessed March 2014).

Ball, S. J. (2013) *The Education Debate: Policy and politics in the twenty-first century*, Bristol, UK: Policy Press.

Bennett, N. (1976) *Teaching Styles and Pupil Progress*, London: Open University Press.

Blair, T. (2005) Education and regeneration, speech at Sedgefield, 18 November. Available at: http://collections.europarchive.org/tna/20060123125816/number10.gov.uk/page8547 (accessed March 2014).

Department for Children, Schools and Families (2009) *Independent Review of the Primary Curriculum* (The Rose Review). Available at: http://webarchive.nationalarchives.gov.uk/20100202100434/ http://publications.teachernet.gov.uk/eorderingdownload/primary_curriculum_report.pdf (accessed March 2014).

Department for Education (2004) *Final Report of the Working Group on 14–19 Reform* (The Tomlinson Report). Available at: www.education.gov.uk/publications/standard/publicationdetail/Page1/DfE-0976–2004 (accessed March 2014).

Department for Education (2010) White Paper *The Importance of Teaching*, Norwich, UK: TSO. Available at: www.gov.uk/government/uploads/system/uploads/attachment_data/file/175429/CM-7980.pdf (accessed March 2014).

Department for Education (2013) *The National Curriculum in England: Key Stages 1 and 2 framework document*. Available at: www.gov.uk/government/uploads/system/uploads/attachment_data/file/260481/PRIMARY_national_curriculum_11-9-13_2.pdf (accessed March 2014).

Department of Education and Science (1981) *The School Curriculum*, London: HMSO.

Dewey, J. (1938, 1963) *Experience and Education*, New York: Pocket Books (reprinted 1997).

Doyle, W. (1977) The uses of non-verbal behaviours – toward an ecological view of classrooms, *Merrill-Palmer Quarterly* 23(3): 179–92.

Expert Panel for National Curriculum Review (2011) *The Framework for the National Curriculum: A report by the Expert Panel for National Curriculum Review*, London: DfE. Available at: www.gov.uk/government/uploads/system/uploads/attachment_data/file/175439/NCR-Expert_Panel_Report.pdf (accessed March 2014).

Fuller, T. (ed.) (1989) *The Voice of Liberal Learning: Michael Oakeshott on education*, New Haven, CT: Yale University Press.

Garner, R. (2013) 100 Academics savage Education Secretary Michael Gove for 'conveyor-belt curriculum' for schools, *The Independent*, 19 March. Available at: www.independent.co.uk/news/education/education-news/100-academics-savage-education-secretary-michael-gove-for-conveyor belt-curriculum-for-schools-8541262.html (accessed March 2014).

Gillard, D. (1987) *Plowden and the Primary Curriculum: Twenty years on.* Available at: www.educationengland.org.uk/articles/04plowden.html (accessed March 2014).

Gove, M. (2009) What is education for? Speech to the RSA, 30 June. Available at: www.thersa.org/__data/assets/pdf_file/0009/213021/Gove-speech-to-RSA.pdf (accessed March 2014).

House of Commons Children, Schools and Families Committee (CSFC) (2009) *National Curriculum: Fourth Report of Session 2008–09 Volume 1*, HC 344-I, House of Commons Children Schools and Families Committee, London: TSO.

Moon, B. (2002) The origins of the national curriculum, in B. Moon, A. Shelton-Mayes and S. Hutchinson (eds) *Teaching, Learning and the Curriculum in Secondary Schools: A reader*, London: RoutledgeFalmer.

Mortimore, P. (2009) Missed opportunities and mad ideas: The government's legacy, *The Guardian*, 7 July. Available at: www.theguardian.com/education/2009/jul/07/peter-mortimore-education-schools (accessed October 2014).

Oakeshott, M. (1991) *Rationalism in Politics and Other Essays*, University Park, IL: Liberty Fund.

Plowden (1967) *Children and Their Primary Schools: Report of the Central Advisory Council for Education (England)*, London: HMSO.

Thomas, G. (2013) *A Very Short Introduction to Education*, Oxford, UK: Oxford University Press.

Wilby, P. (2008) Jim'll fix it, *The Guardian*, 5 August. Available at: www.theguardian.com/education/2008/aug/05/ofsted.primaryschools (accessed October 2014).

3 Inequality and education

All men are created equal but some are more equal than others.

(Popular saying based on the American Declaration of Independence)

There are still pockets of real inequality in education, despite the efforts of successive governments and the fact that the UK is considered the ninth wealthiest country in the world (although the UK is not a country) (World Bank 2014). Governments have long seen schools as the key to tackling social inequality, but the UK has a poor record when it comes to helping children from disadvantaged backgrounds achieve as well as their more advantaged peers – schooling outcomes appear to reflect or even magnify social differences.

> Children enter the school system from different backgrounds, have different experiences of education, and leave with very different results. Children from the poorest and most disadvantaged homes are most likely to attend the lowest performing schools and to achieve the poorest academic outcomes. Finding ways of breaking this chain of disadvantage, educational failure and restricted life chances remains a fundamental challenge. Despite extensive efforts by UK policymakers and practitioners, the weight of evidence still suggests that their strategies have not achieved a desired impact.
>
> (Kerr and West 2010, p. 7)

The Programme for International Student Assessment (**PISA**) is a worldwide study by the Organisation for Economic Co-operation and Development (OECD) in member and non-member nations of 15-year-old school pupils' performance in mathematics, science and reading, with a view to improving education policies and outcomes. It was first performed in 2000 and then repeated every 3 years; 520,000 15-year-old students, representing seventy-four nations and territories, participated in PISA 2010.

Exactly what we mean by social inequality and how to deal with it are very complex issues, but it is clear that children from different backgrounds leave school with different results. Looking into social inequality involves trying to understand how differences in individual or family or community circumstances can shape lives. These differences can relate to a range of factors – ethnicity, religion, gender, income, health, access to services, for example – and these factors can interact in complex ways.

Some data

In the foreword to *The Importance of Teaching*, Prime Minister David Cameron pointed out that, in relation to international competitors, we are not doing very well in terms of educational achievement:

> The truth is, at the moment we are standing still while others race past. In the most recent OECD PISA survey in 2006 we fell from 4th in the world in the 2000 survey to 14th in science, 7th to 17th in literacy, and 8th to 24th in mathematics.
>
> (Department for Education 2010, p. 3)

According to a report by the Department for Work and Pensions (DWP) (2011):

- 5.3 million people suffer from multiple disadvantages;
- 1.9 million children live in workless households in the UK;
- parents' income is a major predictor of children's future income, more so than in a number of other OECD countries.

Based on the targets in the Child Poverty Act, the latest statistics show:

- 2.8 million children (22 per cent) were in relative income poverty in 2008–9;
- 2.2 million children (17 per cent) were in both low income and material deprivation in 2008–9;
- 1.6 million children (12 per cent) were in absolute poverty in 2008–9;
- around 12 per cent of children lived in persistent low income (i.e. in relative poverty for 3 out of 4 years) between 2005 and 2008.

In 2009, the UK was in the bottom two-fifths for overall inequality, as rated by the OECD, and had a higher proportion of children living in workless households than almost any other European country (Department for Work and Pensions 2011).

Early years

Children born in black and minority ethnic families are almost twice as likely to live in poverty as children born into white families (Department for Work and Pensions 2011).

The EYFS profile requires practitioners to make an assessment of whether children are emerging, expected or exceeding against seventeen early learning goals (ELGs). Children are assessed to see whether they have reached a good level of development (GLD) in the prime areas of learning (personal, social and emotional development, physical development and communication and language) and the specific areas of mathematics and literacy (twelve of the seventeen ELGs). Scores across all seventeen ELGs are also recorded.

According to the figures for 2013 (Department for Education 2013), 52 per cent of pupils achieved a GLD; 60 per cent of girls achieved a GLD, compared with 44 per cent of boys. Compared with

The Child Poverty Act 2010 sets four income-based, UK-wide targets to be met by 2020. The targets are based on the proportion of children living in households with:

- relative low income (this measures whether the incomes of the poorest families are keeping pace with the growth of incomes in the economy as a whole) – the target is less than 10 per cent;
- combined low income and material deprivation (this is a wider measure of living standards) – the target is less than 5 per cent;
- absolute low income (this measures whether the poorest families are seeing their income rise in real terms) – the target is less than 5 per cent; and
- persistent poverty (this is defined by the Act as living in relative poverty for at least 3 of the last 4 years) – the target is to be set in regulations.

55 per cent of other pupils, 36 per cent of pupils eligible for FSM achieved a GLD – the difference was particularly evident in the literacy areas of learning.

For all ethnic groups, girls significantly outperformed boys; 47 per cent of Asian, 49 per cent of Chinese and 51 per cent of black pupils achieved a GLD. Pupils of Irish, Indian and mixed white and Asian ethnicity had the highest proportion achieving GLD, and Gypsy/Roma and travellers of Irish heritage had a significantly lower proportion.

The gap between children with SEN and others is 42 percentage points – the biggest difference is in communication and language, particularly the speaking ELG.

Fifty-four per cent of pupils whose first language is English achieved a GLD, compared with 44 per cent of others. Of pupils whose first language is not English, 50 per cent of girls achieved a GLD, compared with 37 per cent of boys.

Of children born in the autumn, 63 per cent achieve a GLD, compared with 40 per cent of those born in the summer (Department for Education 2013).

GCSE

Low educational attainment

Only one in three poor children (children who receive FSM) achieved five A*–C grades at GCSE in 2010, compared with the national average of approximately 60 per cent (Department for Work and Pensions/Department for Education 2012).

The 2013 GCSE results showed that 24.8 per cent of exams sat by girls were graded A* or A, compared with 17.6 per cent of those taken by boys. The gap of 7.2 percentage points was larger than at any time since the introduction of GCSEs in the late 1980s. Girls also achieved 72.3 per cent of papers graded C or better, compared with 63.7 of boys' papers – the biggest disparity in a decade. Following these results, the government launched a major inquiry into boys' education (Paton 2013).

A study in 2010 found that a child's social class is more likely to determine how they perform in school if they are white than if they come from an ethnic minority (Kapadia 2010). Analysing data from 2003 to 2007 showed that 31 per cent of white pupils on FSM achieved five A*–C grades, compared with 63 per cent of white pupils not eligible for FSM. This gap between social classes – 32 percentage points – is far higher for white pupils than for other ethnic groups. The gap is 7 percentage points for Bangladeshi pupils and 5 for Chinese pupils.

In 2009, around half of schools entered no pupils at all for the three sciences: schools in disadvantaged areas suffer most from this trend, as schools struggle to attract good teachers of academic subjects (Department for Education 2010).

A levels

According to research in 2009 (Garner 2009), scores of state schools have become 'no-go' areas for pupils taking traditional

A-level subjects such as maths, science, history, geography or languages. One in seven schools failed to enter a single candidate for A-level physics or geography that summer, one in thirteen failed to enter candidates for history, and one in seventeen failed to enter candidates for maths. There were warnings of a major class divide in the take-up of A-level subjects. Professor Alan Smithers, of the Centre for Education and Employment Research at Buckingham University, said the damaging impact of league tables was partly to blame. Schools in deprived areas were also more likely to have difficulty in recruiting high-quality maths, science and language teachers. The analysis of A-level results, carried out for the Conservative Party, showed most of the schools where no one studied history were in the poorest areas of the country and had twice the national average number of pupils receiving FSM.

At the same time, a study by Cambridge Assessment, which runs three exam boards, including Oxford, Cambridge and RSA Examinations (OCR), showed that children from the higher social classes were more likely to opt for subjects such as biology, further maths, English literature and languages, whereas those from lower-class backgrounds opted for subjects such as ICT, media studies, law and health and social care (Garner 2009). The Russell Group universities were open (Sinclair 2011) about how taking so-called 'soft' subjects at A level could affect a student's chances of admission to particular subjects or universities.

In the last year for which figures are available, of the 80,000 children eligible for FSM, only forty went to Oxbridge. More children from an individual public school, such as Winchester, went to top universities than from the entire population of young people eligible for FSM (Department for Education 2010).

Adults

Becoming unemployed

Children who grow up in poverty are up to 7 per cent less likely to be employed when in their 30s.

Being poor as an adult

People who were poor teenagers in the 1980s are almost four times more likely than their better-off peers to be poor as adults.

People with five or more good GCSEs earn on average 9–11 per cent more than similar people without these qualifications. Returns on A levels are higher, with a 14 per cent wage advantage for those who hold two or more. Parental income is an important predictor of child attainment, and child attainment is an important predictor of future income, and so society entrenches disadvantage (Department for Work and Pensions/Department for Education 2012).

Over the course of a lifetime, a graduate from a Russell Group university will earn on average £371,000 more than someone who left school without five good GCSEs. Young people with no qualifications are more likely to be NEET (not in education, employment or training), which is a major predictor of unemployment, low income, depression and poor mental health later in life. Apart from the link with health and well-being, educational inequality is linked to crime rates and the economy. In 2008, over 50 per cent of all males and 70 per cent of all females in the adult prison population had achieved no qualifications.

A baby born in Kensington and Chelsea has a life expectancy of 85 years, whereas, for a baby born in Islington, less than 5 miles away, it is around 75 years (Department for Work and Pensions 2011).

Social disadvantage

Defining and measuring poverty, or social disadvantage, is very difficult. According to the DWP (2011, p. 12), 'Poverty is about more than income; it is about a lack of opportunity, aspiration and stability'. A key issue is whether poverty describes an absolute state or relative inequality. Absolute definitions are based on access to the basic resources needed to sustain life – for example, food and shelter. Absolute poverty is a fairly rare phenomenon in richer countries, and so most indicators of poverty in such areas are based on relative indicators. Relative definitions are based on access to goods or activities that are thought essential or appropriate to particular societies at particular points in time. In the OECD study *Social Disadvantage and Educational Experiences* (Machin 2006), reducing the impact of social disadvantage on educational attainment was highlighted as a key area for action. The impact of socio-economic circumstances on young people's attainment was said to be more marked in the UK than in any of the other fifty-two countries surveyed.

Poverty is not just a cost to individuals. In 2013, a report by Hirsch estimated that child poverty costs the UK at least £29 billion each year. Of this, £20.5 billion is a direct cost to government, resulting from additional demands on services and benefits, as well as reduced tax receipts.

There is a sizeable body of evidence that educational achievement is significantly lower for children from disadvantaged backgrounds. A paper by Schütz *et al.* (2005) uses cross-country data from the Third International Mathematics and Science Study from 1995 and 1999. In fifty-three out of fifty-four countries, the family background effect was found to be statistically significant, with very large effects in some countries. The largest family background effect was found in England.

In a large-scale study in the UK and USA, Waldfogel and Washbrook (2011) divided families into quintiles by income. The typical family in the top quintile was found to have income of more than four times the poverty line in the UK and more than six times in the USA. The study found that children from the lowest income families in both countries were less likely to be 'school ready' than those from families with higher incomes. There were a number of reasons for this, including parenting styles, and because children from poorer families are less likely to attend nursery before starting school. The study found that early interventions such as Sure Start can be effective in giving children a better start.

In 2011–12, 2.3 million UK children (17 per cent) lived in homes with substantially lower than average income. This rises to 27 per cent (3.5 million) if measured after housing costs are paid. Children's campaigners say the true figure is even higher, and 300,000 more children were living in poverty than the previous year. The difference is due to the debate about measuring poverty. Both the government and the Labour Party prefer the measure of relative poverty, defined as when families have a net income below 60 per cent of median net disposable income, currently £250 a week or less. Using this measure, there has been no change in child poverty on the previous year, and the number of working-age adults in poverty also remained about the same level. The absolute measure of poverty is adjusted for inflation, and, on this measure, one in five children in the UK lives in poverty, and 300,000 more children fell below the poverty line compared with the year before (*BBC News*, 13 June 2013).

Child poverty is associated with living in particular regions or localities. A study by Hirsch (2004) found that 70 per cent of the most deprived areas of the UK are in the cities of Glasgow, London, Liverpool and Manchester. They contain 128 of the 180 wards where more than half of families are out of work and living on benefits. (A ward is a subdivision of a local authority area.) Evidence from such wards suggests young people most at risk of living in severe and persistent poverty are those in single-parent families, with parents working part-time or unemployed, in families with four or more children and with a mother aged under 25. Other high-risk groups in terms of living in poverty are those from ethnic minorities, disabled people, local authority housing association tenants and those with no formal educational qualifications (Department for Work and Pensions 2006).

Staying in education after the compulsory age – which is known to significantly enhance life chances and adult success – is also linked to social disadvantage and family background. People from poorer backgrounds who do enter post-compulsory education are less likely to study at 'elite' universities and more likely to enrol on vocational than academic courses. Even later in life, those who have low basic skills tend to be those who left school at the school-leaving age, have no educational qualifications and come from poorer and more disadvantaged social backgrounds. Participation rates in adult education across all countries are higher for the most educated, so that lifelong learning is biased towards those who already have education and reinforces educational inequalities.

Evidence has shown that there are clear differences between children from different backgrounds even before they start school, which has led to programmes such as Head Start in the US and Sure

Start in the UK (Machin 2006). As Machin points out, because cognitive and non-cognitive skills are key drivers of subsequent economic and social success or failure, and because these skills can be tracked to the early years, some have concluded that this is when education interventions need to occur; for example, Heckman and Wax (2004) stated, 'Like it or not, the most important mental and behavioural patterns, once established, are difficult to change once children enter school'. This is obviously a very controversial idea, as it seems to be suggesting that, if interventions do not take place at a very young age, they may be pointless. One thing we do not yet know conclusively is whether gains from interventions in the early years will be maintained if they are not supplemented by further interventions.

It is well known that family income affects education, but there is debate over whether it is the level of income itself that affects children's life chances or the factors that cause parents to have low incomes. Because we know that there is lower participation in higher education from those who grow up in poorer or disadvantaged circumstances, the reason is almost irrelevant, except that the reason matters when determining an appropriate policy response. Lower levels of participation in higher education from some groups may also come from different attitudes towards debt and concerns about having to repay student loans.

One of the problems is that many of the educational interventions have been relatively short term, often include small samples and have not been fully evaluated, or perhaps have been evaluated after a short time, so that we have little real information about benefits or impact. There are exceptions, and Machin (2006) mentions work by Lavy and Schlosser (2005) and Lavy (2002) evaluating a programme of remedial education for underperforming high school students in Israel. The programme was intended to improve 'matriculation' rates by providing more contact time with teachers and was found to be highly effective. This was in contrast to schemes in the US designed to reduce school dropout rates that were found to be ineffective, mainly because the funding was spread too thinly across a number of schools.

In 2012, the government launched a consultation to find a better way of defining poverty, saying that looking at child poverty simply in terms of income was not sufficient. The report (Department for Work and Pensions/Department for Education 2012) said:

> Income matters, but there is more to poverty and its impact on children than just the income of the household in which they live. Despite being the sixth wealthiest country in the world, in the UK in 2010, there were still children who experienced:
>
> - Material poverty – children whose families' incomes are squeezed by debts, who go to school hungry and who live in houses too cold to do homework, play and sleep well. 1.5 million children live in households where the adults say they cannot afford to keep the house warm.
> - Poverty of opportunity – children who have no access to books at home, fall behind at school, and can't afford to join in the school trips, sports and other activities which provide critical opportunities for children to learn. Five hundred thousand children live in households where the adults say they cannot afford to pay for their children to take part in school trips once a term.
> - Poverty of aspiration – there were 1.84 million (15.8 per cent) children in workless households in 2011. In addition to this, many children will never have known anyone who went onto higher education and, in some cases, they will have never been out of their immediate neighbourhood.

The role of policy

In its 2006 report (Machin 2006), the OECD argued that educational policies can be designed to offset the key aspects of social disadvantage that hold children back. There are various types of strategy or intervention that target all schools, or schools in disadvantaged areas, neighbourhoods and communities, or families, school systems and particular groups of pupils. Interventions that target all schools aim to improve the quality and effectiveness of schooling, particularly leadership and teaching. The underlying assumption is that some groups of children achieve less than others because of the limited effectiveness of some schools – improving schools will help all children. Examples are the National Literacy and Numeracy Strategies. It was announced in 2009 that these would be phased out in England, as improvements in test scores had tailed off, and the effectiveness of such approaches was being questioned.

Interventions that target schools in disadvantaged areas are also built on the assumption that ineffective schools contribute to low attainment, and children in these areas are doubly disadvantaged, with socio-economic disadvantage compounded by poor-quality schools. These interventions involve identifying areas where schools face challenging circumstances and then implementing additional programmes and targeting resources. Examples over recent years include Education Action Zones (EAZs), the Excellence in Cities (EiC) programme and the Leadership Incentive Grant. EAZs ran for 5 years and were designed to enable schools and local authorities in specific areas to work with community members and public and private sector organisations to tackle poor attainment levels. They sought to improve the quality of teaching and learning, address non-attendance and poor behaviour, increase parents' involvement in education and develop links with local businesses.

EAZs were followed by the EiC programme, which focused on practice within schools, using a range of activities around teaching and learning, behaviour and leadership. These included providing learning mentors and programmes for 'gifted and talented' students. Perhaps the best-known example is the London Challenge, which ran from 2003 to 2011. In 1997, only 16 per cent of pupils in London achieved five A*–C GCSEs, and there were real concerns about the differing levels of achievement between ethnic minority groups. By 2005, London's performance was above the national average and it has continued to improve: in 2010, Ofsted said London had a higher proportion of good and outstanding schools than anywhere else in England.

Other interventions focus on specific groups of children – white boys from working-class backgrounds, for example – and aim at closing the achievement gap. Interventions for younger children tend to be concerned with basic literacy, numeracy and social skills, but, for older pupils, may be about making the curriculum more likely to engage disaffected pupils or encouraging children from disadvantaged backgrounds to go to university.

Structural interventions come from the belief that restructuring schools and school systems can help to remove inequality. An example of this is the abolition of the 11 plus in Northern Ireland to equalise young people's access to opportunities at secondary school, but this has proved controversial. Examples in England are the creation of academies, free and trust schools, and forming schools into federations or chains.

Interventions that go beyond school recognise that children's academic performance cannot be seen in isolation from other aspects of their development and their family and community. Examples are the *Children's Plan,* which set out a framework for organising child and family services to support the values set out in *Every Child Matters* – namely, that all children should be healthy, stay safe, enjoy and achieve, make a positive contribution and achieve economic well-being. The Sure Start programme aims to tackle the factors that may disadvantage children in school before they reach school age. Extended, full service or community schools provide a wide range of services for children, families and the community, such as after school homework clubs and classes for adults (Kerr and West 2010).

There is an inherent difficulty in that many of these interventions have been (relatively) short term, and evaluations have been carried out based on relatively short periods of time. Most school-improvement research suggests that a period of at least 3–5 years is needed for interventions to really make a difference. If evaluations are carried out over a much longer period, the school population may have changed dramatically, and so it is difficult to separate out any impact from the intervention (Kerr and West 2010). In government terms, impact is usually measured in test scores. Some researchers suggest that results can be manipulated, for example by making changes to the school population or careful selection of which courses students follow. Critics say that, even if small improvements are achieved, they do not necessarily result in children from disadvantaged backgrounds going on to further or higher education (particularly to the so-called elite universities) or to high-status jobs, as attainment is only a proxy for improved life chances.

Results of evaluations can be contradictory, according to Kerr and West (2010), who give the example of the early evaluations of the literacy and numeracy strategies in England. Some studies showed positive results, seeing improvements in teacher effectiveness and student outcomes, but others were:

> sharply critical, seeing the strategies as encouraging impoverished teaching, being based on poor and limited evidence of what constitutes effective classroom practice, and widening the gap between low and high attaining pupils. For example, the 2009 Cambridge Primary Review argued that: improvements were 'negligible' in primary literacy, and 'relatively modest' in numeracy; gains in reading skills were at the expense of children's enjoyment of reading; the emphasis on testing was 'distorting' children's experiences of schooling; and that a much bigger gap persisted in England between high and low attaining children in reading, maths and science, than in many other countries.
>
> (Kerr and West 2010, p. 30)

According to Machin (2006), the evaluation evidence for EAZs is mainly qualitative (see Halpin *et al.* 2004, Ofsted 2003), and findings are largely negative. The report by Ofsted (2003) suggests that this was owing to an over-ambitious programme of activities that did not always focus specifically or radically enough on the challenges faced by schools in their areas. In contrast, evaluation evidence for the EiC programme shows that the policy has been effective in raising pupil attainment in examinations and increasing attendance at school. Initial results suggested that the EiC programme had a modest positive impact after about 2 years (Machin *et al.* 2004). In conclusion, available evidence suggests that some school-based policies can be effective in raising the performance of disadvantaged students and that this can be done cost-effectively. However, for programmes to be successful, it matters greatly how the extra resources are spent and that they are appropriately targeted.

In the report for the OECD, Machin (2006) argues that, although education can be a way out of social disadvantage, leading to better job prospects for young people and reducing income poverty in adulthood, educational failure can reinforce it. Students' test scores in lower secondary education are strongly shaped by family characteristics, and the expansion of university education most often benefits households with better-educated parents. Rather than equalising opportunities, education can be a powerful driver of social selection, leading to persistence of poverty and less equality of opportunities.

There is a lot of evidence to show that formal education plays a significant role in enhancing economic growth at the societal level and, at the individual level, raising employment probability and earnings, and it significantly impacts upon health, crime rates and other social outcomes. This evidence, however, looks at average effects and can mask individual outcomes.

Young people who live in poverty, however defined, are more likely not to enrol or to stay in education and are more likely to achieve poorer educational outcomes. Those who do not enrol or stay in education and those who achieve poor educational outcomes are more likely to experience poverty. These findings are consistent from one generation to the next (Bynner and Joshi 2002).

Theoretical perspectives

A review of research on the links between education and poverty (Raffo *et al.* 2007) identifies two broad theoretical perspectives – functionalist and socially critical (see Tables 3.1 and 3.2) – and three focus points:

- *micro-level* explanations focus on the individual;
- *meso-level* explanations focus on social contexts – family, school, community;
- *macro-level* explanations focus on social structures and inequality.

The functionalist perspective assumes that education plays an important role in the proper functioning of society, but the supposed benefits often do not materialise for individuals or groups from poorer backgrounds. The socially critical perspective assumes that education is potentially beneficial – the question is whether its benefits can be realised just by overcoming specific problems. The ability to engage with social and economic development is

Table 3.1 Theoretical perspectives

	Functionalist	**Socially critical**
Macro-level	Explanations tend to see the relationship between poverty and education resulting from underlying social structures mediated by meso- and micro-level factors	Education can challenge existing power structures and enable democratic development, but education in its form is implicated in creating, reproducing and enhancing inequality. Education is viewed as not having been developed to be enabling and educative for young people in a manner that might challenge existing structures
Meso-level	Focus is on (a) socially and culturally mediating impacts of peer group, family and neighbourhoods on young people and their understanding of, aspiration to and capability within schools and (b) processes of schooling and delivery of public services that have aided or constrained educational achievement for young people	Focus on neighbourhoods, community radicalism and different school curricula and cultures and the potential these have for changing power relations in education
Micro-level	Concerns about (a) individual identity and links to action and (b) notions of hereditary difference, especially around IQ	Focus is on the social, not the individual
Integration	Can be integrating explanations. May start at micro-level but integrate with factors at meso- and macro-level. Often focus on biopsychological perspectives that focus on human and self-development and interactive influences of genetics and environment	Perspective does not really integrate different levels of analysis

Note: Based on Raffo *et al.* 2007

Table 3.2 Research approaches that come from these perspectives

	Functionalist	**Socially critical**
Macro-level	Analysis of the impact of globalisation and resulting forms of social exclusion reflected in aspects of social ghettoisation, health inequalities, high levels of unemployment, poor housing, poor infrastructures for such individuals/communities. These factors are linked to and compound poor educational attainment Research evidence to show how taxation and reduction in levels of child poverty have contributed to educational investments by families experiencing poverty	Identification of global and national social and economic structures that determine educational provision and achievement Studies examine how power structures impact on the lives and educational experiences of particular groups Development of a critical analysis of functional policy interventions such as educational choice and the market
Meso-level	Globalisation has had an impact on the way families and communities living in poverty experience life. Of particular importance is the ghettoisation of particular neighbourhoods, with a lack of employment and effective public services that is likely to impact on self-esteem and lack of resources that results in poor health and diet, all of which, taken together, impact on the ability of families to support young people with education Different neighbourhoods and communities can provide differential levels of social and cultural capital that can alleviate some of the material aspects of poverty and provide improved opportunities for educational success for certain groups of young people	Studies that provide an account of the lives of people in neighbourhoods and communities Studies that have emphasised more radical and democratic approaches to running schools and classrooms that have challenged and changed existing power relations through, for example, the way pupils and teachers interact and the way school governance relates more directly to community needs

	Effective parenting linked to notions of educational aspirations of parents, educational support and stimulation for young people in the home. Secure and stable home environments and participation within school are central to young people's educational success	Interventions that focus on community radicalisation in 'answering back' and creating equitable educational opportunities
	Schools with particular strategies and approaches can make a difference in areas of 'challenge'. This is heavily influenced by the compositional make-up of schools, the constraints that poverty exerts on schools, the capability of teachers	
	Improved public-sector service delivery can improve families' and young peoples' access and achievement within school, but the ability to develop effective multi-agency working is constrained by professional and organisational boundaries	
Micro-level	Individuals are seen as having much greater levels of individual choice through enhancement of forms of social capital that might provide 'bridges' for young people into experiencing and valuing education. Recognises the importance of appropriately developed and culturally embedded mentoring programmes to provide opportunities for broadening networks of influence for young people	
	Focus on notions of constrained inherited capabilities and intelligence that pre-ordain an individual's ability to succeed in society. Provides few opportunities to ameliorate the position an individual has owing to the inherited capabilities with which they are born. The approach has been heavily criticised methodologically, theoretically and morally	

inherently inequitable, and education currently reflects unequal distribution of power and resources. Explanations from a socially critical perspective tend to focus on the macro-level, showing how privileged groups within society sustain a range of social structures, including the education system, to maintain their position, or the meso-level, exploring the ways that schools systematically marginalise certain groups of learners. Studies from a socially critical perspective often support activist approaches, for marginalised groups to 'answer back' and to recognise the contribution that those categorised as poor can and do make.

Current interventions

The pupil premium was introduced by the coalition government in April 2011 to raise the attainment of disadvantaged pupils and close the gap between them and their peers. It is additional funding allocated to schools to work with pupils who have been registered for FSM at any point during the last 6 years (known as 'Ever 6 FSM') or who have been in care for 6 months or longer. The premium is worth £935 per eligible child in primary school and £900 per eligible child in secondary school for 2013–14, increasing to £1,300 and £935, respectively, for 2014–15.

An analysis by think tank Demos of 2012–13 GCSE results (Demos 2014) found that government policies were failing to reduce educational inequality and the attainment gap was increasing, despite the pupil premium. Inequality was found to be rising in 72 out of 152 local authorities, with 66 having a larger attainment gap than before the pupil premium was introduced. In the last 2 years 1 in 12 local authorities has seen successive increases in its attainment gap, although 17 of the 20 local authorities with the narrowest attainment gaps are in London. The study found a 0.3 per cent increase in the national attainment gap, to 26.7 per cent. This jumps to 29.5 per cent when London schools are excluded from the data. The figure is based on the difference in educational attainment (the numbers achieving five or more GCSEs at A*–C) between pupils who receive FSM and their peers.

According to Demos, the study shows the scale of the challenge facing policymakers and raises questions about how best to use funding to improve standards. A spokesman for Demos said:

> The Pupil Premium is a good policy in theory. Targeting funds towards disadvantaged pupils makes sense and, given that the national attainment gap at primary school level is already around 20 per cent, the Government's decision to increase the amount going to primary schools is welcome.
>
> It will take time to see how successful the Pupil Premium will be. But we can't just throw money at the problem and expect these differences in attainment to disappear. Schools and local authorities need proper guidance – backed by robust research – on what works in closing the gap, including how to tackle the underlying causes both in and outside of school.

In an Ofsted survey of 262 school leaders in 2012, only 1 in 10 said that the pupil premium had significantly changed the way that they supported pupils from disadvantaged backgrounds. Funding was commonly being used to maintain or enhance existing provision, rather than to put in place new initiatives: more than two-fifths of the schools had used the pupil premium at least in part to fund new or existing teaching assistants, and more than one-quarter to fund new or existing teachers. A third of all schools said that they had used the funding to subsidise or pay for educational trips or residential visits. Around 1 in 6 said that they had used the funding to subsidise or pay for uniforms and equipment. It was clear to inspectors that, in some schools, spending was not entirely focused on the needs of the pupils for whom it was intended. A common view was that the pupil premium did not recognise the complexity of pupils' needs. Key recommendations were that school leaders should ensure pupil premium funding is not absorbed into mainstream budgets but targeted at designated children, so that they can clearly identify how the money is being spent. They should evaluate their pupil premium spending and spend it in ways known to be most effective. Schools should continue to encourage parents to apply for FSM, particularly where pride or stigma act as barriers.

A poll by the National Foundation for Education Research for the Sutton Trust in 2013 found that 67 per cent of school leaders – up from 52 per cent in 2012 – said their school consults research in deciding their pupil premium priorities (National Foundation for Education Research 2013). Two-fifths (43 per cent) of school leaders whose schools consider research evidence use the Sutton Trust/EEF Toolkit. However, fewer than 5 per cent say that they use the strategies shown by research to be most effective.

In 2011, the government announced pupil premium summer schools, designed to support disadvantaged children in the transition from primary to secondary school. Each participating secondary school was funded £250 per eligible pupil per week, for up to a 2 week programme. A survey of 21,065 Year 7 pupils from schools that had or had not been part of the summer school scheme found that most of the pupils who had attended a summer school made new friends, had fun and felt more confident about starting secondary school. Pupils from Asian backgrounds or those with English as an additional language (EAL) were significantly less likely to attend. Of those responding to the survey, 83 per cent of those offered a place at summer school had taken it up. Pupils who lived in deprived areas rated the summer schools more highly, and girls rated them more highly than boys. Recommendations from the survey included thinking about how the offer could be targeted for boys, and how children with SEN could be included more, as this group of pupils can find the transition between schools particularly challenging (Martin *et al.* 2013).

References

Bynner, J. and Joshi, H. (2002) Equality and opportunity in education: Evidence from the 1958 and 1970 birth cohort studies, *Oxford Review of Education* 28(4): 405–25.

Demos (2014) *A Tale of Two Classrooms: London results skew national picture as educational inequality on the rise.* Available at: www.demos.co.uk/press_releases/ataleoftwoclassroomslondonresultsskewnationalpictureaseducationalinequalityontherise (accessed March 2014).

Department for Education (2010) White Paper *The Importance of Teaching*, Norwich, UK: TSO. Available at: www.gov.uk/government/uploads/system/uploads/attachment_data/file/175429/CM-7980.pdf (accessed March 2014).

Department for Education (2013) Early Years Foundation Stage Profile Attainment by Pupil Characteristics, England 2013, SFR 47/2013.

Department for Work and Pensions (2006) *Households Below Average Income 1994/5 to 2004/5*, National Statistics Bulletin, March, Norwich, UK: TSO.

Department for Work and Pensions (2011) *A New Approach To Child Poverty: Tackling the causes of disadvantage and transforming children's lives*, Norwich, UK: TSO. Available at: www.gov.uk/government/uploads/system/uploads/attachment_data/file/177031/CM-8061.pdf (accessed March 2014).

Department for Work and Pensions/Department for Education (2012) *Child Poverty in the UK: The report on the 2010 target*, Norwich, UK: TSO. Available at: www.gov.uk/government/uploads/system/uploads/attachment_data/file/192213/child_poverty_in_the_uk_the_report_on_the_2010_target.pdf (accessed March 2014).

Garner, R. (2009) Scandal of class divide at A level, *The Independent*, 19 August.

Halpin, D., Power, S., Whitty, G. and Gerwirtz, Z. (2004) Area-based approaches to educational regeneration: The case of the English Education Action Zones experiment, *Policy Studies* 25: 75–85.

Heckman, J. and Wax, A. (2004) Home alone, *Wall Street Journal*, 23 January, p. A14.

Hirsch, D. (2004) *Strategies Against Poverty: A shared road map*, York, UK: Joseph Rowntree Foundation.

Hirsch, D. (2013) *An Estimate of the Cost of Child Poverty in 2013*. Report for the Child Poverty Action Group. Available at: http://cpag.org.uk/sites/default/files/Cost%20of%20child%20poverty%20research%20update%20(2013).pdf (accessed March 2014).

Kapadia, R. (2010) *Ethnicity and Class: GCSE performance*. Paper presented at BERA conference, University of Warwick, 1–4 September.

Kerr, K. and West, M. (eds) (2010) *Social Inequality: Can schools narrow the gap?* (Insight 2). Macclesfield, UK: BERA.

Lavy, V. (2002) Evaluating the effect of teachers' performance incentives on pupils' achievements, *Journal of Political Economy*, 110(6): 1286–317.

Lavy, V. and Schlosser, A. (2005) Targeted remedial education for underperforming teenagers: Costs and benefits, *Journal of Labour Economics*, 23(4): 839–74.

Machin, S. (2006) *Social Disadvantage and Education Experiences*, OECD. Available at: www.oecd.org/els/soc/36165298.pdf (accessed March 2014).

Machin, S., McNally, S. and Meghir, C. (2004) Improving pupil performance in English secondary schools: Excellence in Cities, *Journal of the European Economics Association*, 2(2–3): 396–405.

Martin, K., Sharp, C. and Mehta, P. (2013) *The Impact of the Summer Schools Programme on Pupils*, DfE Research Brief. Available at: www.nfer.ac.uk/publications/ESSP04/ESSP04researchbrief.pdf (accessed March 2014).

National Foundation for Education Research (2013) *Teacher Voice Omnibus: Spending priorities for the pupil premium*, March. Available at: www.suttontrust.com/our-work/research/item/nfer-teacher-voice-omnibus/ (accessed March 2014).

Ofsted (2003) *Excellence in Cities and Education Action Zones: Management and impact*, London: Ofsted.

Ofsted (2010) *London Challenge*, London: Ofsted. Available at: www.ofsted.gov.uk/resources/london-challenge (accessed March 2014).

Ofsted (2012) *The Pupil Premium: How schools are using the Pupil Premium funding to raise achievement for disadvantaged pupils*, London: Ofsted. Available at: www.ofsted.gov.uk/resources/pupil-premium (accessed March 2014).

Paton, G. (2013) GCSE results 2013: Girls stretch to record lead over boys, *The Telegraph*, 22 August.

Raffo, C., Dyson, A., Gunter, H., Hall, D., Jones, L. and Kalambouka, A. (2007) *A Review of Research on the Links Between Education and Poverty*, York, UK: Joseph Rowntree Foundation.

Schütz, G., Ursprung, H. and Woessman, L. (2005) *Education Policy and Equality of Opportunity*, CESifo Working Paper 1518.

Sinclair, J. (2011) Russell Group universities shun 'soft' subjects, *The Independent*, 4 February. Available at: www.independent.co.uk/news/education/education-news/russell-group-universities-shun-soft-subjects-2204296.html (accessed March 2014).

Waldfogel, J. and Washbrook, E. (2011) Early years policy, *Child Development Research*: 1–12. Available at: http://eprints.lse.ac.uk/43728/1/Early%20years%20policy(lsero).pdf (accessed March 2014).

World Bank (2014) *Purchasing Power Parities and Real Expenditures of world economies: Summary of results and findings of the 2011 International Comparison Program*. Available at: http://siteresources.worldbank.org/ICPINT/Resources/270056–1183395201801/Summary-of-Results-and-Findings-of-the-2011-International-Comparison-Program.pdf (accessed March 2014).

4 Special educational needs and inclusion

Inclusion should mean being involved in a common enterprise of learning, rather than being necessarily under the same roof.

(Mary Warnock)

Ideas around SEN and inclusion have been, and still are, at the root of many debates in education. Inclusion is a difficult concept, as it tries to reconcile providing a common entitlement to all children with accommodating individual differences, particularly difficult in an education system with an emphasis on standards and outcomes.

In 2012–13, 1.55 million children in the UK had SEN, and 229,390 of these had statements of SEN. Boys are two and a half times more likely than girls to have a statement at primary school, and nearly three times more likely at secondary school. Pupils with SEN are much more likely to have FSM than others. Black pupils are more likely, and Chinese pupils less likely, to have SEN than other ethnic groups. In January 2012, 71.5 per cent of the 29,020 looked-after children had SEN, compared with 19.8 per cent of all pupils, meaning that looked-after children were approximately three and a half times more likely to have SEN compared with all children. Looked-after children were more than ten times more likely than all pupils to have statements of SEN (Department for Education 2013).

A pupil has a **statement** of SEN when a formal assessment has been made. A document setting out the child's needs and the extra help they should receive is in place.

What are special educational needs?

Children with SEN are those whose educational needs *are not met adequately by ordinary provision.* This is about 16–20 per cent of children in the school system. SEN has recently come to be more associated with disabilities – physical and sensory disabilities and also cognitive, language and emotional/behavioural difficulties. There are other children whose needs may not be met by ordinary provision, such as those with EAL or those with high abilities or talents who are considered 'gifted and talented'. Although these children may also have particular needs in terms of their education, the term SEN does not apply to them.

Current legislation says that a child has SEN when they have a 'learning difficulty' that calls for 'special provision'. 'Special provision' is something different from, or additional to, what is normally provided in schools. Historically, special provision was found in special and separate settings, such as special schools, classes or units. Today, with moves towards inclusion, the provision tends to mean support for learning in mainstream classes or inclusive settings and making the curriculum and teaching meet the needs of a range of learners.

Some educationists argue that we should not refer to educational needs but barriers to learning. To take a very simple example, if a child who uses a wheelchair cannot access a school building, the building access is a barrier, and the problem is with the building, not the child. There are issues around labelling children – in the *Index for Inclusion,* Booth and Ainscow (2011 [2002]) argue that the term 'special educational needs' has considerable limitations, confers a label that can lead to lowered expectations and deflects attention away from difficulties experienced by others who do not have this label.

Models of disability

The two models that have most influenced recent thinking about disability are the medical (or deficit) and social models. The medical model sees disabled people as the problem – the problem is within them, and they need to change and adapt to the circumstances in which they find themselves. In contrast, the social model sees disability as being caused by the barriers in society and the way society is organised, so that society discriminates against people and excludes them from involvement and participation.

Other models are the administrative model, which focuses on disability as an assessment process for identifying needs, and the charity model, which sees disability as a personal tragedy. The bio-psychosocial model recognises the complexity of definition and includes social, biological and psychological factors.

Inclusion

Although the current policy in England is that, as far as possible, all children should be educated in a mainstream school, there is no agreed definition of inclusion – a concept that can be debated at many levels. At the theoretical level, Low (1996, p. 2, in Croll and Moses 2000) makes the point that: 'Inclusion as an educational ideal has the "moral high ground", but at the day to day level of the thinking that informs educational policy its position is much less secure'.

Mary Warnock suggests that, although the idea of inclusion comes from 'hearts in the right place', it may have difficulties in practice: for example, if an emotionally disturbed child in a mainstream class frequently disrupts the learning of others, or if a child with Asperger's Syndrome is subject to bullying, so that he feels emotionally excluded, even though he is in the same classroom.

Expressed in the simplest way, there are three viewpoints on inclusion as it relates to children with SEN:

- children with SEN should be educated in special schools, which can best meet their needs;

- most children should be educated in mainstream schools, but with some children in special schools that can meet the severest needs;
- all children should be educated in mainstream schools.

Lunt and Norwich (1999, p. 32) highlighted a range of perspectives:

- Bailey's (1998) view that it is about learning in the same place, on the same curriculum as others;
- Tomlinson's (1997) view that it is not necessarily about being in the same place and on the same curriculum;
- Booth and Ainscow's (1998) view that it is not a state at all, but an unending process of increasing participation;
- Thomas's (1997) view that it is about accepting all children;
- Sebba and Sachdev's (1997) view that it is about schools responding and restructuring their provision;
- Florian's (1998) view that opportunity to participate in inclusion is about active involvement and choice and not something done to the disabled.

The first two of these points highlight a continuing argument, which is to what extent the place where a child is educated defines whether practice is inclusive. From a human rights approach that recognises the rights of all children to inclusive education, which goes with the responsibility of governments to provide it, Rustemier (2002) argues that the existence of special schools is a form of institutional discrimination. Others argue that inclusion is not just about location.

> The concept of inclusion springs from hearts in the right place. Its meaning, however, is far from clear, and in practice it often means that children are physically included but emotionally excluded. . . . Inclusion should mean being involved in a common enterprise of learning, rather than being necessarily under the same roof.
>
> (Warnock 2005, p. 36)

Farrell's (2000) preferred alternative was for 'educational inclusion', as this removes the emphasis on where education takes place and focuses instead on engagement in an appropriate educational experience, implying that the child's SEN are met and s/he is part of the educational community.

Ainscow *et al.* (2006) suggest that inclusion can be defined in two ways – a descriptive definition of inclusion reports on the variety of ways inclusion is used in practice, whereas a prescriptive definition indicates the way the concept is used. They developed a typology of six ways of thinking about inclusion:

- inclusion as a concern with disabled students and others categorised as 'having special educational needs';
- inclusion as a response to disciplinary exclusion;
- inclusion in relation to all groups seen as being vulnerable to exclusion;
- inclusion as developing the school for all;
- inclusion as 'education for all';
- inclusion as a principled approach to education and society.

(Ainscow *et al.* 2006, p. 15)

The Green Paper *Excellence for all Children* stated:

> There are strong educational, as well as social and moral grounds for educating children with special educational needs with their peers. We aim to increase the level and quality of inclusion within mainstream schools, while protecting and enhancing specialist provision for those who need it.
>
> (Department for Education and Employment 1997, p. 43)

However, according to Croll and Moses (2000, p. 2), in declaring a commitment to inclusion but preserving the role of special schools, the Department for Education and Employment (DfEE) was perhaps guilty of 'expressing strong support for the principle of inclusion while, at the same time, qualifying this support to the point where it is hard to see any particular policy direction being indicated'.

In 2004, *Removing Barriers to Achievement* was clear that there was a continued role for special schools that could provide 'education for children with the most severe and complex needs and sharing their specialist skills and knowledge to support inclusion in mainstream schools' (Department for Education and Skills 2004, p. 26). It also made it clear that inclusion is not just about location: 'Inclusion is about much more than the type of school that children attend: it is about the quality of their experience, how they are helped to learn, achieve and participate fully in the life of the school' (Department for Education and Skills 2004, p. 25).

There is confusion, particularly for practitioners, in the duality of mainstream and special provision. As Evans and Lunt (2002, p. 3) ask:

> But what does inclusion mean in practice? Does it mean that the local school should provide for 100 per cent of its local pupils, for 99 or 98 per cent, or some other proportion? Does it mean that all pupils should be educated together in the same class or in the same school, and with the same teacher? Should particular schools include particular pupils, thus enabling pupils to attend mainstream though not their local school? Does it include on-site or off-site units?

As Cole (2005, p. 31) points out, 'If there is no consensus about what inclusion means then it is to be expected that the aims and motivations of various parties may differ and even conflict'.

There is also an issue in relation to inclusion about who is being included. Corbett (2001) argues that inclusion means responding to individual needs, not special needs, and suggests that, in the past, there has been a view that, 'Inclusion meant bringing those outside ("the special") into the privilege of mainstream without acknowledging that many mainstream learners can feel excluded by a restricted curriculum, inflexible pedagogy and hierarchical ethos' (Corbett 2001, p. 1).

Booth (1999, p. 164) similarly argued:

> The concept [SEN] focuses attention on the difficulties experienced by some learners and deflects attention from those experienced by others and deflects attention from those experienced by others as well as the developments in school

> cultures, policies, curricula and teaching approaches that will minimise educational difficulties for all. It deskills teachers by encouraging them to think that many learners need specialist teaching. Its use helps to marginalise inclusion policies from general education policies and to further fragment them in documents about special education needs, social inclusion and exclusion and ethnic minority education.

In relation to schools and education, inclusion is a term that still causes much debate. For many people, inclusion refers to all children and their rights and entitlement to education, but, for others, inclusion is still very much rooted in SEN. There is a strong argument that, if schools are inclusive and cater for the needs of children with SEN, they will be better schools for all children. Ofsted defines inclusion as the process of educating children with SEN alongside their peers in mainstream schools (Ofsted 2003), but a focus on children who are seen as having SEN can ignore or marginalise the needs of other children, for example those from minority ethnic groups, those whose first language is not English or traveller children. The National Curriculum views inclusion as the creation of 'learning environments . . . which respond to pupils' diverse needs' and provide opportunities:

> for all pupils to achieve, including boys and girls, pupils with special educational needs, pupils with disabilities, pupils from all social and cultural backgrounds, pupils of different ethnic groups including travellers, refugees and asylum seekers, and those from diverse linguistic backgrounds.
>
> (Department for Education and Employment/Qualifications and Curriculum Authority 1999, p. 31)

In *Evaluating Educational Inclusion* (2000), Ofsted defined inclusion as being far broader than pupils with SEN:

> Educational inclusion is more than a concern about any one group of pupils such as those pupils who have been or are likely to be excluded from school. Its scope is broad. It is about equal opportunities for all pupils, whatever their age, gender, ethnicity, attainment and background. It pays particular attention to the provision made for the achievement of different groups

of pupils within a school. Throughout this guidance, whenever we use the term different groups it could apply to any or all of the following:

- girls and boys;
- minority ethnic and faith groups, travellers, asylum seekers and refugees;
- pupils who need support to learn English as an additional language (EAL);
- pupils with special educational needs;
- gifted and talented pupils;
- children 'looked after' by the local authority;
- other children, such as sick children, young carers, those children from families under stress, pregnant schoolgirls and teenage mothers; and
- any pupils who are at risk of disaffection and exclusion.

(Ofsted 2000, p. 4)

In other words, almost all children.

Inclusion in education cannot be considered in isolation, as it sits within a political and societal context. Loxley and Thomas (2001) suggest that the notional commitment to inclusion in England and Wales, at both national and local (school) level, sits within a larger scenario, 'which many would interpret as antithetical to inclusion' (p. 291), producing a central tension and inconsistencies. There is a particular problem in some schools caused by a policy to admit and work with any child, whatever their difficulties or level of ability, and the pressure to achieve results and do well in league tables.

Because of these debates, some writers have started to talk about the concept of 'inclusive education', which has its roots in the idea of comprehensive schooling, where pupils are not selected on the basis of ability, gender or ethnicity. Inclusive education involves:

- the participation of all children in local schools;
- school-wide modifications and restructuring of the curriculum, teaching and the school culture;
- encouraging a sense of belonging and acceptance of all children;
- not being about where children are educated but how, in social and curriculum terms.

How did we get here?

Looking back at where we have come from helps us to understand where we are now and the continuing debates. We have come a long way – though many would say, not far enough – since the Egerton Commission pronounced in 1889 that:

> The blind, deaf and dumb and the educable class of imbecile . . . if left uneducated, become not only a burden to themselves but a weighty burden on the state. It is in the interests of the state to educate them, so as to dry up, as far as possible, the minor streams which must ultimately swell to a great torrent of pauperism.
>
> (Riddell 2002, p. 4)

It is uncomfortable to note that the 1921 Education Act required local authorities to record the numbers of 'feeble-minded' and 'backward' children, so that separate education could be provided.

In 2010, Hodkinson said that special education in England had been subject to rapid development over the previous 25 years, particularly in relation to inclusion. He suggested that the 'current push for the implementation of inclusive education' could be an example of policy development and philosophical thought outpacing practice, so that the most vulnerable learners might be 'crushed by the weight of political policy, philosophical thought and ideological doctrine that seemingly dominate the current educational discourse' (Hodkinson 2010, p. 61).

In the nineteenth century, there were four levels of special condition – idiot, imbecile, feeble-minded and moral-defective. Idiots were seen as ineducable and excluded from the education system, imbeciles were placed in asylums, and the others were placed in special schools. Discourses on education at that time produced the medical and charitable models of disability. The medical model viewed children's development and behaviour in terms of internal biological differences, so that conditions were within-child defects or deficits, and external factors such as poverty had no bearing on the disability. The charitable model saw disabled children as tragic figures to be pitied.

At the beginning of the twentieth century, ideas were emerging that it was not just children with very evident disabilities – the blind and the deaf, for example – who needed special education, but any children who were 'different'. The legal context for integration and inclusive education in England and Wales began with the Education Act 1944, which stipulated that children with severe disabilities were to be educated in special schools wherever possible, although those with less serious disabilities could be educated in mainstream schools. It also gave an entitlement to education for all, except those deemed ineducable. It was not until 1971 that all school age children in England and Wales were entitled to an education.

The Committee of Inquiry chaired by Baroness Warnock, which reported in 1978, was a landmark, following the longest-ever investigation into special education in England, Wales and Scotland. The Committee noted that the labelling of children requiring special education used negative terms – *educationally sub-normal* in England, and in Scotland *mentally handicapped*. Definitions of special education, according to the Warnock Committee, ignored the fact that many children, at some time during their school career, need extra help: the Warnock Report was important because it stated that about one in six children at any time and one in five children at some point in their school careers would need some kind of special educational provision. It emphasised that SEN and the provision required to meet these are not fixed. The Committee's research suggested that only 2 per cent of children needed separate, specialist education provision, with a further 18 per cent requiring special provision in mainstream schools. The Committee was the first to use the term *special educational needs*, which had the more positive effect of moving the emphasis to needs rather than within-child defects and deficits, saying:

> We have adopted the concept of SPECIAL EDUCATIONAL NEED, seen not in terms of a particular disability, which a child may be judged to have, but in relation to everything about him, his abilities as well as his disabilities – indeed all the factors which have a bearing on his educational progress.
>
> (Department of Education and Science 1978, p. 37)

When the Warnock Committee was set up in 1974, it was not to include in its deliberations dyslexia, or children 'who suffered from nothing except social deprivation' (Warnock 2005, p. 25) or who did not have English as their first language. At that time, dyslexia was thought to be an invention of the middle classes to cover up the fact that their children had difficulties with reading or writing. The issue around speaking English was partly that there was a Home Office scheme to fund the teaching of English as a second language, and also that being designated as having SEN was still thought derogatory, and so using this status for someone just because they were not a native English speaker would be racist. There was a belief at that time that the social conditions in which a child lived were not a matter for education. It was held that true educational equality could only come if schools treated all children as the same, each a *tabula rasa* on which good teaching could make its mark. Margaret Thatcher's Secretary of State for Education, John Patten, later caused an uproar when he said that a child's background was totally irrelevant to his or her educational potential. It is easy to see what he meant, and clearly teachers must not allow what they know of a child's background to colour their view of the child's potential, but we know now that socially deprived children tend to have more educational difficulties than other children. This is why, for example, the education of looked-after children now has more focus, but the refusal to consider social deprivation among the causes of SEN is firmly embedded in the 1981 Act (Warnock 2005).

The Education Act 1981 reflected the findings and recommendations of the Warnock Report and heralded a period of rapid educational change. Between 1980 and 2005, thirty-four Education Acts were passed, with hundreds of accompanying circulars, regulations and statutory instruments. The 1981 Act required local authorities to provide suitable support and resources to meet needs identified in a statement of SEN. For the first time, this imposed a duty on local authorities to ensure that children with SEN were educated in mainstream schools, so long as:

- this was in accord with their parents' wishes;
- the child's SEN could be met in the mainstream school;

- the education of other children in the school would not suffer;
- the placement was compatible with the efficient use of resources.

(Hornby *et al.* 1995, p. 3)

A national survey in 1985 (Centre for Studies on Inclusive Education 1986) found that, in their literature, only 11 per cent of English LEAs referred to the need to integrate children with SEN in mainstream schools, only one-third of LEAs told parents/carers that they had a right to be fully consulted, and only 14 per cent referred to parents/carers in the assessment process. In these and other areas of LEA information for parents/carers, the government's intention had been that all figures would be 100 per cent.

According to Roaf and Bines (1989), the changes following the Warnock Report illustrated a shift in emphasis from medical or psychological criteria of assessment towards an 'educational, interactive and relative approach' (p. 6), taking into account all factors that have a bearing on educational progress. This social model of disability sees SEN not in individual or deficit terms, but in relation to the requirements of the curriculum and schooling, meaning that inappropriate teaching materials and techniques could be seen as having generated, or at least exacerbated, learning difficulties experienced by learners.

In contrast to the American system, which stresses disability, since Warnock the UK education system has tended to focus on need. Norwich, for example, suggests children can have a range of different needs:

- *individual needs* arising from characteristics which are unique to the child and different from all others
- *exceptional needs* arising from characteristics shared by some children (eg visual impairment or high musical abilities)
- *common needs* arising from characteristics shared by all (e.g. the need to belong).

(Norwich 1996; original emphasis)

The Warnock Committee's emphasis on need was intended to bring an end to the categorisation that had existed previously, but the idea of needs is still deficit based (Tomlinson 1982). In the event,

SEN became a label in itself, a way of categorising children as if they were a homogeneous group. As long ago as 1989, Pumfrey and Mittler wrote an article suggesting that 'the concept of SEN has now outgrown its usefulness and should be laid to rest', taken up again by Mittler (2000). It is also open to interpretation, so that what is defined as SEN (and thus requiring additional support) in one school or area is not so defined in another. A report by the Centre for Studies on Inclusive Education (CSIE) in 2005 found 'disturbing' local variation – pupils with statements of SEN in one local authority area were twenty-four times more likely to be placed in segregated education than those in another area. Although it is often thought that the Warnock Committee strongly promoted the idea of integration or inclusion, it did not. Its clear support for special schools is seen by some as at least partly to blame for the slow progress in integration and inclusion.

The *Salamanca Statement* (UNESCO 1994) went beyond SEN and was a catalyst for much of the education policy in the UK that supported more inclusive practices in schools:

> The guiding principle that informs this Framework is that schools should accommodate all children regardless of their physical, intellectual, social, emotional, linguistic or other conditions. This should include disabled and gifted children, street and working children, children from remote or nomadic populations, children from linguistic, ethnic or cultural minorities and children from other disadvantaged or marginalised areas or groups.
>
> (UNESCO 1994, p. 6)

The *Salamanca Statement*'s connection with the UN gives it an influential human rights context. This could be seen as problematic (for example, Low 1996), because the 'moral high ground' of the human rights approach could be said to have limited debate – inclusion is morally and socially right and thus incontestable. The stance taken by the CSIE, for example, is that all children have a right to an inclusive education. The notion of rights, however, is controversial. Others would argue, for example, that children in mainstream education have a right not to have their education disrupted by a child with behaviour problems.

The *Code of Practice on the Identification and Assessment of Special Educational Needs* was published in 1994 (Department for Education 1994). It sought to establish a national policy, with schools taking responsibility for as many children with SEN as possible, and LEAs undertaking their statutory duties, although there was a problem, as many LEAs did not have the money to fund demands for additional resources. The Code established a continuum of needs and re-emphasised that all children were to have access to a broad and balanced curriculum, including the National Curriculum, and most children should be in a mainstream school. It established the need for an SEN co-ordinator (SENCo) in every school. Each child with SEN was to have an individual education plan (IEP) – combined with the introduction of a five-stage model, this placed a very significant administrative and bureaucratic burden on teachers and schools.

The Disability Discrimination Act 1995 did not mention inclusion or access to education, leading to a major debate about the government's continuing tolerance of discrimination against disabled children and young people. It was not until 2001 that the Act was amended by the Special Educational Needs and Disability Act to cover every aspect of education (Ellis *et al.* 2008). In 2001, *Inclusive Schooling* (Department for Education and Skills 2001a) provided statutory guidance, including 'Mainstream education cannot be refused on the grounds that the child's needs cannot be provided for within the mainstream sector' (p. 9), placing a duty on schools to be able to accommodate every child.

The *Special Educational Needs Code of Practice* (Department for Education and Skills 2001b), which was revised from the Code published in 1994, emphasised a stronger right for children with SEN to be educated in a mainstream school and replaced the stages from the original Code with Early Years/School Action, Early Years/School Action Plus and Statements of Special Educational Need.

The Code (Department for Education and Skills 2001b) suggests that all schools will make provision for increased curriculum differentiation, curricular adaptations and pastoral or disciplinary procedures, dependent on the child's strengths and weaknesses, through their cycle of observation, assessment, planning and

Table 4.1 Three levels of SEN

SEN level	Level of action	Approx. % of school population
School action	Usually arises from concern expressed by class teacher or form tutor. Responsibility for extra support lies with class teacher, who works out action to be taken with SENCo. Additional provision comes from within school's resources	9% in mainstream schools
School Action Plus	IEP drawn up with the support of outside support services, e.g. social services, educational psychologists. SENCo will work with class teacher, parents, external agencies to draw up IEP. Additional provision comes from within school's resources	6% in mainstream schools
Statement	Multi-professional assessment prepared by LEA after being triggered by school or parents/carers. Wide involvement of parents, teachers, external agencies. Statement is a legal contract between LEA and parents and involves additional funding to support the child in school, often through the provision of a teaching assistant	1.7% in mainstream schools; 1.3% in special schools

review. These arrangements apply to all children and are not part of special provision. The Code states:

> The assessment process should always be fourfold. It should focus on the child's learning characteristics, the learning environment that the school is providing for the child, the task and the teaching style. It should be recognised that some difficulties in learning may be caused or exacerbated by the school's learning environment or adult/child relationships. This

> means looking carefully at such matters as classroom organisation, teaching materials, teaching style and differentiation in order to decide how these can be developed so that the child is enabled to learn effectively.
>
> (Department for Education and Skills 2001b, p. 44)

This acknowledges the ecological perspective (see Chapter 4) that it is the structure of schools as organisations rather than the differences between individual pupils that creates SEN. It places an emphasis on schools and teachers examining and developing their policy and practice, recognising that human strengths and weaknesses can only be understood in the context in which they occur. The language of School Action (Plus) emphasised that the focus was on the school's response necessary to ensure pupils are making adequate progress.

Every Child Matters, published in 2003, followed the inquiry into the death of Victoria Climbié and made a commitment to reform children's services to prevent vulnerable children 'falling through the cracks between different services' (Department for Education and Skills 2003, p. 5). Taking a more holistic view of the lives of children and young people, it identified five outcomes all children should achieve:

- being healthy;
- staying safe;
- enjoying and achieving;
- making a positive contribution;
- economic well-being.

(Department for Education and Skills 2003, pp. 6–7)

In 2005, Baroness Warnock made what was widely publicised as a U-turn when she said that: 'There is increasing evidence that the ideal of inclusion, if this means that all but those with the most severe disabilities will be in mainstream schools, is not working' (Warnock 2005, p. 32).

And so, inclusion should be rethought:

> If it is too much to hope that it will be demoted from its present position at the top of the list of educational values, then at least

> let it be redefined so that it allows children to pursue the common goals of education in the environment within which they can best be taught and learn.
>
> (Warnock 2005, p. 50)

Stating that, 'Inclusion should mean being involved in a common enterprise of learning, rather than being necessarily under the same roof' (2005, p. 36), Warnock suggested that the government should consider the definition of inclusion suggested by the National Association of Head Teachers in 2003:

> Inclusion is a process that maximises the entitlement of all pupils to a broad, relevant and stimulating curriculum, which is delivered in the environment that will have the greatest impact on their learning. All schools, whether special or mainstream, should reflect a culture in which the institution adapts to meet the needs of its pupils and is provided with the resources to enable this to happen . . . Inclusive schooling is essential to the development of an inclusive society. It involves having an education service that ensures that provision and funding is there to enable pupils to be educated in the most appropriate setting. This will be the one in which they can be most fully included in the life of their school community and which gives them a sense both of belonging and achieving.
>
> (Warnock 2005, p. 1)

This change of heart just serves to illustrate that inclusion cannot work unless it is both driven and supported by policy and properly resourced. It does work effectively in countries such as Canada, where money that would be spent on expensive special schools is directed towards the mainstream.

In September 2010, Ofsted published a review of SEN and disability (Ofsted 2010), commissioned to evaluate how well the legislative framework and arrangements served children and young people with SEN and/or disabilities. The review found both widespread weaknesses in the quality of what was provided for children with SEN and evidence that the way the system is currently designed contributes to these problems. In common with the earlier study by the CSIE, mentioned above, the review team found that, despite extensive statutory guidance, the consistency of the identification of SEN varied widely, not only between different local areas but also within them, and children and young people with similar needs were not being treated equitably and appropriately. Across education, health services and social care, assessments were different and the thresholds for securing additional support were at widely varying levels. The report recommends, inter alia, that evaluation should focus on outcomes for children and young people, not on whether they have received the services prescribed, and schools should stop identifying pupils as having SEN when they simply need better teaching and pastoral support. It calls for a review of the statutory framework for SEN, particularly the *Code of Practice*.

The following year, the coalition government published its Green Paper *Support and Aspiration: A new approach to special educational needs and disability* (Department for Education 2011). Among its proposals were simplification of the system and a reduction in bureaucracy, more control for parents over support for their child and family, a revised *Code of Practice* and tackling the 'problem of over-identification' in schools by having a single category for children whose needs exceed what is normally available in schools. Of concern to many was the intention to remove what the Green Paper described as the 'bias towards inclusion' – parents of children with statements of SEN would be able to express a preference for any state-funded school. The government would also 'prevent the unnecessary closure' of special schools, giving parents and community groups the power to take them over.

In a letter to *The Guardian* published on 12 March 2011, ten professors of special and inclusive education said that the Green Paper implies that inclusion is a privilege to be earned, rather than a 'socially just and fair approach to schooling with benefits for all'. This, they suggest, will mean, for many, likely exclusion from mainstream schools and, thus, from the 'big society' the government intends to create. This was disputed in a response from minister Sarah Teather (*The Guardian,* 14 March), who emphasised the need for parents' choice over schools for their children. However, the Green Paper certainly appears to focus on needs and disabilities, thus turning the clock back to the medical model of disability, and away from a focus on inclusion.

At the time of writing, the coalition government's plans included abolishing School Action and School Action Plus and IEPs. The *Code of Practice* was to be revised and was to be published in September 2014, reflecting the view that SEN was over-identified in schools. The proposal was for individual children with SEN to have an Education Health and Care Plan, but this led to concerns that children with less serious difficulties might be overlooked. It was anticipated that there might be geographical differences too, as local authorities published local offers. The plans were set out in the Children and Families Bill.

The changes came from the view that schools were over-identifying SEN, often because they thought this was the only way to obtain additional support for a child. The rationale behind the proposed changes was said to be that the current system was not working well because the emphasis was on labelling children's needs according to how support was to be provided, rather than the outcomes sought for the child and how to reach them. The current categories were also said to lead to children being unnecessarily labelled as having SEN, with little or no appropriate action taken to support them. The Lamb Inquiry (2009) had reported that SEN can sometimes be 'unhelpfully collated' with falling behind, which was thought to have contributed to increased numbers of pupils at School Action (Plus). At the end of KS2, August-born pupils were found to be 60 per cent more likely to be identified as having SEN than September-born pupils, a relationship strongest for those in the School Action category. The Inquiry also found a risk that the use of the SEN label led to lower expectations or less vigorous intervention. The Ofsted review (2010) found that additional provision for children identified at School Action level was often 'an inappropriate response to inadequacies in whole-class teaching or pastoral support'. Nearly a fifth of the schools visited by Ofsted suggested they provided additional SEN support, when this was regarded as the norm in other schools. Often, this provision became the justification for defining a pupil as having SEN, and identifying SEN was sometimes viewed as the only legitimate route to gaining additional provision. Ofsted found that, 'as many as half of all pupils identified for School Action would not be identified as having special educational needs if schools focused on improving teaching and learning for all, with individual goals for improvement' (Ofsted 2010).

The proposal was to have one category:

> A simplified, rigorous approach will focus the system on the impact of the support provided to that individual child, rather than how children access support according to the category they fit into. It will also challenge schools to improve the quality of teaching and learning for all pupils, rather than inappropriately and inaccurately labelling some pupils as having SEN.

Debates

Debates centre on addressing the credibility gap between the rhetoric and reality of inclusive education (Clark *et al.* 1998). Barton (1998) suggests that 'special needs' is a euphemism for school failure, and Richmond (1979) expresses concern over the use of the term 'special'. Richmond suggests there is nothing special about schools ensuring they are teaching effectively, that children are learning, that the curriculum is appropriate, and that there is a suitable environment, with advice and support. This resonates with current debates around the existence of distinctive SEN pedagogy (in Ellis *et al.* 2008). According to Kershner (2007), training and professional development need to address:

- the fundamental importance of understanding child development in context, as a basis for understanding the identification of SEN;
- the value of knowing that you do not know everything and believing that change is possible;
- the need to communicate understanding and resolve differences between people who have useful knowledge;
- the need to recognise the school as a site for the development of teaching expertise and the creation of knowledge.

Two consistently emerging areas for debate concern the 'right' and 'might' of inclusive education: the 'right' is centred around philosophical issues and the human rights agenda, with a belief that meeting individual children's needs overrides an ideological commitment to inclusion concerns (Croll and Moses 2000). The 'might' is politically led and tends to focus on the educational context, with a perceived tension between the development of inclusive practices and the continuation of national academic attainment targets. Governments have supported apparent paradoxes in policy and practice, including selective education based on academic ability for some, exclusion from mainstream education based on behaviour for others, the continued use of the term special educational needs and IEPs, and the option for parents to choose special school placement. Whereas some contend that segregation and exclusion are socially constructed and, thus, can logically be deconstructed to promote full inclusion, others argue that this reasoning is flawed (Fuchs and Fuchs 1994; Zigmond and Baker 1996).

Dyson argues that there is a fundamental contradiction within the UK education system between 'an intention to treat all learners as essentially the same and an equal and opposite intention to treat them as different' (2001, p. 25). A similar argument has been put forward by Rustemier (2002), who says that the aims and purposes of education in the UK are at odds with human rights concerns for inclusion and with education that should develop 'respect for human rights and fundamental freedoms' (p. 23).

In this chapter, it has been possible to give only a very brief overview of the background to SEN and inclusion, mentioning some of the main developments and policy documents. It is a confusing picture, not least because there are no agreed definitions of 'special educational needs' or 'integration' or 'inclusion', and the interpretation of these terms can depend on the context in which they are used.

There are a number of dilemmas and contradictions. Trying to implement a philosophy of inclusion means a conflict with other features of the education system – competition, league tables and academic attainment, for example – and so there is a rhetoric versus reality situation that comes down to issues of resourcing, teacher confidence, and so on.

As education generally takes place in groups, the school system does not always see or appreciate learners as individuals. Robinson

(2011 [2001], p. 57) compares schools with factories and says that schools are based on principles of standardisation and conformity, with children moving through the system by age group, with all 5-year-olds together, all the 6-year-olds together, and so on, 'as if the most important thing that children have in common is their date of manufacture'. Because of this, the concepts of inclusion and individuality can have an uneasy relationship – rather like adolescents who want to be different, but at the same time need to belong. There must be a balance, but, once policy and law become involved, the balance becomes socially defined, and thus there can be winners and others who do not fare so well.

Further reading

Inclusive Education: Readings and reflections
Gary Thomas and Mark Vaughan, 2004, Open University Press
An unusual format, as the book includes many extracts from policy documents and key texts from across the world, as well as a very interesting commentary – a very useful book.

Special Educational Needs and Inclusion: Reflection and renewal
Simon Ellis, Janet Tod and Lynne Graham-Matheson, 2008, NASUWT, available at: www.nasuwt.org.uk/TrainingEventsandPublications/NASUWTPublications/AccessiblePublications/Education/ReflectionandRenewalSENandInclusion/ (accessed March 2014)
A useful guide to the literature and main theories, debates and concepts.

Special Educational Needs: The basics
Janice Wearmouth, 2013, Routledge
A useful and up-to-date introduction for beginning teachers and other professionals.

Theories of Inclusive Education: A student's guide
Peter Clough and Jenny Corbett, 2000, Paul Chapman

Traces the major stages of thinking in the development of inclusive education, including personal reflections by influential thinkers.

Special Educational Needs: A new look
Mary Warnock and Brahm Norwich, 2010, Continuum
A dialogue between two leading but different thinkers in the field, looking at why past policies have not worked.

References

Ainscow, M., Booth, T., Dyson, A., Howes, A., Gallannaugh, F., Smith, R., Farrell, P. and Frankham, J. (2006) *Improving Schools, Developing Inclusion,* London: Routledge.

Bailey, J. (1998) Australia: Inclusion through categorisation, in T. Booth and M. Ainscow (eds) *From Them to Us: An international study of inclusion in education,* London: Routledge.

Barton, L. (1998) *The Politics of Special Education,* Lewes, UK: Falmer Press.

Booth, T. (1999) Viewing inclusion from a distance: Gaining perspective from comparative studies, *Support for Learning* 14(4): 164–8.

Booth, T. and Ainscow, M. (eds) (1998) *From Them to Us,* London: Creative Print Design.

Booth, T. and Ainscow, M. (2011 [2002]) *Index for Inclusion: Developing learning and participation in schools,* Bristol: CSIE.

Centre for Studies on Inclusive Education (1986) *Caught in the Act,* Bristol, UK: CSIE.

Centre for Studies on Inclusive Education (2005) Are LEAs in England abandoning inclusive education? Press release, 8 July, CSIE. Available at: www.csie.org.uk/resources/segregation-trends.shtml (accessed 14 August 2014).

Clark, C., Dyson, A. and Millward, A. (1998) Theorising special education: Time to move on? In C. Clark, A. Dyson and A. Millward *Theorising Special Education,* London: Routledge.

Cole, B. (2005) Mission Impossible? Special educational needs, inclusion and the re-conceptualisation of the role of the SENCO in England and Wales, *European Journal of Special Needs Education,* 20(3): 287–307.

Corbett, J. (2001) *Supporting Inclusive Education*, London: Routledge Falmer.

Croll, P. and Moses, D. (2000) Ideologies and utopias: Education professionals' view of inclusion, *European Journal of Special Needs Education*, 15(1): 1–12.

Department for Education (1994) Code of Practice on the identification and assessment of pupils with special educational needs, London: DfE.

Department for Education (2011) Green Paper *Support and Aspiration: A new approach to special educational needs and disability*, London: TSO.

Department for Education (2013) *Special Educational Needs in England, January 2013* (SFR30/2013). Available at: www.gov.uk (accessed March 2014).

Department for Education and Employment (1997) Green Paper *Excellence for All Children: Meeting special educational needs*, London: DfEE.

Department for Education and Employment/Qualifications and Curriculum Authority (1999) Inclusion: Providing effective learning opportunities for all children, in *The National Curriculum Handbook for Primary/Secondary Teachers in England*, London: DfEE/QCA.

Department of Education and Science (1978) *Special Educational Needs: Report of the Committee of Inquiry into the Education of Handicapped Children and Young People (The Warnock Report)* (Cmnd 7212). London: HMSO.

Department for Education and Skills (2001a) *Inclusive Schooling*, Annesley, UK: DfES.

Department for Education and Skills (2001b) *Special Educational Needs Code of Practice*, Annesley, UK: DfES.

Department for Education and Skills (2003) Green Paper *Every Child Matters*, London: DfES.

Department for Education and Skills (2004) *Removing Barriers to Achievement: The government's strategy for SEN*, Annesley, UK: DfES.

Dyson, A. (2001) Special educational needs in the 21st century: Where we've been and where we're going, *British Journal of Special Education*, 28(1): 24–9.

Ellis, S., Tod, J. and Graham-Matheson, L. (2008) *Special Educational Needs and Inclusion: Reflection and renewal*, Birmingham, UK: NASUWT.

Evans, J. and Lunt, I. (2002) Inclusive education: Are there limits? *European Journal of Special Needs Education*, 17(1): 1–14.

Farrell, M. (2000) Educational inclusion and raising standards, *British Journal of Special Education*, 27(1): 35–8.

Florian, L. (1998) Inclusive practice: What why and how? in C. Tilstone, L. Florian and R. Rose (eds) *Promoting Inclusive Practice*, London: Routledge.

Fuchs, D. and Fuchs, L. (1994) Inclusive school movement and the radicalisation of special education reform, *Exceptional Children*, 60(4): 294–309.

Hodkinson, A. (2010) Inclusive and special education in the English educational system: Historical perspectives, recent developments and future challenges, *British Journal of Special Education*, 37(32): 61–7.

Hornby, G., Davis, G. and Taylor, G. (1995) *Special Educational Needs Co-ordinator's Handbook*, London: Routledge.

Kershner, R. (2007) What do teachers need to know about meeting special educational needs? in L. Florian (ed.) *The Sage Handbook of Special Education*, London: Sage.

Lamb, B. (2009) *The Lamb Inquiry: Special educational needs and parental confidence*, Annesley, UK: DCSF.

Low, C. (1996) Sense and nonsense relocated, in Special Educational Needs Policy Options Group (ed.) *Provision for Special Educational Needs From the Perspectives of Service Users*, Tamworth, UK: NASEN.

Loxley, A. and Thomas, G. (2001) Neo-conservatives, neo-liberals, the New Left and inclusion: Stirring the pot, *Cambridge Journal of Education*, 341(3): 291–301.

Lunt, I. and Norwich, B. (1999) *Can Effective Schools be Inclusive Schools?* London: Insitute of Education.

Mittler, P. (2000) *Working Towards Inclusive Education: Social contexts*, London: David Fulton.

Norwich, B. (1996) Special needs education or education for all: Connective specialisation and ideological impurity, *British Journal of Special Education*, 23(3): 100–4.

Ofsted (2000) *Evaluating Educational Inclusion*, London: Ofsted.

Ofsted (2003) *Special Educational Needs in the Mainstream*, London: Ofsted.

Ofsted (2010) *The Special Educational Needs and Disability Review: Report summary*, Manchester, UK: Ofsted.

Pumfrey, P. and Mittler, P. (1989) Peeling off the label, *Times Educational Supplement*, 13 October.

Richmond, R. (1979) Warnock: Found wanting and waiting, *Special Education – Forward Trends*, 693: 8–10.

Riddell, S. (2002) *Special Educational Needs* (Policy and Practice in Education series), Edinburgh, UK: Dunedin Academic Press.

Roaf, C. and Bines, H. (eds) (1989) *Needs, Rights and Opportunities*, London: Falmer.

Robinson, K. (2011 [2001]) *Out of Our Minds: Learning to be creative*, Chichester, UK: Capstone.

Rustemier, S. (2002) *Social and Educational Justice: The human rights framework for inclusion*, Bristol, UK: CSIE.

Sebba, J. with Sachdev, D. (1997) *What Works in Inclusive Education?* Ilford, UK: Barnardo's.

Thomas, G. (1997) Inclusive schools for an inclusive society, *British Journal of Special Education*, 24(3): 103–7.

Tomlinson, J. (1997) Inclusive learning: The report of the Committee of Inquiry into Post-school Education of Those with Learning Difficulties and Disabilities in England 1996, *European Journal of Special Needs Education*, 12(3): 184–6.

Tomlinson, S. (1982) *A Sociology of Special Education*, London: Routledge and Kegan Paul.

United Nations Educational, Scientific and Cultural Organisation (UNESCO) (1994) *The Salamanca Statement and Framework for Action on Special Needs Education*, adopted by the World Conference on Special Needs Education: Access and Quality, Salamanca, Spain, 7–10 June.

Warnock, M. (2005) *Special Educational Needs: A new look*, London: Philosophy of Education Society of Great Britain.

Zigmond, N. and Baker, J. (1996) Full inclusion for students with learning disabilities: Too much of a good thing, *Theory into Practice*, 35(1): 26–34.

5 Child development

The teacher–organizer should know not only his own science but also be well versed in the details of the development of the child's or adolescent's mind.

(Jean Piaget)

People develop and change physically and psychologically throughout their lives, but more changes take place in the first few years of life than at any other time. Before the age of 2, for example, a child will grow to half his or her adult height and learn enough language for basic communication, although there is a lot of variation in the ages at which children learn basic skills, such as walking and talking, and developmental psychologists have tried to understand what influences this process. We know, for example, that children brought up in institutions where they receive little attention and have few opportunities to play develop at a slower rate than children in more stimulating environments. It seems that, when there are poor opportunities for exercise and movement, there is delay in cognitive and motor development, as if playing helps a child to think. The opportunity to play for as little as an hour a day, though, can help overturn the effects of understimulation.

Development is usually shown in stages. Basically, everyone has to go through the same stages and in the same order, reaching later stages by going through the earlier stages – you have to be able to count and understand the idea of numbers before you can add and subtract – but there is some variation. Some babies, for example, do not learn to crawl, but go straight to walking.

The best-known theorists are listed below. Today, many children's professionals take an eclectic approach to theory – all of these theorists have valid and useful views. By understanding each theoretical approach, you can pick and use parts of theories, if they seem appropriate to the context (see summary of theories in Table 5.1).

Arnold Gesell

Gesell was an early proponent of maturational theory, which sees development as a biological process occurring automatically in predictable, sequential stages. He developed a timetable of developmental events that we still use today. There is a long-running debate about whether nature or nurture is more important to development. Nature is our biological inheritance – our genes determine what colour eyes we have and when we start walking. Nurture is the environment we are brought up in, everything external that affects our development, including such things as parenting style. Gesell identified the role of nature or heredity in children's development. He gathered normative data on a range of children and concluded that each child's development unfolded according to a genetic timetable.

According to maturationists, all healthy young children are ready for school when they can perform tasks such as reciting the alphabet and counting. If a young child's development lags behind his peers, this is interpreted as the child needing more time to acquire the knowledge and skills required. Maturationists tend to think that any difficulties children experience come from within the child. This can be used to explain anything from difficulties with reading to attention deficit hyperactivity disorder (ADHD). It is a very simplistic view and suggests any support a child could be given is pointless. It can also be used as an explanation – which becomes a self-fulfilling prophecy – by teachers, saying that they knew a child would have problems because s/he has a late birthday and is very young in the year.

Table 5.1 Development theories and theorists

Theoretical approach/ Principles of the approach	Theorist
Maturation	
Growth and development occur in orderly stages and in sequence. The child's genetic timetable affects the rate of maturation	Arnold Gessell (1880–1961)
Psychodynamic	
Behaviour is controlled by unconscious urges. The id, ego and superego are the three components of the mind	Sigmund Freud (1856–1939)
Psychosocial	
Personality develops in stages over a lifetime. Development is influenced by interactions with family, friends and culture	Jean Piaget (1896–1980), Lev Vygotsky (1896–1934)
Cognitive	
There are qualitative changes in the way children think. The child is an active learner going through stages	Erik Erikson (1902–94)
Behaviourist	
Learning is gradual and continuous. Development is a sequence of specific conditional behaviours. The main emphasis is on the environment, not heredity. Observable behaviours are thought to be the most important	John Watson (1878–1958), B. F. Skinner (1904–90), Albert Bandura (1925–)
Ecological	
There is a balance between nature and nurture and emphasis on both environment and heredity. The child is influenced by a number of concentric factors	Urie Bronfenbrenner (1917–2005)

Sigmund Freud

Freud proposed a staged theory of what he termed psychosexual development. The five stages were the oral, anal, phallic, latent and genital stages. According to Freud, development occurs as we struggle to balance the demands of the id (the pleasure-seeking, instructive part of our personality) with the demands of the superego (our conscience, which develops from the values of our parents and the wider society). The ego, the third part of the personality, tries to maintain a balance, preventing us from acting antisocially and helping us to find socially acceptable ways to satisfy the id. Most psychoanalytic theorists did not work in school settings, but a central aspect of the theories is that children must be supported in working through emotional and psychological crises, so that they develop emotional well-being and mental health. Freud saw the development of females from a male perspective. He saw girls' motivation as 'penis envy' and labelled the third stage of development phallic. His theories are based on methods such as dream analysis, which are not rigorous or open to verification.

Erik Erikson

Erikson was interested in the influence of culture and society on child development, and his book *Childhood and Society* (1950) is considered a classic. Erikson's theory, the Eight Ages of Man, covers the whole lifespan (see Table 5.2). His idea was that each stage of development has a task that must be completed. Successful resolution of each stage affects the next stage. People form personality strengths and weaknesses depending on their development at each stage, and he believed it was always possible to go back and renegotiate issues from a previous stage of development. Erikson gave us the idea of the identity crisis – he considered it was inevitable that young people would experience conflict as they develop into adults.

Erikson's theory is important for education, because it shows how children develop a foundation for emotional and social development and mental health. He thought the early childhood years were important for developing trust, autonomy and initiative.

Table 5.2 Erikson's developmental stages

Stage	Conflict	Significant relationships	Outcome
Infancy, 0–18 months	Trust vs mistrust	Main caregiver, parents	Children develop a sense of trust when caregivers provide care, affection and reliability. Lack of this will lead to mistrust
Early childhood, 2–3 years	Autonomy vs shame and doubt	Parents	Children need to develop a sense of personal control over physical skills and a feeling of independence. Success leads to a sense of autonomy and self esteem, failure leads to feelings of shame and doubt
Pre-school, 3–5 years	Initiative vs guilt	Family	Children need to begin exploring, asserting control and power over the environment. Success leads to a sense of purpose. Children who try to exert too much power experience disapproval and a sense of guilt
School age, 6–11 years	Industry vs inferiority	Family, school, neighbours	Children have to cope with new social and academic demands. Success leads to a sense of competence, failure leads to feelings of inferiority
Adolescence, 12–18 years	Identity vs role confusion	Peers, groups	Teens need to develop a sense of self and identity. Success leads to an ability to stay true to oneself, whereas failure leads to role confusion and a weak sense of self
Young adulthood, 19–40 years	Intimacy vs isolation	Friends and lovers	Young adults need to form intimate loving relationships with other people. Success leads to strong relationships, failure leads to loneliness and isolation
Middle adulthood, 40–65 years	Generativity vs stagnation	Shared household	Adults need to create or nurture things that will outlast them, by having children or doing something positive that benefits others. Success leads to feelings of usefulness and accomplishment, failure leads to shallow involvement in the world
Maturity, 65 years to death	Ego integrity vs despair	Extended family, mankind	Older adults need to look back on life and feel a sense of fulfilment. Success leads to feelings of wisdom, whereas failure results in regret, bitterness and despair

Note: Erikson later added a further, ninth stage, to represent very old age

Erikson's theory can be related to teaching young children by recognising the need for them to feel that the adults around them are reliable and will meet their needs. To develop autonomy, they need to do things for themselves whenever possible. Young children, according to Erikson, struggle between holding on and letting go in things such as sharing with friends, independent toileting, relationships and making choices. Letting go and holding on can both lead to destructive behaviours – being uncooperative, tantrums, hitting or biting when angry – and constructive behaviours – attachment to special people, persistence in getting something done, sharing. Adults around them need to recognise and support children's growing demands for independence and not shame them for behaviour that is developmentally appropriate. Rather than being controlled, which can lead to more frustration and becoming controlling in later life, children need to have appropriate opportunities for choice and control, within consistent, firm and necessary limits. So, in a classroom, shelves and storage at child height mean children can choose books and pencils for themselves. Although young children cannot make a choice from a broad range of options, they can decide when given a limited choice – whether they would like to look at a book or draw a picture, perhaps.

Actions based on Erikson's theory can support healthy development:

- *Stage of trust/distrust*:
  - holding babies close, physical contact, particularly when feeding;
  - responding quickly when babies cry.
- *Awareness of autonomy/shame or doubt*:
  - give children simple but real choices;
  - set clear, consistent and reasonable boundaries;
  - accept and understand swings between independence and dependence.
- *Initiative/guilt*:
  - encourage children to be independent;
  - focus on what children can do, not on mistakes made;

- set realistic expectations;
- make the curriculum relevant, based on action.

Jean Piaget

Piaget began his career working at the Alfred Binet Laboratory School in Paris, standardising the French version of a British intelligence test. He noticed similarities in the incorrect answers children gave to questions at particular ages, and began to wonder how they arrived at the answers – this research question became his life's work. He was interested in *how* children arrive at what they know, rather than *what* they know or *when* they know it. To an extent, Piaget's work has been discredited in recent years – much of his work uses unfamiliar terminology and is difficult to read, and it has been criticised for limitati[illegible] ged by current research. Some say that he foc[illegible] ught processes and not enough on c[illegible] ionships, and, because a lot of his c[illegible] children, critics say his work is [illegible] er, just as Erikson's stages have he[illegible] develop socially and emotionally, Pi[illegible] nent (see Table 5.3) have helped us [illegible] nk. Although his theories may no[illegible], Piaget's work is still used as a bas[illegible]

It was thought [illegible] was either intrinsic, coming from the ch[illegible], taught by adults. Piaget argued that neither was co[illegible], and that learning is created through the child's interaction with the environment: children construct their own knowledge by finding meaning in the people, places and things in their world. He said, 'construction is superior to instruction' (Hendrick 1992), meaning that children learn best when they do the work themselves, rather than being given explanations by adults. Like Dewey, Piaget believed that children's curiosity drives their learning – children need to learn through being given problem-solving challenges, rather than information. On this basis, a teacher is someone who fosters enquiry and supports the child's search for answers. Like Montessori, Piaget believed that children need to be given every opportunity to do things for themselves. So, for

Table 5.3 Piaget's stages of cognitive development

Age	Stage	Behaviours	
Birth–2 years	Sensorimotor	Learn through senses Learn through reflexes Manipulate material	Knowledge mainly comes from the senses. Children become aware of object permanence but are egocentric. It is the age when children show separation anxiety – they understand that when a parent or other important person is out of sight they are somewhere else, so children try to bring them back by crying
2–7 years	Pre-operational	Form ideas based on their perceptions Can only focus on one variable at a time Over-generalise based on limited experience	During this stage, children learn to manipulate the environment and to use words to represent objects, which helps them play with ideas. Their logic comes from incomplete knowledge
7–11 years	Concrete operational	Form ideas based on reasoning Limit thinking to objects and familiar events	Logical thought develops during this stage, and the child can categorise or classify things according to similarity or difference. Logic is usually only applied to things that are tangible or can be seen
12 years and older	Formal operational	Think conceptually Think hypothetically	This stage is characterised by orderly thinking and mastery of logical thought. Children can use abstract ideas, make hypotheses and understand the implications of thinking (theirs or other people's)

Note: Based on Piaget 1976

example, it is better for a child to make bread and see how yeast works and the dough develops, rather than being told how it happens. Piaget also thought that play was very important: as children take part in pretend play – 'cooking' with sand or playing hospitals – they make sense of the world around them and how things work.

Piaget's theory was that all children pass through the same stages when developing their thinking skills. Children develop at their own rate, and there can be wide variation, but a child has to be at a particular stage of development to understand a new concept. He thought that intellectual development was partly based on physical development and on interaction with the environment. Piaget did not think it was possible to teach a young child to understand a concept, but that children would build their own understanding through their activities.

Piaget said that, for very young children, when an object is out of sight, they think it has gone and do not look for it. When they are older, and an object is hidden, they will look for it. This is Piaget's theory of object permanence – realising that objects have their own existence, whether or not we can see them.

Piaget thought that young children were egocentric, in that they could only see things from their own point of view. In a series of experiments, he showed pre-operational children a model of three mountains and moved a doll around on the mountains. The children were shown photographs of the mountains and asked which of the photographs showed what the doll would be able to see from different viewpoints. Most of the children could not choose the correct photograph, choosing the one that gave their point of view, leading to Piaget's theory of egocentrism.

Piaget carried out a series of conservation experiments with children under 7. Children could be presented with two balls of plasticine, both the same size. One ball would be flattened, and the children would be asked whether the two balls now weigh the same or not. Or they might be shown two short, fat beakers, both the same size and containing identical amounts of liquid. The liquid from one beaker would be poured into a tall, thin container, and the children would be asked to say which beaker contained more liquid. Younger children tend to assume that the amounts of liquid have changed, but, as they get older, they realise that the amounts stay the same, although they appear different.

Margaret Donaldson thought that things were not as simple as this. Donaldson, who briefly worked with Piaget, has led post-Piagetian thinking in the UK. According to Hughes (2001), Donaldson returned from working with Piaget, 'impressed by his methods and the scale of his theorising, but not convinced he was necessarily right' (p. 176). Central to Donaldson's theory is the idea of embedded and disembedded theory. Thinking that is embedded, or situated, in a familiar context makes sense and so is more easily understood by children. When children are asked to think in unfamiliar, unrealistic or abstract contexts, their thinking is disembedded and does not make sense to them (Donaldson 1978).

According to Donaldson, Piaget's mountains test is disembedded and so presents difficulties and does not allow children to demonstrate their understanding. Martin Hughes devised a test where models of a policeman and a naughty boy were placed on a board with intersecting walls. Children were asked to place the boy where he could not see the policeman. Because this was embedded in a context the children could understand, far more of them showed that they could think in a non-egocentric way than in Piaget's experiments. Donaldson describes experiments by James McGarrigle based on Piaget's conservation tasks. In one of the classic tasks, children are shown two lines of ten counters. When they have agreed that the two lines are the same, one line is extended so that it is longer than the other. Although they know that both lines have ten counters, young children tend to say that the longer line has more. McGarrigle devised variations on this test involving a teddy bear, which gave a context for the question, and more children were able to respond correctly. Donaldson suggests that children's errors or misunderstanding come about because they are not simply responding to what they are being asked to do, but are trying to understand the meaning of the test, to make sense of the situation. Piaget's theories led many practitioners, especially in the 1960s, to think that children's thinking has a limit, or ceiling. Donaldson's work emphasises what children are able to do, rather than concentrating on what they cannot do. She stresses that thought and feelings are of equal value.

Urie Bronfenbrenner

Bronfenbrenner was born in Russia, but his family emigrated to the US when he was a young child. He is remembered both for his theory of development and as a co-founder of Head Start in 1965. Head Start supported the achievement of disadvantaged children and led to Sure Start in the UK, persuading politicians that early intervention could make a difference.

Bronfenbrenner was interested in the links between culture and ecology and development. His Ecological Systems Theory is presented as a series of concentric circles (see Figure 5.1). In the centre is the microsystem – the child (or developing person, according to Bronfenbrenner) and the objects s/he comes across or people s/he interacts with on a daily basis. The mesosystem is all the settings and links between them that are a part of the child's life – school, the local community, church or other place of worship, extended family. The exosystem includes people and places the child may not interact with directly, but that still impact on the child. These interactions may be two-way. For example, if a child is disabled, the exosystem may include organisations that support him or her without coming into contact with the child him/herself. In addition, what the child needs – special resources perhaps – could have an impact on the organisation. The outside ring is the macrosystem, or wider sociocultural context, with global similarities and inter-societal contrasts. To illustrate, schools and supermarkets and cafes in the UK vary, but there are many similarities. The same is true of the US, but, in both places, 'homes, day care centres, neighborhoods, work settings and the relations between them are not the same for well-to-do families as for the poor'. Bronfenbrenner later added a fifth element – the chronosystem (the evolution of the external systems over time). This is not represented as one of the rings but shows the way changes over time in the cultures or mesosystems can impact on the developing child. An example given by Bronfenbrenner is divorce, where the impact may not be felt for a while, may be different for boys and girls and may vary between cultures.

Bronfenbrenner's work on child development is hugely important and influential. Development is not just confined to childhood,

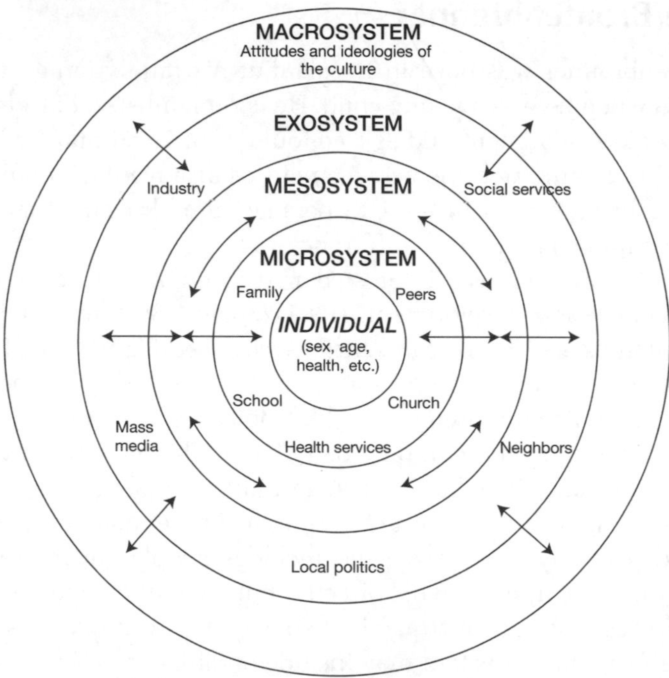

Figure 5.1 Model of Bronfenbrenner's theory

Source: Bronfenbrenner 1979

and practitioners are now far more likely to consider a child's context when looking at his or her learning and development. Links have been made between the various social science disciplines, and so it is possible to look at the key elements in the wide social structure and across societies as models for human development, although critics say that the theory places too much emphasis on the environment, with too little on biological and cognitive factors.

In Bronfenbrenner's obituary, it says that, before him, 'child psychologists studied the child, sociologists examined the family, anthropologists the society, economists the economic framework of the times and political scientists the structure', but, 'as the result of Bronfenbrenner's groundbreaking concept of the ecology of human development, these environments – from the family to economic and political structures – are viewed as part of the life course, embracing both childhood and adulthood' (Lang 2005). Few people would argue that these various influences are important, but using this effectively and fully can be difficult – how is it possible to account for all the interactions and variables affecting a child?

Attachment theory

After the Second World War, psychiatrist John Bowlby (1907–90) was commissioned by the World Health Organisation to study the mental health needs of orphaned and homeless children. He said that their distress could not be explained by then current theories. The concept of cupboard love was meant to explain their unhappiness – to meet their need for food, warmth and safety, children would attach themselves to an adult who would provide for them. The main purpose was sustenance and protection, with attachment secondary, but Bowlby thought the response of children to separation from adults went beyond this. Bowlby turned to the work of others to try to understand. James Robertson, a psychiatric social worker, had filmed young children reacting to short separations from their parents, and his work had a significant impact on the debate about the impact of separation on young children. American scientist Harry Harlow had been studying rhesus monkeys and used wire models as substitute mothers to show that, when frightened, young monkeys were more interested in a comforting 'mother' than a feeding one.

Attachment theory has continued to develop since Bowlby first wrote about it in the 1960s, but the main features are:

- children need to feel safe and secure and show a preference for being close to a small number of adults;
- children are born with a number of behaviours – crying, laughing, gurgling – that encourage others to pay attention to them;
- attachment behaviour – what the child does to bring about attachment – increases when s/he is frightened or anxious and decreases when s/he feels safe and secure;

- the need for attachment figures lessens as we grow up, but, even as adults, at times of difficulty we still seek comfort and support from loved ones;
- attachment of the child and parent develops over time and usually comes through the routine tasks in which parents and children are involved.

Studies generally suggest, as might be expected, that children who are securely attached are better able to cope with new experiences and relationships, whereas poor attachment can lead to difficulties later. Many studies show that the harmful effects of early experiences can be overturned, especially if the child is still young when conditions improve, and researchers have been struck by children's resilience, as there is a tendency to normal development in all but the most adverse circumstances.

Bowlby's work has been very influential. It was a gift to post-war politicians, who were dealing with the issue of what to do about women who had been doing men's work while the men were away at war. Nurseries that had taken children full-time during the war now only had part-time places. It was argued that this was because children should be at home with their mothers, but this both reduced the number of women seeking work, thus creating more jobs for the returning men, and doubled the number of nursery places, to cater for the baby boom as fathers returned. The work of Bowlby's students, who produced a film showing the effects on children when they were hospitalised and separated from their parents, shocked the nation and was instrumental in change to make it possible for parents to stay in hospital with their children.

Although things are slowly changing, mothers are still usually portrayed as central to their child's development, a uniqueness that can make it difficult for fathers to play a key role in children's lives, as well as separating the worlds of work and childcare. As other researchers, for example Tizard (1991), have pointed out, although children in residential care are separated from their mothers, they are separated from fathers and other family too. Even in the 1980s, when challenged to address criticisms of his work, Bowlby remained firmly of the view that motherhood and career could not be combined.

Moral development

The National Curriculum includes an aim for schools 'to promote the spiritual, moral, social and cultural development of all pupils and prepare them for the opportunities, responsibilities and experiences of adult life'. The Department for Education's (2011) definition of moral development is as follows:

> Pupils' moral development involves pupils acquiring an understanding of the difference between right and wrong and of moral conflict, a concern for others and the will to do what is right. They are able and willing to reflect on the consequences of their actions and learn how to forgive themselves and others. They develop the knowledge, skills and understanding, qualities and attitudes they need in order to make responsible moral decisions and act on them.

Moral or values education is becoming even more important, as concerns about violence and antisocial behaviour increase – although morality is a lifelong issue, concerns about antisocial behaviour are often related to young people. Moral development is central to all human growth, and values or moral education can be traced back to Confucius and Aristotle.

For Thomas Aquinas, the only authentic goal of education was to be realised in practical virtue, and Thomas More similarly saw education as being about achieving personal integrity and conforming one's actions to the common good. This 'true education' contrasted with the piling up of facts, which was mere instruction (Lovat 2012).

Psychoanalytic theorists suggest the roots of morality are relationships, motives, emotions, individuality and psychopathology. Freud said that the quality of the child's relationship with his parents affects the child's moral development. The id is the pleasure-seeking part of our psyche, and the superego is our conscience, with the ego helping us to find a balance, to find morally and socially acceptable ways to satisfy the id.

Social learning theory developed from behaviourism and assumes that children learn how to behave morally by being rewarded or punished and by imitating adult behaviour. Bandura (1961) carried out several studies of aggression. The best known of these involved a bobo doll (a life-size inflatable figure designed to be knocked over and then stand up again). An adult acted aggressively towards the doll and then left the room. Children copied the adult's behaviour, but they were less likely to copy the behaviour if they had seen the adult being punished for it (see www.youtube.com/watch?v=zerCKolRjp8; accessed March 2014). Bandura's studies have been criticised – experiments with dolls that are designed to be knocked over do not necessarily mean that children are acting aggressively, or that they would use the same behaviour with another person.

Jean Piaget looked at children's moral development through the rules they developed and used in their games. Young children played for enjoyment and ignored the rules. Six-year-olds tended to be inflexible in applying rules, but, by the age of 10, children realised that rules could be manipulated. Piaget told children stories that included a moral dilemma and then analysed their responses. He said that, for young children, the naughtiness of an action depended on the amount of damage done – moral realism. Older children would take personal, cultural and social factors into account – moral relativism. So, if one child's actions did a lot of damage, and another child's actions did less damage but involved something he was forbidden to do, younger children would say that the first child was naughtier, because of the damage. Older children would say that the second child was naughty, because of his motives.

Lawrence Kohlberg is perhaps the best-known theorist of moral development. Kohlberg was a constructivist and built on Piaget's work. Like Piaget, he was interested in how people think.

He thought it was impossible to separate school goals – academic skills – from moral development, and his work has had a profound effect on education and teacher education. Kohlberg posed a series of moral dilemmas – an example might be a man stealing a drug that would save his wife's life, when he could not afford to buy the drug and the pharmacist would not give it to him. Should he be punished? From subjects' responses to questions, he identified three main stages of moral development, each with two sub-stages.

Kohlberg's stages

Kohlberg's stages are as follows:

- *Preconventional* – children up to about the age of 10 are mainly concerned with avoiding punishment and meeting their own needs.
- *Conventional* – older children are concerned with meeting other people's expectations of moral behaviour. The second stage at this level is the concern with doing the right thing for people or groups with whom you are concerned. In between these levels, there may be a stage of questioning what is right and wrong around things that had previously been accepted.
- *Postconventional* – moral behaviour is part of a social contract, and individuals' behaviour is influenced by the values and opinions of people they live and interact with. The final stage is when the individual adheres to universal moral principles.

There has been criticism of the various theories, for example that Piaget and Kohlberg are culturally biased in their views, and that we do not all necessarily develop in stages.

Further reading

Several of the books in this section are primarily psychology books and so also contain chapters on motivation, etc.

The Story of Childhood: Growing up in modern Britain
Libby Brooks, 2006, Bloomsbury
A really interesting book, featuring interviews with nine children and giving an insight into what it is like to be a child today.

How Children Learn: From Montessori to Vygotsky – educational theories and approaches made easy
Linda Pound, 2006, Practical Pre-school Books
Probably aimed more at early years specialists than teachers,

but a very useful book, giving a brief introduction to the theories and ideas of pioneers in education.

How Children Learn 3: Contemporary thinking and theorists. An overview of contemporary educational and psychological theorists
Linda Pound, 2009, Practical Pre-school Books
As above, but concentrates on contemporary theories and theorists.

Theories of Childhood: An introduction to Dewey, Montessori, Erikson, Piaget and Vygotsky
Carol Garhart Mooney, 2000, Redleaf Press
A slim volume, a useful introduction to these theories and theorists, though the practical examples in the book are American.

Psychology and Education
Susan Bentham, 2002, Routledge
A useful book that covers a range of topics, from learning and assessment through to teaching and learning.

The Developing Child
Helen Bee and Denise Boyd, 2013, Pearson
Now in its thirteenth edition, arguably the definitive book on child development.

Principles of Developmental Psychology
George Butterworth and Margaret Harris, 1994, Lawrence Erlbaum
Reviews the history of developmental psychology and introduces the major theorists and ideas.

Life-span Development: Frameworks, accounts and strategies: theories, concepts and interventions
Léonie Sugarman, 2001, Routledge
Primarily aimed at psychology students, looks at development through the lifespan, discussing major theories and ideas.

Growing Critical: Alternatives to developmental psychology
John R. Morss, 1996, Routledge
Not a critique of developmental psychology but an analysis of critical psychology and a new look at some of the main theories and concepts.

References

Bronfenbrenner, U. (1979) *The Ecology of Human Development: Experiments by nature and design*, Cambridge, MA: Harvard University Press.

Department for Education (2011) *Spiritual, Moral, Social and Cultural Development*. Available at: www.education.gov.uk/schools/teachingandlearning/curriculum/a00199700/spiritual-and-moral (accessed March 2014).

Donaldson, M. (1978) *Children's Minds*, London: Fontana.

Erikson, E. (1950) *Childhood and Society*, London: Paladin.

Hendrick, J. (1992) *The Whole Child*, Englewood Cliffs, NJ: Merrill.

Hughes, M. (2001) Margaret Donaldson, in J. A. Palmer (ed.) *Fifty Modern Thinkers on Education*, Abingdon, UK: Routledge.

Lang, S. S. (2005) Urie Bronfenbrenner, father of Head Start program and pre-eminent 'human ecologist', dies at age 88, *Cornell Chronicle*, 26 September. Available at: www.news.cornell.edu/stories/2005/09/head-start-founder-urie-bronfenbrenner-dies-88 (accessed 14 August 2014).

Lovat, T. (2012) Values education, in J. Arthur and A. Peterson (eds) *The Routledge Companion to Education*, London: Routledge, pp. 380–8.

Piaget, J. (1976) *The Child and Reality*, London: Penguin.

Tizard, B. (1991) Employed mothers and the care of young mothers, in A. Phoenix, A. Woollett and E. Lloyd (eds) *Motherhood: Meanings, practices and ideologies*, London: Sage.

6 How children learn

Learning and development are interrelated from the child's very first day of life.

(Lev Vygotsky)

This chapter looks at theories of learning. Remember that learning in the classroom involves two people, two processes – teachers and pupils, teaching and learning. So, as well as thinking about how children learn, you also need to think about pedagogy and your role as the teacher.

Children are not just empty vessels into which teachers can pour their knowledge. Learning takes place when experiences cause a permanent change in knowledge, attitude, belief, perception or behaviour, and so, after we learn something, we may act differently, perform differently with a new skill, learn to see something in a new way, or change our attitudes or behaviour. Learning can be formal or informal. Formal learning is deliberate, intended learning – as in the classroom. Informal learning is unintended, for example, from watching television or listening to friends.

Early thinkers on learning

In a volume of this size, it is not possible to include everyone who has had a major influence on education. The companion volumes, *Fifty Major Thinkers on Education* and *Fifty Modern Thinkers on Education*, published by Routledge, give an introduction to the key thinkers. Dewey is included here because he is arguably one of the greatest influences on modern education – the progressive education movement of the early twentieth century owes a lot to him, and his influence can be seen in the Hadow and Plowden Reports (see Chapter 1). Montessori and Steiner both established schools that we still have today.

John Dewey (1859–1952) was interested in philosophy, psychology and educational theory. His Laboratory School established the University of Chicago as the centre of thought on progressive education (see Chapter 2), and much of his thinking influences what we do today. *My Pedagogic Creed*, published in 1897, sets out many of his ideas. In his early work, he struggled to answer questions such as how do we best introduce children to new material? How can we best plan? And how can teachers and support staff best work together? – questions that are still pertinent today. His revolutionary ideas – similar to those of Piaget and Montessori – were that children learn by doing, and education should involve real-life experiences and encourage independent thinking and experimentation. Dewey believed that teachers need to have confidence in their skills and experience and must:

- have a strong general-knowledge base as well as knowledge of their pupils;
- be willing to use their knowledge and experience to help children make sense of the world;
- spend time observing children and plan, organise and document children's work;
- want to continue learning.

Dewey criticised traditional formal teaching, believing that learning should be fun, while stating that fun is not enough to make an experience educational – when planning an activity, teachers need to ask themselves:

- How will this build on what children already know and help them grow?
- What skills are being developed?
- How does this activity help children know more about their world and prepare them to live more fully?

According to Dewey, an experience can only be described as educational if it:

- is based on children's interests and grows out of their knowledge and experience;
- supports children's development;
- helps children develop new skills;
- adds to children's understanding of their world and prepares them to live more fully.

Maria Montessori (1870–1952) was the first woman in Italy to graduate from medical school, was nominated for the Nobel Peace Prize three times and developed an approach to education for the youngest children that still bears her name. Montessori's interest in young children began when she was responsible for visiting insane asylums and selecting people for treatment. She was a keen observer and realised that, where children had been diagnosed as unteachable, the problems were often not with the child, but with adults, their approaches and the environment. In 1907, Montessori was offered a building in the slums of Rome to open her first *casa dei bambini* (children's house), to reduce vandalism and keep the children of working parents off the streets. She wanted to create an environment that would compensate for the conditions in which the children lived. Many of her ideas are so fundamental to the way we teach young children today that we take them for granted, but at the time they were radical. Montessori thought that young children needed furnishings their own size and tools that would fit their hands; because such materials were not available, Montessori made them herself. For Montessori, environment meant not only the space and the equipment within it, but also the adults and children. She believed that children learn language and other skills without conscious effort, from the environments where they spend their time. Environments need to be beautiful and orderly, so children can learn from them and through sensory experiences. Montessori thought teachers should provide real tools (knives, scissors, woodworking tools) that work, keep materials and equipment organised and accessible so that children can find and put away what they need, and create beauty and order in the classroom.

In a classroom designed around Montessori's ideas, a teacher would think about the way that colours work together and how children's work is displayed, the furniture, lighting and music, flowers, what is available to touch or smell. Shelving would be at child height, with materials well organised so that children can find what they need without having to ask. Tools such as scissors would be real tools, so that children can carry out their tasks and learn how to use tools safely, rather than struggling with blunt tools that can make tasks more difficult, and even less safe. Montessori believed that children want and need to care for themselves and their environment – adults should spend less time looking after children but should provide the environment and materials and step back to allow children to structure their own time. The teacher is responsible for increasing each child's competence whenever possible. Children should be involved in real-life tasks – children can be asked to sort and put away materials in the classroom, or given a bowl of soapy water and a brush and asked to clean a painting table.

Montessori's theory was that, when children were engaged in serious work, they were less likely to be disruptive. If teachers allowed children to choose what they wanted to do and how and when they did it, teachers would then have more time to assist individual children. Teachers had to be on hand to provide materials and to plan purposeful, self-directed activities. The key, for Montessori, was observation, to determine what children were interested in and what they needed to learn. If children were not learning, then adults were not watching or listening carefully enough. Montessori brought her scientific skills into the classroom, believing that you needed to know all you could about the children you were going to teach, and the way to do that was to carefully observe them.

Rudolf Steiner (1861–1925) was born in what is now Croatia. He became very interested in spirituality and established a 'science of the spirit' that he called anthroposophy. Concerned with the human struggle for inner freedom, there is still a World Anthroposophical Society, with its headquarters in Switzerland. Workers at the Waldorf–Astoria cigarette factory in Stuttgart asked Steiner to open a school for their children, and the first Steiner Waldorf school opened in 1919. Today, there are over 1,000 schools, 2,000 early years settings and around 60 teacher training institutes in 60 countries. There are 35 schools in the UK and 14 early years settings. Steiner Waldorf schools are state funded in most European countries, Australia, New Zealand and the USA; most schools in the UK are privately funded but aim to make their schools as accessible as possible. Steiner Waldorf schools are all non-selective, multicultural and co-educational, offering a comprehensive curriculum. They are independent, self administered community schools, without internal hierarchical management structures.

Steiner education takes account of the needs of the whole child – academic, physical, emotional and spiritual – is based on an understanding of the relevance of the different phases of child development, develops a love of learning and an enthusiasm for school and sees artistic activity and the development of the imagination as integral to learning. Steiner thought there were three 7-year cycles of development that connect with the human qualities of thinking, feeling and willing:

- From birth to 7, the active or will predominates.
- From 7 to 14, the affective or feeling predominates.
- From 14 to 21, the cognitive or thinking ability predominates.

Education needs to work with the needs and abilities of the child at each stage: Steiner believed that children who were pressured to succeed intellectually at too early an age often lacked the motivation to learn for themselves. Within the Steiner philosophy, children are not introduced to print (books) until formal schooling begins at the age of 7. There is a focus on the spoken word and on learning through play. Learning is cross-curricular, without subject boundaries, and children learn through creativity and practical activity, such as gardening and cooking. Mathematics, for example, is learned through practical work such as cooking. The physical environment, such as the colour and furnishing of the classroom, is important, as is the structure and rhythm of the teaching day, week and year, so that children have a routine and know what to expect. Steiner believed that working with rhythm helped children to understand the past, present and future and to find their place in the world. Children usually have the same class teacher from 6 to 14, with specialist teachers. Each day includes a quiet time.

There is a central place for structured movement, the outdoor environment and learning through doing across the entire age range. The school timetable may include traditional games, sports, eurythmy, gymnastics, drama productions and an extensive programme of handicrafts and the development of manual skills. Social and emotional skills are fostered in a variety of ways: by the recognition of childhood as a time of wonder, by the family-like environment of the extended early years, by the provision of clear adult authority and guidance and by the exploration of global and social perspectives at secondary level. Whole class teaching is combined with individualised and differentiated learning. Imaginative engagement with the lesson material allows all learners, regardless of strengths, weaknesses and learning styles, to work at different levels within their class group.

Learning through play

This is not a new idea – Plato said that children should learn through play. It has increasingly been recognised that play is very important for children's learning, although research for the DfES found that few early years practitioners could explain why (Moyles *et al.* 2002). According to *The Statutory Framework for the Early Years Foundation Stage* (Department for Education 2012, p. 6):

> Play is essential for children's development, building their confidence as they learn to explore, to think about problems, and relate to others. Children learn by leading their own play, and by taking part in play which is guided by adults.

The *Early Years Foundation Stage Profile Handbook 2014* (Department for Education 2013, p. 20) says that:

> *Finding out and exploring* is concerned with the child's open-ended hands-on experiences which result from innate curiosity and provide raw sensory material from which the child builds concepts, tests ideas and finds out.

Using what they know in their play describes how children use play to bring together their current understandings, combining, refining and exploring their ideas in imaginative ways. Representing experiences through imaginative play supports the development of narrative thought, the ability to see from other perspectives, and symbolic thinking.

Being willing to have a go refers to the child finding an interest, initiating activities, seeking challenge, having a 'can do' orientation, being willing to take a risk in new experiences, and developing the view of failures as opportunities to learn.

Children do not make a distinction between work and play – Isaacs (1933) said, 'Play is the child's work'. Play can be difficult to define. It is complex and unpredictable, it is pretend, but to a child it is very real, it is active and focuses on doing. Lindon (2001) defines play as, 'a range of activities, undertaken for their own interest, enjoyment or the satisfaction that results'. Children's play always has a purpose, although this may not be clear to adults. It should be open-ended, with no outcomes or requirements for achievement, and controlled by children. Play can be difficult for parents and practitioners, because they may not see learning taking place – parents may be keen to have evidence of learning on paper, but children may learn far more about number when setting up and running a shop, for example, than when filling in a work sheet. Play is important for motivation – in play, children can see the point of what they are doing and thinking about and can concentrate for long periods. They can feel confident and in control, they can meet their own needs and explore at their own pace, making sense of the world.

Children can learn a great deal through play: the cognitive processes of learning, thinking and understanding; the affective area of development, learning about relationships, emotions and self-esteem; creativity; attitudes to life such as independence, curiosity, risk-taking, flexibility; and the development of psychomotor skills, such as hand–eye co-ordination and moving around skilfully. Sometimes, play can be helped along by adults modelling an activity, or asking open-ended questions to extend children's thinking, but adults must always be responsive to the child, not the other way round. There is a continuum of play, from completely child directed to completely teacher directed, which may apply more to older students. It is perhaps ironic that, as children grow up and become more skilled at play, they get less opportunity at school to learn this way.

Play is particularly important in today's society, when children tend to have less freedom to play out of doors and to socialise with other children away from an adult, and have more input from television, computers and videos, and therefore fewer opportunities to use their own creativity and imagination (Pound 2006).

Through observing pre-school children, Mildred Parten (1932) identified different stages of social play, although these are not necessarily followed in a linear way by all children:

- *Unoccupied play*: generally, very young infants will engage in this type of play. They tend to look at their hands or other parts of their body, do not seek contact with others or appear to have a purpose.
- *Solitary play*: infants tend to play by themselves, unaware of others around them. They move quite quickly from one activity to another.
- *Onlooker play*: this can occur across development stages. Onlooker play is when children are near a group of children and are following their activities or copying what they are doing. They usually do not want to participate or are waiting for someone to help them.
- *Parallel play*: during parallel play, toddlers play alongside each other and with similar materials, but do not interact.
- *Associative play*: usually seen in pre-school years. Children will begin to play and talk with each other and perhaps take on roles, but the roles are not sustained for very long, and there does not seem to be a common purpose.
- *Co-operative play*: this type of play occurs in the later pre-school years. Children take on roles and sustain them for the duration of play. Children have agreed goals and roles.

Parten (1932) argued that, as children grow older and they have more opportunities for mixing with their peers, they spend less time on their own in solitary or onlooker play, and more time in associative and co-operative play.

Play has been linked to theories of learning. For example, behaviourism suggests that children deserve to play after learning, and so play is a reward, and cognitive theories emphasise play's contribution to problem-solving, creativity and communication, mainly linked to the work of Piaget and Vygotsky. Pound (2006, p. 74) suggests the different views and arguments for play are as follows:

- *The romantic argument*: the child is considered as a whole; play is part of children's nature and children are happy when playing and learning. This view is linked to Froebel's theory.
- *The behaviourist argument*: linked to Skinner's theory. It suggests that after learning children deserve to play. Play is used as a reward.
- *The therapeutic argument*: as in the psychoanalytical theories of Freud and others, children seen as struggling with fears. Play helps children to deal with fears and anxieties but it can also help them to learn to empathise with others. This can help children develop awareness of how others feel and how to manage their own emotions.
- *The cognitive argument*: more recent theories of play emphasise its contribution to the development of problem-solving creativity, communication and developing understanding of social rules. These ideas are most firmly linked to Piaget and Vygotsky. However, neuroscience and current developmental psychology is underlining this argument.
- *The economic argument*: Marie Guha (a former teacher trainer who worked at Goldsmiths College, London) proposes that if practitioners take all these arguments into account then it makes sense to support play – learning will be more effective if we use effective and relevant approaches which include play.
- *The biological argument*: scientists and psychologists are coming to the view that since playfulness is present in all humans it must have a biological function. It has been suggested that play supports the development of creativity and imagination which is essential to the development of the flexible and adaptable human brain.

Theories of learning

Behaviourism

Behaviourism began in the early twentieth century and has been fiercely criticised, but it is very well known and still has its supporters. Behaviourism says that we cannot understand the inner workings of the mind, but can only study observable events – input (stimulus), output (response) and a black box in the middle, where things happen, but we cannot study them.

Behaviourist theories began with the work of Ivan Pavlov (1849–1936) and classical conditioning. He discovered that dogs could be trained (conditioned) to salivate when a bell rang, if the bell consistently came before food. Salivating at the sight of food is a natural response – pairing a natural response with an artificial one is conditioning.

John Watson (1878–1954) did similar work with children. Watson saw children as an empty vessel and famously believed that he could shape any child's development and turn them into whatever he wanted them to be. He moulded behaviour by controlling the stimulus and response. Watson suggested that operant conditioning controls actions through providing a stimulus after rather than before an action, and then providing a reward to reinforce behaviour. If an adult reinforces a child's behaviour – by saying 'well done' or giving a smile – the child is more likely to repeat it. Edward Thorndike (1874–1949) developed the law of effect, which says that behaviour leading to positive consequences will be repeated. He found that repetition improves the ability to solve patterns through experiments with animals.

Burrhus Skinner (1904–90) is perhaps the best-known behavioural theorist, who applied ideas from his work with rats and pigeons to children. He thought animals and humans were all organisms, but humans were more sophisticated. Skinner thought punishment was counter-productive and emphasised reward. He broke tasks down into small steps, reinforcing each step as it was learned.

Behaviourists discourage unwanted behaviour through punishment, although this is not as effective in changing behaviour as rewards. This approach of operant conditioning had a huge influence on child psychology and teaching in its day. Even though they may not call it behaviourism, many teachers hold similar views and use praise and rewards to shape behaviour. Behaviour modification is used in schools particularly where students show challenging behaviour – it uses a combination of conditioning and modelling to reinforce desirable behaviour.

Behaviourism is sometimes called learning theory, with learning and development seen in terms of nature versus nurture. Behaviourism is at the nurture end of the debate, with behaviourists believing that all behaviour is learned and can be shaped. Behaviourist theory is behind teaching methods that focus on repetition of words and completing rows of sums. Star charts rewarding children for behaviour or the advice not to pick babies up when they cry because this reinforces behaviour come from behaviourism.

Critics of behaviourism say that its focus on animals leads to a simplistic view of human learning and motivation. Humans are treated as if they have no mind of their own, just a brain that responds to external stimuli. Studies have shown that, if young children are rewarded for a particular behaviour, they may no longer exhibit that behaviour unless they are rewarded. Behaviourism also does not explain language learning, which is not explained through stimulus response: children make up words and may fail to say words for which they are rewarded, such as please or thank you. Although behaviourists thought the environment was important in children's learning, critics thought this was too narrow a view.

Social learning theory came from behaviourism – it built on the idea of conditioning and reinforcement but saw learning by observing and imitating as important. Modelling is important – watching other children and receiving feedback on their behaviour means children can develop personal standards and self-efficacy. In a poor learning environment, they can also develop low self-esteem and poor habits and standards. Social learning theory, in practice, means that children need positive role models, to observe and practise behaviours and build strong relationships.

Cognitive development

Piaget is best known for suggesting that children progress through stages of development (see previous chapter), and he believed that children construct knowledge: it is not imposed by conditioning and reinforcement.

His ideas on development are based on the idea of biological adaptation – just as animals adapt to their environment, so the mind adapts its structures to cope with observations and experiences through the processes of accommodation (the ability to take in new experiences and information) and assimilation (the mind modifying itself in the light of new experiences). These processes – accommodation and assimilation – allow the learner to develop equilibrium, or balance, between new information and experiences and internal mental structures, or schemata. So, cognitive development involves taking new experiences into a child's cognitive structures. If these are in conflict, the mind's schemata or structure have to change to accommodate the new information. This

Table 6.1 Piaget's stages of cognitive development

Age	Stage	Learning
Birth–2 years	Sensorimotor	Learning comes from actions: touching, grabbing, sucking, feeling, picking up and dropping
2–7 years	Pre-operational	Children begin to use symbols to represent their discoveries; language and pretend play develop; thinking is not yet logical
7–11 years	Concrete operational	Reasoning is more logical; children can classify and organise things into groups; thinking is still not abstract
12 years and older	Formal operational	Abstract thought begins, and children can reason with symbols that do not refer to concrete objects, e.g. they can think about a range of solutions to a problem

cognitive conflict is said to be a useful part of learning in the classroom. Piaget's work has been criticised, but it is difficult to deny his influence on learning theory and what happens in classrooms, particularly in subjects such as maths and science.

Constructivist theory says that learners are not empty vessels into which knowledge can be poured, but they come with knowledge already organised. Learners will hang new information on to their existing knowledge and ways of understanding the world. For effective learning, new knowledge must be integrated into an existing conceptual structure. Constructivism focuses on the learner and the personal meanings they make based on their prior knowledge. Piaget is probably the best-known constructivist, but George Hein (1998) has proposed a set of nine learning principles of constructivism, in the context of museum education:

1 Learning is an active process in which the learner constructs meaning out of sensory input.
2 People learn to learn as they learn: people learn about the process of learning as well as the content.
3 Learning happens in the mind.
4 Learning and language are inextricably linked – learning involves language: the language we use influences learning.
5 Learning is a social activity and happens with others.
6 Learning is contextual: we do not learn isolated facts and theories in some abstract, ethereal land of the mind, separate from the rest of our lives: we learn in relationship to what else we know, what we believe, our prejudices and our fears.
7 One needs knowledge to learn: it is not possible to assimilate new knowledge without having some structure developed from previous knowledge to build on.
8 It takes time to learn: learning is not instantaneous. For significant learning, we need to revisit ideas, ponder them, try them out, play with them and use them.
9 Motivation is essential for learning.

Constructivism is a significant influence on classrooms today, but, in terms of teaching and learning, perhaps the most useful theory is sociocultural theory and the work of Lev Vygotsky.

Sociocultural theory

Vygotsky said that learning is strongly shaped by the social context (the class, the child's family), culture and the tools used by the teacher. Vygotsky agreed with Piaget that learners are active, constructive beings, and he thought language was important, so that children's talk in the classroom should go alongside practical activity. Pupils who are working together, sharing ideas and supporting each other are being taught within socioculturalism. Vygotsky also thought that teachers and other adults were important for children's learning, because the development of children's higher level thinking comes from co-operation with a teacher.

Vygotsky proposed the idea of a 'zone of proximal development' (the ZPD). The ZPD is the zone between the pupil's actual level (where they are) and the potential level (where they could be), or the difference between the most difficult task a child can do alone and the most difficult task they can do with help. Just as a builder will use scaffolding to help reach the highest points of a building, so teachers and peers can help a child to reach a new idea or skill.

Vygotsky's ideas were controversial, but, had he not died at the age of 38, they would probably have been even more influential. He realised that, in a group of children at the same developmental level, some children were able to learn with a little help, whereas others were not, which formed the basis of his theory. He did not approve of assessment of children's abilities being based on intelligence tests: he thought there should be both quantitative and qualitative data, with observation of children being at least as important as test scores. His most important contribution to our understanding of children's learning is the importance of interaction with teachers and other children. Vygotsky thought that good scaffolding could only come from good observation by teachers, by teachers knowing their children really well and planning the curriculum accordingly – similar to Dewey's idea that teachers use their knowledge of the world to help make sense of it for children.

Based on Piaget's theories, educators had viewed children's knowledge as constructed from personal experiences, but Vygotsky's work showed that social and cognitive development work together, so that personal and social experience cannot be separated. A child's world is shaped by their family, community, socio-economic status and culture. Their understanding of the world comes from the values and beliefs of the adults and other children in their lives – children learn from each other, developing new language skills and understanding new concepts as they speak and listen to each other. Like Piaget, Vygotsky believed that much learning takes place when children play – they use language, they discuss rules and roles and directions, correcting each other and learning about new situations. Where learning used to be something we do on our own, Vygotsky showed how much we learn through working and discussing with others.

Curriculum planning is perhaps the area Vygotsky has had most influence on. Particularly in the US, before Vygotsky, educators who worked with Piaget's theory were reluctant to push children. Piaget believed that, as cognitive development is tied to physical development, children at a particular stage of development are incapable of the reasoning they will grow into at the next stage, and so teachers planned a curriculum that supported children at their current level of development, without stretching them or extending their learning. Vygotsky showed that children's cognitive development is affected by physical development but also by their environment and interactions with others. His ideas are more flexible than Piaget's, because he sees developmental readiness as including skills and ideas that children have not yet reached, but that they can get to with support from teachers and peers, encouraging teachers to plan lessons that scaffold learning and extend children's knowledge. Teachers need to develop skills of observing and questioning, really know their children and encourage peer interactions that will support them, know when to let children work on their own and when to step in with suggestions or ideas.

Communities of learners

One criticism of learning theories is that they tend to focus on individuals, rather than seeing individuals in their environment. We all experience learning in a particular context and often as a group

– a group of student teachers perhaps – and we learn by becoming more involved in our community. The early phase of becoming involved in a community has been called 'legitimate peripheral participation'.

> Learning viewed as situated activity has as its central defining characteristic a process that we call legitimate peripheral participation. By this we mean to draw attention to the point that learners inevitably participate in communities of practitioners and that the mastery of knowledge and skill requires newcomers to move toward full participation in the sociocultural practices of a community. 'Legitimate peripheral participation' provides a way to speak about the relations between newcomers and old-timers, and about activities, identities, artifacts and communities of knowledge and practice. A person's intentions to learn are engaged and the meaning of learning is configured through the process of becoming a full participant in a sociocultural practice. This social process includes, indeed it subsumes, the learning of knowledgeable skills.
>
> (Lave and Wenger 1991, p. 29)

Legitimate peripheral participation means that newcomers do more than observe – they begin to absorb and be absorbed in the 'culture of practice'. After time, learners make the culture of practice theirs. This means, for example, that apprentices begin to know who is involved, what they do, how they talk, work and conduct their lives, what other learners are doing, and what learners need to know to become full practitioners.

Ecological systems theory

Bronfenbrenner's ecological systems theory (see Chapter 4) sees learners as inseparable from their environment – the environment is portrayed as layers, like the rings of an onion. The child's immediate environment – usually his or her family – is the microsystem, and a caring, praising, encouraging environment will support the young child's learning. The mesosystem is where the connections between home, school and community take place. The exosystem does not directly involve the child but still affects them – perhaps the parents' working arrangements or their community connections. The macrosystem is the cultural values, laws and resources of the country – its wealth and institutions will have an impact on the child's experience and all layers of their environment.

In this model, the child is both product and producer of the environment, and the theory stresses the equal importance of the inner child and the environment – nature and nurture – in learning.

Multiple intelligences

Howard Gardner (1943–) developed multiple intelligence theory in the 1980s because he believed that the dominant ideas of intelligence and learning, particularly IQ, were unsatisfactory. The IQ model was based on the idea that intelligence is a measurable, constant entity. This model was discredited for a number of reasons, notably that the tests designed to measure intelligence were often culturally and racially biased in favour of middle-class, white people. Gardner did not think intelligence could be seen or measured and described as an IQ score. His focus is on *how* people are intelligent, rather than how much intelligence they have. He defines intelligence as, 'the ability to solve problems or to create products that are valued within one or more cultural settings'. Gardner saw the emergence of intelligences coming from the opportunities offered to children in a particular context or culture.

Gardner praised Piaget as the single dominant thinker in his field, but thought he placed too much emphasis on logic and number in learning and too little on emotions and motivation. He also criticised the notion of staged development, because, as learners move from one stage to another, they leave behind earlier development. Gardner (and Bruner) said that earlier aspects of development – such as thinking and exploring through play – are not left behind, but can be drawn on to support new skills or experiences.

The idea of multiple intelligences is that our ability is made up of a number of different intelligences that may be present in differing degrees. Each intelligence has its own set of mental operations, and there is no single, overarching mental ability. Traditional views of intelligence focused on certain types of problem-solving (mathematical, logical intelligence) and language abilities (linguistic intelligence). Gardner said that these were just two types of intelligence, and identified eight kinds of intelligence in all:

1 *interpersonal*: the intelligence of social understanding, appreciating and responding to the feelings, intentions and motivations of others;
2 *intrapersonal*: self-knowledge, recognising one's strengths, weaknesses, desires, understanding one's behaviour and feelings;
3 *naturalist*: being able to identify and classify things in the natural world, i.e. plants, animals, minerals;
4 *verbal/linguistic*: relating to words, speech and language;
5 *musical/rhythmic*: relating to tone, rhythm, pitch and timbre;
6 *visual/spatial*: pictures and images;
7 *bodily/kinaesthetic*: of the whole body and hands;
8 *logical/mathematical*: relating to numbers and reasoning, detecting logical and numerical patterns, skill with long chains of logical or mathematical reasoning.

Gardner says that evidence of multiple intelligences comes from the following:

- Damage to specific areas of the brain causes specific difficulties or impairment, for example, with language.
- People can show specific gifts in particular areas, such as music or maths prodigies.
- Specific areas, such as spatial awareness, can be tested in different ways, and correlations between tests can be shown.
- Behaviour can be encoded in a system of symbols – language and maths can be written as well as spoken and read.

Multiple intelligences theory is useful for children who do not excel in the maths or linguistic areas: teachers can use different types of intelligence to support children's learning and can highlight and celebrate particular strengths and abilities, raising confidence and self-esteem. A negative aspect of the theory could be that children are labelled or stereotyped – for example, boys as visual learners, girls as skilled with language. In practice, schools and teachers may not be equipped to deal with multiple intelligences. Children from lower socio-economic backgrounds may not have many opportunities to explore music, for example, even though this might be an area where they could thrive.

Critics suggest the theory is too narrow and has little empirical or scientific evidence to support it. Intelligence is largely a result of experience, and the theory ignores emotional intelligence and the affective domain, which are important aspects of learning. It is a useful theory, however, for encouraging policymakers and teachers to think about personalised learning and individual learners' needs.

Bloom's taxonomy

The thinking skills approach to learning suggests that thinking skills are not just innate and unchanging – things we are born with that remain at one level – but skills that can grow and develop in the right environment and with the right teaching and learning interventions. There does not seem to be agreement on exactly what thinking skills are, but many people refer to Bloom's taxonomy of educational objectives, developed in 1956 (see Figure 6.1). This shows skills in a hierarchy, from simple recall of information at the bottom to making judgements about the usefulness and reliability of an idea at the top. Each of the levels is broken down into different skills: knowledge includes listing, defining and recalling; synthesis includes reorganising, arranging, speculating and hypothesising, and so on.

In the 1990s, a former student of Bloom's, Lorin Anderson, worked with a new group of psychologists to update the taxonomy and make it more relevant (see Figure 6.2). Note the change to verbs.

Other lists have related to the information society and included skills such as finding, organising and analysing information. Still others include problem-solving, brainstorming ideas, finding evidence or dispositions and attitudes towards learning, such as being flexible and listening to others. These relate more to the affective domain of Bloom's taxonomy (attitudes, motivation and emotion) rather than the cognitive, learning domain.

Metacognition can be defined as looking down and reflecting on cognition – thinking about thinking, being aware of one's own

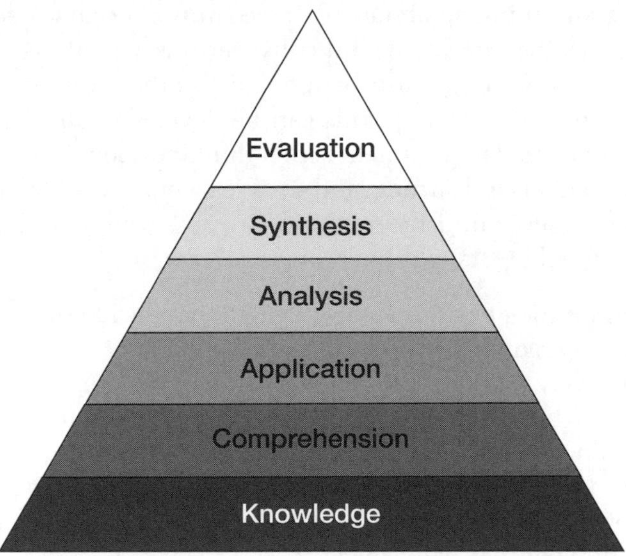

Figure 6.1 Bloom's taxonomy

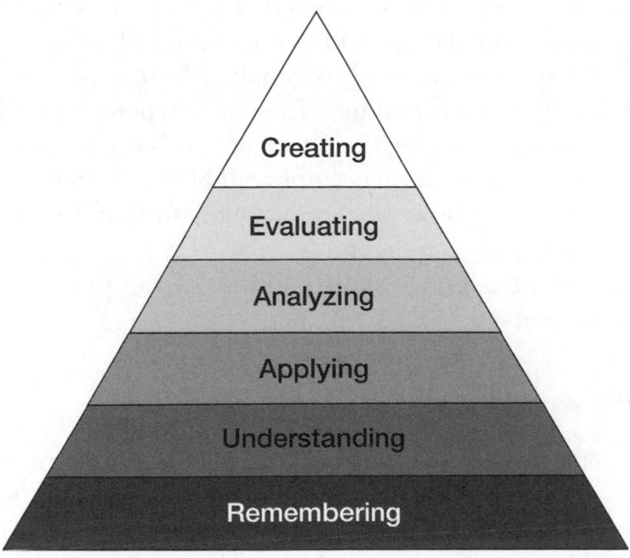

Figure 6.2 Updated taxonomy

thinking and thinking about it. Metacognition occurs if someone is aware that they are having difficulty learning something and start to wonder why. It can also be applied to other contexts, so, for example, problem-solving skills can be developed and applied to many situations. The argument is that thinking about how we think and learn enhances learning, and so, if learners know how to study and learn, they will achieve more. Ormrod (1995) suggests that learners should be taught how to:

- monitor their existing knowledge, so that they know what they know already;
- effectively recall previously learned knowledge;
- know which strategies are or are not effective for their own learning, and how to use those that are effective;
- plan an approach to a learning task that is likely to be effective;
- know their own learning and memory abilities and be realistic about what they can achieve.

Arguments for adopting the thinking skills approach include the following:

- The information society means that no one can know all there is to know about a topic, and so the important skill is to be able to find, organise, evaluate and apply information.
- A thinking skills curriculum is a better preparation for life and employment than a curriculum that is subject based.
- Subject knowledge soon becomes out of date in today's society, and so knowing how to learn and how to find information is more important than learning facts.
- These are transferable skills and can lead to improved examination results.

Learning styles

The concept of learning styles is that people can learn in many different ways, but, for each learner, there are special, individual conditions that promote learning – each of us has our own learning style. The idea developed in the 1970s. There are many versions of learning styles, but one of the best known is Kolb's (1984), from which he developed a learning style inventory. Kolb's model involves four stages:

1. *concrete experience*: the learner encounters a new experience or situation or reinterprets existing experience;
2. *reflective observation of the new experience*: inconsistencies between experience and understanding are particularly important;
3. *abstract conceptualisation*: the reflection leads to a new idea or a modification of an existing concept;
4. *active experimentation*: the learner applies the concepts to the world around them to see what results.

Learning is a cyclical process, with each stage supporting and feeding into the next. Learners can enter the cycle at any stage and follow the sequence, but must go through all four stages for effective learning to occur (see Figure 6.3).

Another common model of learning styles is Fleming's VARK model:

- Visual learners
- Auditory learners
- Reading–writing preference learners
- Kinaesthetic or tactile learners.

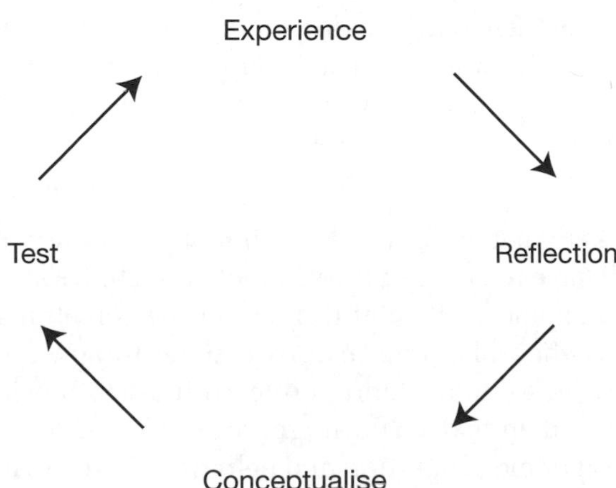

Figure 6.3 Learning styles model

The idea behind the model is that visual learners have a preference for seeing – for example, pictures and visual aids such as diagrams. Auditory learners learn best through listening (lectures, discussions), and kinaesthetic learners learn best through experience (moving, touching, experiments and projects). Students can identify their preferred learning style and focus on what suits them best to maximise their learning. There is obviously a difference between having a preferred learning style and saying that students can only learn in a particular way.

There are those who say that teachers should assess the learning styles of their students and adapt their teaching methods to best fit each student's learning styles. Critics will say that, although there is a lot of evidence for differences in individual thinking and ways of processing information, few studies have reliably tested the validity of using learning styles in education, and there is little evidence that identifying individual learning styles leads to better outcomes. In 2005, the think tank Demos produced a report on learning styles that said the evidence was highly variable, and practitioners were 'not by any means' frank about the evidence for their work (Hargreaves 2005).

There are a number of researchers who wonder why we are even still talking about learning styles, for example:

> The contrast between the enormous popularity of the learning-styles approach within education and the lack of credible evidence for its utility is, in our opinion, striking and disturbing. If classification of students' learning styles has practical utility, it remains to be demonstrated.
>
> (Pashler *et al.* 2008)

It is unlikely that, within a classroom of up to thirty children, a teacher will have the time to think about each child's learning style and how to exploit it. It might, however, be something that you think about when planning lessons – some things, for example, might be easier to understand and learn if set to music, or using images rather than texts. You might also consider learning styles in the context of metacognition and helping children to understand and learn how they learn, developing learning skills for life. An article published in *The Guardian* (Revell 2005) sets out some of the arguments around learning styles and also gives examples where they are used in schools.

Further reading

Helping Young Children to Play
T. Bruce, 2001, Hodder & Stoughton
Now out of print, but this is a useful book, written for childcare students, that concentrates on the practical aspects of play.

Learning Through Play: For babies, toddlers and young children
T. Bruce, 2011 (2nd edn), Hodder Education
Professor Bruce is an acknowledged expert on play. This is a useful book for its guide to the values behind play and the relationship between play and child development. It is interesting to read alongside Moyles' work (see below).

Metacognition in Young Children
S. Larkin, 2009, Routledge
This book brings together international research to look at how we might encourage metacognition in primary-aged children.

The Excellence of Play
J. Moyles, 2010 (3rd edn), Open University Press
Now an Emeritus Professor, Janet Moyles is well known for her work on the early years and play. It is interesting to read her work alongside that of Tina Bruce, as Moyles stresses the use of play to support learning, whereas Bruce talks about free-flow play, which is child initiated.

Rethinking Play and Pedagogy in Early Childhood Education: Concepts, contexts and cultures
S. Rogers (ed.), 2010, Routledge
This book brings together a collection of papers from international experts to examine how play is important in the early years.

Play, Learning and the Early Childhood Curriculum
E. A. Wood, 2013 (3rd edn), Sage
Now in its third edition, the book has been updated to reflect current thinking about the importance of play and includes work from practitioners to show how theory and practice can be linked.

References

Department for Education (2012) *The Statutory Framework for the Early Years Foundation Stage*. Available at: www.education.gov.uk/aboutdfe/statutory/g00213120/eyfs-statutory-framework (accessed March 2014).

Department for Education (2013) *The Early Years Foundation Stage Profile Handbook 2014*. Available at: www.gov.uk/government/publications/early-years-foundation-stage-profile-handbook-2014 (accessed March 2014).

Hargreaves, D. (2005) *About Learning: Report of the Learning Working Group*, London: Demos. Available at: www.demos.co.uk/publications/aboutlearning (accessed March 2014).

Hein, G. E. (1998) *Learning in the Museum*, London: Routledge. (Hein's principles are also available at: www.exploratorium.edu/ifi/resources/research/constructivistlearning.html [accessed March 2014].)

Isaacs, S. (1933) *Social Development of Young Children*, Abingdon, UK: Routledge.

Kolb, D. (1984) *Experiential Learning: Experience as the source of learning and development*, Englewood Cliffs, NJ: Prentice Hall.

Lave, J. and Wenger, E. (1991) *Situated Learning: Legitimate peripheral participation*, Cambridge, UK: Cambridge University Press.

Lindon, J. (2001) *Understanding Children's Play*, Cheltenham, UK: Nelson Thornes.

Moyles, J., Adams, S. and Musgrove, A. (2002) *Study of Pedagogical Effectiveness in Early Learning (SPEEL)*, Research report 363, London: DfES.

Ormrod, J. E. (1995) *Human Learning*, London: Prentice Hall.

Parten, M. (1932) Social participation among preschool children, *Journal of Abnormal and Social Psychology*, 28(3): 136–47. Available at: http://dx.doi.org/10.1037%2Fh0074524 (accessed March 2014).

Pashler, H., McDaniel, M., Rohrer, D. and Bjork, R. (2008) Learning styles: concepts and evidence, *Psychological Science in the Public Interest*, 9(3). Available at: www.psychologicalscience.org/journals/pspi/PSPI_9_3.pdf (accessed March 2014).

Pound, L. (2006) *How Children Learn*, London: Practical Pre-school Books.

Revell, P. (2005) Each to their own, *The Guardian*, 31 May. Available at: www.theguardian.com/education/2005/may/31/schools.uk3 (accessed March 2014).

7 Theories of motivation

Motivation is the art of getting people to do what you want them to do because they want to do it.

(Dwight D. Eisenhower)

Motivation is seen as the key to learning: the affective (emotional) domain of humans should be given as much attention as the cognitive (knowledge and skill) domain. How would you define motivation? Is it what gets you out of bed in the morning? Drive, interest, enthusiasm, commitment, 'hunger'? Simply, motivation is about the 'whys' of behaviour. For scientists, it is an internal state that arouses, energises and directs behaviour. Motivation is vital for learning, because it can lead to enthusiasm, risk-taking, perseverance and commitment from pupils. Lack of motivation can lead to (or come from) fear of failure, low self-esteem and low self-expectations, which lead to poor performance and a downward spiral. Teachers cannot control the motivation of a student but can act in ways that are most likely to influence motivation, whether positively or negatively.

Few books for teachers look at motivation in any detail. They might look at tips and hints for motivating children, but not at the theories of motivation, probably because these are concerned with adults and are usually work-related. There is also a view that we do not need to think about motivation in relation to young children, because they have a natural curiosity, enthusiasm for learning and discovering and a desire to please their teachers, and so they are already motivated.

Under the heading of 'active learning – motivation', the *Early Years Foundation Stage Profile Handbook 2014* (Department for Education 2013) describes the following:

- Being involved and concentrating describes the intensity of attention that arises from children concentrating on following a line of interest in their activities.
- Keeping on trying refers to the importance of persistence even in the face of challenge or difficulties, an element of purposeful control which supports resilience.
- Enjoying achieving what they set out to do refers to the reward of meeting one's own goals, building on the intrinsic motivation which supports long-term success, rather than relying on the approval of others.

Theories of motivation are based on the idea that there is no random behaviour: whatever we do, we do for a reason. Freud would say that, although there are always motives for behaviour, we are not necessarily consciously aware of why we do what we do. Theorists are making connections between behaviour and the reasons or motives behind it.

Humanistic theories

Probably the most famous theory of motivation is Maslow's hierarchy of needs (1943). This is always presented as a triangle, although the words can differ (see Figure 7.1). Maslow's theory is that human beings have needs that they are driven, and want, to meet.

During the 1960s and 1970s, Maslow added additional layers for aesthetic, cognitive and transcendence needs.

He argued that we have to satisfy needs lower in the hierarchy before the higher level needs of esteem and self-actualisation can be met (part of the theory was that very few people, perhaps one in a hundred, achieve self-actualisation, although that is not relevant here as we are focusing on children). Meeting those needs is what motivates us. So, unless our needs for warmth and food and shelter are met, and we feel secure and meet our social needs, we are unlikely to be successful. Critics of the theory argue that these things

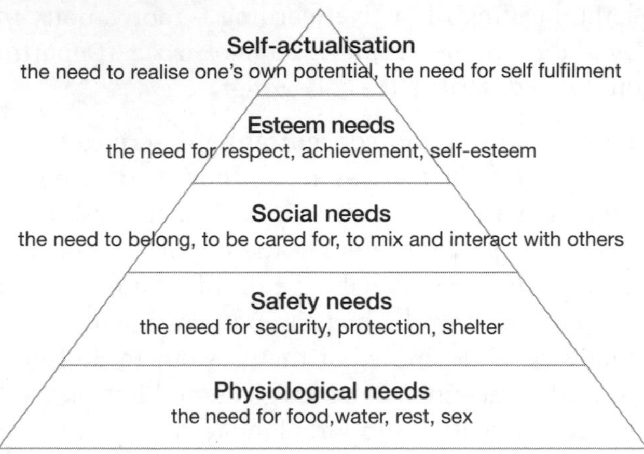

Figure 7.1 Maslow's hierarchy of needs

are not hierarchical and we could aim to satisfy several needs at once. In a classroom situation, however, the hierarchy makes a lot of sense. You will know that it is difficult to learn if the classroom is cold, or you missed breakfast and desperately need a cup of coffee, or you cannot stop thinking about a problem at home. So, children are unlikely to learn if they are hungry or thirsty, cold, tired or feeling insecure. This is one reason why some schools have started breakfast clubs, to make sure that children have something to eat and drink at the beginning of the day. Maslow (1970) suggests that teachers should make sure classrooms are supportive environments. Students need to be shown that they are valued and respected and feel emotionally and physically safe and secure within the classroom, before they can learn.

The main criticism of Maslow's theory concerns his ideas of self-actualisation, because his methods were not rigorous. He looked at eighteen individuals he considered to be self-actualised, a biased sample of highly educated, mostly white males (including Abraham Lincoln, Albert Einstein, Gandhi and Beethoven). His methodology was biographical analysis, which is subjective.

Other theorists refer to other needs – Rogers (1961) says we have a need for self-regard, whereas Harré (1979) says we need social respect.

Expectancy theory

Following on from Maslow, Vroom created his expectancy theory (1964). This relates to the workplace, but attempts to show why people follow a particular course of action. Three variables affect how you feel and how you perform:

- *Value* is the importance attached to the particular outcome of a situation.
- *Expectancy* is the belief that there is a link between your output and the success of the situation.
- *Instrumentality* is the belief that the success of the situation is linked to the expected outcomes.

Vroom said that all three factors had to be in place for motivation to occur: if they were not, then the chances were that you would not engage in any new learning or behaviour, and you would struggle to maintain your motivation. So, for example, for you to be successful with a job application, you would have to believe that you would be offered the post, the increased salary would be worth having, and the job would satisfy your career goals.

Vroom believed that expectancy theory could be applied to any situation where someone does something because they expect a particular outcome. Vroom said that how motivated you are depends on whether you want a reward for doing a good job, and whether you believe making more effort leads to that reward.

Attribution theory

Weiner (1974) proposed attribution theory, built on earlier work by Rotter (1966), who developed the concept of locus of control. Someone with an internal locus of control would assume personal responsibility for what happened to them and would see the consequence of their behaviour – reward or punishment – as entirely a result of their own actions. An individual with external locus of control would not see the results of their behaviour, whether good or bad, as a result of their own actions. The consequences of their behaviour would be the result of chance, fate, luck or the actions of others.

Attribution theory is about explanation and expectations. Students attribute particular characteristics to themselves to explain their success or failure. A student with low motivation and low self-esteem will blame his lack of success on his lack of ability, which he sees as fixed, so that, when he does have some success, he will attribute this to luck or something else outside his control, not to his effort or ability. A highly motivated student has confidence in his ability and the importance of making an effort, and so he will attribute any success he has to his ability and hard work. This is called self-efficacy, our belief that we can control our own learning and achievement and future. Success is not put down to luck, nor failure to a difficult exam. Self-efficacy contrasts with learned helplessness, the feeling that our lack of success is outside our control and we cannot do anything to change things. Self-efficacy was a concept from Bandura (1986). Students with a high estimation of their personal effectiveness show greater persistence, effort, motivation and interest in their education. Self-efficacy is really important, because it determines what an individual chooses to do, the amount of effort and persistence they put into a task. The more self-efficacy someone has, the more they try to succeed in difficult circumstances.

The concept of learned helplessness has come from work by Seligman and Maier (1967). They carried out studies with dogs, exposing them to unavoidable electric shocks over a period of time. Even when the conditions changed and the dogs could escape from the electric shocks, they did not do so. The dogs had learned that whatever they did had no effect on their environment, and so they did nothing. People with very low self-esteem may exhibit learned helplessness, as they believe that whatever they do will have no effect. This shows the importance of expectations – if pupils and teachers have high expectations, this can often lead to higher achievement. If teachers have low expectations of pupils, and if pupils have low expectations of themselves, this can lead to a downward spiral of achievement. This is a self-fulfilling prophecy – if teachers believe that a child will perform badly and expect low achievement, this seems to affect both the teacher and the pupil, and the prophecy comes true. It can be important to value independent thought rather than correct answers, and to set challenging work to raise students' view of their abilities. Students need to experience success and failure, so that they can see a link between their actions and the outcomes, but also because students who always succeed may experience learned helplessness in the same way as those who always fail.

It is suggested that the importance of expectations can be seen in gender differences in education – girls expect to do better in 'feminine' areas such as art, writing and literature, whereas boys expect to do better in 'masculine' subjects such as mathematics, technology and science, and these expectations affect their performance.

Intrinsic and extrinsic motivation

Motivation can be intrinsic or extrinsic. Intrinsic comes from within – the learner's interests, curiosity, feelings of interest, personal satisfaction and achievement. Extrinsic motivation comes from rewards, incentives or punishment. Extrinsic motivation can come from payment or thanks, 'carrots' or 'sticks', or avoiding punishment. It is linked to behaviourist psychology, which emphasises using rewards and punishment to shape and condition behaviour. There is debate over which kind of motivation is most important in schools. Learning is not like the behaviour of rats, in that it is important in its own right, not just a way of avoiding punishment or receiving a reward. It is often argued that intrinsic motivation is stronger and more permanent and leads to the highest levels of achievement. It does not have to be 'either or', however – both types of motivation can exist side by side. Just as payment for a job does not mean that the jobholder does not derive fulfilment and satisfaction from it, in schools, extrinsic motivation from stickers, awards, prizes and applause can have an important effect on self-esteem and achievement and may lead to intrinsic motivation. Praise from teachers is vitally important for all students.

Those who support progressive education will say that the only kind of meaningful motivation comes from interest and absorption in the task or subject itself. Children should want to do an activity because it interests them – intrinsic motivation.

On the other hand, formalists will say that life is not like this – a lot of what has to be learned is dull and difficult, but this is just part of the real world. Motivation is extrinsic – encouragement to learn comes from rewards, the praise and approval of teachers, a desire to achieve better grades, reports to parents and other incentives and sanctions.

Recent research

In 2005, Smith *et al.* carried out a systematic literature review looking at what pupils aged 11–16 believe impacts on their motivation to learn in the classroom.

> A **systematic literature review** focuses on a research question and tries to identify, appraise, select and synthesise all high-quality research relating to that question. The review aims to provide an exhaustive summary of current literature relevant to that question.

The review identified six themes as the key to motivation. A summary of the points made under each theme is as follows:

The role of the self

- Pupils make decisions about school subjects as a result of a range of interconnected factors that occur over time.
- Once made, these decisions become the dominant influence on the levels of engagement.
- A belief in innate preferences for particular subjects can be confirmed by parental preferences.
- The dichotomy between performance and mastery goals is too simplistic.
- Group work appears to result in greater engagement by pupils.
- Teacher expectations impact on the effort expended by pupils on school-related work.

- Boys interviewed in one study felt that the adult community held erroneous perceptions about how they saw themselves and how this impacted on their motivation to learn.

Utility

- Students appear to be more motivated by activities that they perceive as useful or relevant.
- Even where students perceive a task to be useful, they are not necessarily motivated to go beyond the requirements of the specified learning task.

Pedagogical issues

- Some pupils perceive schoolwork as boring and repetitive.
- Pupils perceive that a teacher's approach, attitude and enthusiasm influence their engagement.
- Pupils appear to be more engaged with lessons that they perceive to be fun.
- Pupils appear less interested when classroom activity takes a formal, passive form.
- Pupils express a preference for collaborative work.
- Authentic learning tasks are more likely to cognitively engage pupils.

The influence of peers

- Being perceived as clever appears to be socially acceptable and a source of social respect among peers. However, if 'cleverness' is combined with other characteristics that transgress peer-group norms and values, then it is perceived to be less acceptable.
- Pupils perceive that the norms and organisation of 'school' interfere with other, more desirable forms of peer-group interaction.
- Pupils frequently expressed the importance of not being made to appear foolish in front of their peer group.

Learning

- Pupils believe that effort is important and can make a difference.
- Pupil effort appears to be influenced by the expectations of the teacher and expectations of the wider community.
- Pupils suggested that increased self-understanding came from collaboration, varied methodology and active, experiential work.

Curriculum

- Some pupils perceive the curriculum to be restricted in what it recognises and values as student achievement.
- Curricula can isolate pupils from their peers and from the subject matter.
- The way that the curriculum is mediated can send messages that it is not accessible to all.
- The way that assessment of the curriculum is constructed and practised in school appears to influence how pupils see themselves as learners and social beings (Smith *et al.* 2005, p. 3).

One of the conclusions from the review was that there is a real lack of robust studies focusing on pupil views, and more research needs to be undertaken. The researchers found that motivation (as well as demotivation) is complex and the result of causal chains rather than single causes. Teacher expectations can impact positively and negatively on pupil motivation, and teacher expectations can be too low. There are also other factors outside the classroom that impact on motivation, such as parental views and the wider cultural view of the worth of education, so that although teachers can make a difference, they may not by themselves be able to change the motivation of disaffected or disengaged pupils.

The findings suggest that pupil engagement in learning is more likely if:

- lessons are perceived to be fun;
- lessons are varied and participative;

- teachers favour collaborative methodologies;
- pupils perceive activities as useful and authentic.

In 2010, a report by Ofsted (*Learning: Creative approaches that raise standards*) found that pupils' motivation, progress and attainment in primary and secondary schools were improved by creative approaches to learning, such as:

- stimulating pupils with memorable experiences and practical activity;
- allowing pupils to question, explore and challenge ideas;
- encouraging pupils to think creatively;
- supporting pupils to reflect on and evaluate their learning.

Inspectors found that, in schools with good teaching, there was no conflict between the National Curriculum and creative approaches to learning. These schools drew on content and skills specified in the National Curriculum in their planning and good practice. Pupils' motivation was reinforced by the awareness they gained from tracking their own progress. Creative learning was understood to be characterised by:

- questioning and challenging;
- making connections and seeing relationships;
- envisaging what might be;
- exploring ideas, keeping options open;
- reflecting critically on ideas, actions and outcomes.

The report recommends that all schools should:

- from the Early Years Foundation Stage onwards, ensure that pupils are actively encouraged to ask questions, hypothesise and share their ideas, and that these skills extend into their writing;
- in curriculum planning, balance opportunities for creative ways of learning with secure coverage of National Curriculum subjects and skills;
- provide continuing professional development to ensure that teachers and support staff have the knowledge, skills and confidence to encourage pupils to be independent and creative learners, and to monitor and assess the effectiveness with which they develop these capabilities;

- ensure that all pupils develop skills in technology to support independent and creative learning;
- support and sustain partnerships that have the potential to develop pupils of all abilities as confident and creative learners.

Improving motivation

Cox (1991, in Bentham 2002) suggests behavioural techniques such as shaping. His guidelines for improving motivation come from the basic behaviour modification techniques suggested by Skinner, but also include a person-centred approach, recognising the effects of positive and negative motivation. With a focus on the importance of verbal feedback, Cox suggests:

- giving feedback as soon as possible;
- avoiding value statements such as 'that's great', which are unclear and not very helpful; students need to know what is being praised, and praise needs to be genuine;
- any negative feedback should be given privately, so that students are not embarrassed in front of the rest of the group;
- corrective feedback should be framed positively – better to say 'Next time try and do this . . .', rather than, 'Don't do that'.

One way to combat learned helplessness and improve motivation is to increase a student's involvement in learning, through setting goals and targets. If the teacher sets goals and targets, students can see themselves as performing for others, and this could lead to a fear of falling short of others' expectations. Target setting for pupils can boost confidence, encourage them to take responsibility for their own learning and raise achievement. Students should negotiate goals with the teacher that are clear and specific, moderately difficult and achievable in the near future. Achieving the goals and being given praise and feedback should raise self-esteem and motivation. SMART goals are *s*pecific, *m*easurable, *a*ttainable, *r*ealistic and *t*imebound.

Further reading

Essential Motivation in the Classroom
Ian Gilbert, 2002, RoutledgeFalmer
An entertaining read, offers lots of advice and practical tips, many anecdotes.

The Art of Peaceful Teaching in the Primary School: Improving behaviour and preserving motivation
Michelle McGrath, 2000, David Fulton
A very accessible book, practical rather than theoretical, with some useful examples and practical advice for teachers.

References

Bandura, A. (1986) *Social Foundations of Thought and Action*, Englewood Cliffs, NJ: Prentice Hall.

Bentham, S. (2002) *Psychology and Education*, Hove, UK: Psychology Press.

Department for Education (2013) *The Early Years Foundation Stage Profile Handbook 2014*. Available at: www.gov.uk/government/publications/early-years-foundation-stage-profile-handbook-2014 (accessed March 2014).

Harré, R. (1979) *Social Being*, Oxford, UK: Blackwell.

Maslow, A. H. (1943) A theory of human motivation, *Psychological Review*, 50(4): 370–96.

Maslow, A. H. (1970) *Motivation and Personality*, New York: Harper & Row.

Ofsted (2010) *Learning: Creative approaches that raise standards*. Available at: www.ofsted.gov.uk/publications/080266 (accessed March 2014).

Rogers, C. (1961) *On Becoming a Person: A therapist's view of psychotherapy*, London: Constable.

Rotter, J. B. (1966) Generalised expectancies for internal vs external control of reinforcement, *Psychological Monographs*, 80(1).

Seligman, M. E. P. and Maier, S. F. (1967) Failure to escape traumatic shock, *Journal of Experimental Psychology*, 74: 1–9.

Smith, C., Dakers, J., Dow, W., Head, G., Sutherland, M. and Irwin, R. (2005) A systematic review of what pupils aged11–16 believe impacts on their motivation to learn in the classroom, in *Research Evidence in Education Library*, London: EPPI-Centre, Social Science Research Unit, Institute of Education, University of London.

Vroom, V. H. (1964) *Work and Motivation*, New York: Wiley.

Weiner, B. (1974) *Achievement and Attribution Theory*, Morristown, NJ: General Learning Press.

8 Behaviour for learning

No matter how strange, behaviour always has a purpose or function.

(LaVigna and Donellan)

Being able to manage behaviour in the classroom is often what concerns beginning teachers the most. It is important, however, to think about the language we use – the idea of behaviour management carries with it notions of controlling others and issues of power. Behaviour in the classroom can be seen as a continuum – at one end is the authoritarian classroom, where the teacher is in control of the students and punishes them if they misbehave; at the other is a permissive approach, where students do as they please. 'Misguided teachers who constantly tell their pupils to sit down and be quiet imply a preference for working with a group of trees, not a classroom of people' (Robert Sylwester, Professor Emeritus of Education, University of Oregon, cited in Didau 2012).

In 2008, the annual conference of members of the Association of Teachers and Lecturers (ATL) heard the results of a survey of behaviour in UK schools. Of 800 teachers questioned, one in ten said they had been attacked and injured by violent pupils, three out of ten had experienced 'physical aggression', and three-quarters said they had been threatened or insulted by pupils. Almost all reported problems with low-level disruption. ATL general secretary Mary Bousted told the conference, 'No teacher should have to tolerate these unacceptable levels of poor pupil behaviour and certainly no one should be attacked in school' (Taylor 2008). In May 2008, Education Secretary Ed Balls announced that heads were to be granted new powers to search for alcohol, drugs and stolen goods and that there were plans to reform pupil referral units. Every child would have a tailored plan for improving behaviour and school results (*The Guardian*, 21 May).

I am not denying that there are issues, but it is important not to overstate problems around behaviour – a consistent message is that the majority of children and young people enjoy learning, work hard and behave well (Ofsted 2005). A survey by Bate and Moss (1997) found that the older pupils are, the less teachers think there should be a need to teach behaviour skills: teachers in the survey thought that 84 per cent of behavioural skills should have been established at primary level.

In 1989, the Elton Report was a response to media coverage of an apparent decline in standards of behaviour in schools (Department for Education and Science 1989). Commenting on the concerns that had led to the setting up of the Elton Inquiry, the report said:

- Bad behaviour is not a new problem, nor is it confined to England and Wales.
- Reducing misbehaviour is a realistic aim, eliminating it completely is not.
- Persistent, low level disruptive behaviour is the type of behaviour that concerns teachers most, due largely to its frequent, wearing nature.

(Department for Education and Science 1989, p. 65)

The report used the term classroom management, not behaviour management. Group management is an aspect of classroom management, which includes the teacher's subject knowledge and the ability to plan and deliver a lesson that flows smoothly and holds pupils' attention. The report suggested that group management skills included 'the ability to relate to young people, to encourage them in good behaviour and learning and to deal calmly but firmly with inappropriate or disruptive behaviour' (Department for Education and Science 1989, p. 67). The report firmly refuted the idea that the skills could not be taught but were a natural gift: 'The central problem of disruption could be significantly reduced by helping teachers to become more effective classroom managers' (Department for Education and Science 1989, p. 12).

A significant finding of the report was that some schools have a more positive atmosphere than others, and it was these positive schools that tended to have more positive work and behaviour. Although children's home background is important, the role of the school is very influential:

> A child from a disadvantaged background is still likely on average to do less well than a child from an advantaged home when they attend the same school. But if the disadvantaged child attends an effective school he may well do better than a more disadvantaged child attending an ineffective school.
>
> (Department for Education and Science 1989, p. 88)

Furthermore:

> Research evidence suggests that pupils' behaviour can be influenced by all the major features and processes of a school. These include the quality of its leadership, classroom management, behaviour policy, curriculum, pastoral care, buildings and physical environment, organisation and timetable and relationships with parents.
>
> (Department for Education and Science 1989, p. 89–90)

It was, perhaps, unfortunate that the Elton Report was released at the same time as the National Curriculum was introduced.

The Elton Report says that there is general agreement in the literature about the elements of good practice. Teachers should:

- Know their pupils as individuals. This means knowing their names, their personalities and interests and who their friends are.
- Plan and organise both the classroom and the lesson to keep pupils interested and minimise the opportunities for disruption. This requires attention to such basics as furniture layout, grouping of pupils, matching work to pupils'

abilities, pacing lessons well, being enthusiastic and using humour to create a positive classroom atmosphere.

- Be flexible in order to take advantage of unexpected events rather than being thrown off balance by them. Examples would include the appearance of the window cleaner or a wasp in the middle of a lesson.
- Continually observe or 'scan' the behaviour of the class.
- Be aware of, and control their own behaviour, including stance and tone of voice.
- Model the standards of courtesy that they expect from pupils.
- Emphasise the positive, including praise for good behaviour as well as good work.
- Make the rules for classroom behaviour clear to pupils from the first lesson and explain why they are necessary.
- Make sparing and consistent use of reprimands. This means being firm rather than aggressive, targeting the right pupil, criticising the behaviour and not the person, using private rather than public reprimands whenever possible, being fair and consistent, and avoiding sarcasm and idle threats.
- Make sparing and consistent use of punishments. This includes avoiding whole group punishment which pupils see as unfair. It also means avoiding punishments which humiliate pupils by, for example, making them look ridiculous. This breeds resentment.
- Analyse their own classroom management performance and learn from it. This is the most important message of all.

(Department for Education and Science 1989, pp. 71–2)

Following the Elton Report, in 1994, for the only time in its history, the DfE produced a co-ordinated suite of six circulars for schools, offering advice on the education and management of children with challenging behaviour and medical needs, in the light of recent legislation. The set of circulars was entitled *Pupils with Problems*, which, as Ellis and Tod (2009) point out, locates the problem within the pupil, reflecting the prevailing beliefs regarding the causes of learning and behaviour difficulties experienced by pupils.

In 2005, the Steer Report, *Learning Behaviour: The report of the Practitioners' Group on School Behaviour and Discipline,* was, like the Elton Report, prompted by media interest in behaviour in schools (Department for Education and Skills 2005). As Ellis and Tod (2009) point out, the Steer Report outlined ten aspects of effective school practice that contribute to the quality of pupil behaviour. Each of these aspects was also identified in the Elton Report 16 years before: Steer recognised that the key principles about the management of pupil behaviour have been known for a long time. The report listed six core beliefs about behaviour in schools:

- The quality of learning, teaching and behaviour in schools are inseparable issues and the responsibility of all staff.
- Poor behaviour cannot be tolerated as it is a denial of the right of pupils to learn and teachers to teach. To enable learning to take place preventative action is the most effective, but where this fails, schools must have clear, firm and intelligent strategies in place to help pupils manage their behaviour.
- There is no single solution to the problem of poor behaviour, but all schools have the potential to raise standards if they are consistent in implementing good practice in learning, teaching and behaviour management.
- Respect has to be given in order to be received. Parents and carers, pupils and teachers all need to operate in a culture of mutual regard.
- The support of parents is essential for the maintenance of good behaviour. Parents and schools each need to have a clear understanding of their rights and responsibilities.
- School leaders have a critical role in establishing high standards of learning, teaching and behaviour.

(Department for Education and Skills 2005, p. 2)

A follow-up report, *Learning Behaviour: Lessons learned* (Department for Children, Schools and Families 2009), said that good teaching was a prerequisite for good behaviour: 'The need for consistent good quality teaching, as the basis for raising standards and reducing low level disruption, has been highlighted both by Ofsted and fellow practitioners' (Department for Children, Schools and Families 2009, p. 63). The report stressed:

- the importance of early intervention and disseminating good practice to schools;
- appropriate engagement of, and support for pupils; withdrawal from class where appropriate;
- engagement of parents should be supported and strengthened, with more consistent use of parents' contracts;
- the role of local authorities in prioritising support for pupils and making provision for excluded pupils;
- the roles of local authorities and children's trusts in relation to behaviour and attendance partnerships.

The theories

Much of the material in this section is taken from Porter (2006).

Behaviourism

> A major concern within the behavioural approach to teaching is with the identification of things and events which children find rewarding and to structure the teaching environment so as to make access to these rewards dependent upon behaviour which the teacher wants to encourage in his class.
>
> (Wheldall and Merrett 1984, p. 19)

Behaviours usually begin randomly. According to behaviourism, voluntary behaviour (operant behaviour) is controlled by the responses it receives, so that, if you want to increase a particular behaviour, you follow it with a reinforcing consequence, or follow it with a punishing consequence to reduce the behaviour. The environment can make particular behaviours more or less likely to occur. According to behaviourism, the main purpose of managing behaviour is to establish or maintain order, so that students can learn effectively.

Behaviourist interventions begin by observing and defining the behaviour that needs to be increased or decreased – the target behaviour. According to O'Leary (1972), the target behaviours must be significant, not just acts that are inconvenient to others. You then define what the behaviour will look like, following a successful intervention. The advice (Maag 2001) is to think small and keep in mind that children with behavioural difficulties cannot be expected to behave perfectly or better than children without difficulties. The intervention occurs in four phases, which could form the basis of a written 'contract' negotiated with students.

Phase 1: assessment

Observe and record in detail how often the behaviour occurs, under what conditions, and what response follows. When you have the details, you can analyse the information, perhaps by producing a graph or chart. When you have decided on your intervention, you will carry out observation again, so that you can see how effective it is.

Phase 2: adjust antecedents

Antecedents are the conditions under which behaviour occurs. After you have completed your observation and recording, you can interrogate your data, so that you can see if there are any situations in which the behaviour seldom occurs, whether it only occurs with particular teachers, or in particular lessons, or at a specific time of day, and so on. Positive behaviour support says that, as behaviour occurs within specific contexts, you have to adjust the contexts, rather than trying to blame individual students. This could mean looking at the working environment – a young child who is disruptive might feel more comfortable sitting close to the teacher, for example – or altering the pattern of the day, so that more difficult tasks come earlier, or are interspersed with different work. Whatever you do should give pupils more positive attention and help to build their self-esteem and relationships with others.

Phase 3: increase reinforcement for desired behaviours

If a pupil cannot complete a task, you can think about breaking it down into small, achievable steps or giving prompts to help them and gradually withdrawing these (called fading). You can model or demonstrate the behaviour needed to complete the task, or begin by reinforcing performance that is less than desired and then requiring small improvements until performance is at the required level (shaping). When students can perform the desired behaviours, these can be strengthened by reinforcement – this can be for the student or the whole class. There are various types of reinforcement. Activity reinforcement involves, for example, being able to choose the activity for half an hour on a Friday afternoon or hearing a story. Tangible reinforcement is things such as stickers and stars; social reinforcement can be praise from the teacher or time to spend with friends; token reinforcement is something such as putting a marble in a jar when one of the students does something you want to reinforce, and then rewarding the whole class when the jar is full; negative reinforcement is removing something – for example, taking away the need to do homework. To be of use, the reinforcement or reward needs to be achievable. Porter (2006) gives the example of a small boy who received a letter from his teacher telling him that, to attend the end of year party in 2 weeks' time, he would need 72 points. In 2 terms he had achieved 6 points: achieving a further 66 in 2 weeks was impossible. The chances are that a child in this position would feel very disheartened, and negative behaviours could increase.

Phase 4: punishing undesired behaviours

When desired behaviour has been strengthened, other behaviour could be reduced or weakened by using punishment. There are three rules governing the use of punishment:

- the ethical principle that punishment should only be applied to behaviours that cannot be dealt with in any other way;

- these behaviours must be serious enough to warrant the use of punishment, for example, the behaviour is potentially dangerous or interferes with other students' learning;
- it must be linked with a desired behaviour, so that pupils have something else to do in place of an inappropriate behaviour – known as the fair pair principle.

As a teacher, you must be clear about the behaviour you wish to reduce, identifying what actually happens, rather than labelling the student or the behaviour. Punishment can be either delivering an aversive consequence or withdrawing a positive one.

Behaviourist methods have shown some limited success at improving behaviour, particularly for students with SEN. It does take time, and class teachers are unlikely to have the time to manage this kind of programme.

Cognitive-behaviourist theory

Underlying this theory is the idea that students can learn effective ways of dealing with problems independently. Success with a task depends on the environment, students' emotions and self-esteem, their feelings about the task and ability to complete it, and their problem-solving skills. The aim is to support students with their thinking, so that they can understand what they are doing and why. Whereas behaviourism concentrates on what students do, cognitive theory focuses more on their thinking processes. Cognitive theorists see people as possessing the capacity for both good and evil and making choices about their behaviour.

Cognitive theory is implicit in any teaching, involving analysing the task to determine what skills and strategies the students need, analysing their skills to see what they lack and implementing a programme to teach these. The final stage is feedback, from the teacher and from students themselves – evaluating their own performance is important for sustaining motivation. Students need to receive accurate and specific information, so that they can recognise their achievements and correct errors. They need to be shown how to regard poor performance as information about what does not work, not evidence of their failure.

Cognitive behaviourism focuses on students' self-management and also offers support to teachers in planning their own work. The aim is for students to become independent, managing their own behaviour and increasing their motivation. A criticism of the approach, however, is that the behaviourist aspects of the theory mean it has a dual personality – the use of external controls and punishments can undermine students' self-efficacy and the aim of engaging students more actively in their own behaviour.

Humanism

In education, humanism has its roots in the progressive movement and the work of Froebel and Dewey. It is egalitarian, allocating equal worth to all people, with teachers' status coming from their skills and expertise, rather than from having power over students. There are three strands to the humanist view of children:

- Humanism trusts children's innate capacity for growth, as they strive to be all they can be. All children want to learn useful skills, and so, when adults do not threaten them with punishment or bribe them with rewards, they will be motivated and will make constructive choices.
- Humanism says that children are inherently good and are equally capable of considerate behaviour as they are of looking out for themselves.
- Children have a status as human beings. Age is no barrier to human rights, and children are of value now, not for what they may become in the future.

Humanists reject the behaviourist idea that external events dictate our behaviour. All behaviour comes from within – all the external world can give us is information; we choose what we do. Explanations of disruptive behaviour are as follows:

- Students learn by exploring the rules of their social environment, just as they explore the physical world, and sometimes they act in ways that are testing how far they are able to go.
- In childhood and beyond, people make mistakes.

- Children will be motivated to do high-quality work only when it meets their needs. When children have emotional problems in their lives that are beyond their ability to understand and cope with, they display dysfunctional behaviour. This behaviour can take the form of doing whatever they need to do to survive emotionally.
- Reactive behaviour comes when children are reacting against authoritarian attempts to control their autonomy. Reactions can be in the form of resistance, rebellion, retaliation, escape and submission.

The goal of discipline within humanist theory is to develop self-discipline, so that people are humane and compassionate and act in accordance with their own high values. The goal of educators should not be compliance, as controlling others is unethical, ineffective and dangerous. Just as learning facts does not teach students how to think, making students conform does not help them to become good people. Teaching children obedience can make them more vulnerable to sexual abuse, as they are trained to do what adults tell them. Children can be at risk, because they fail to resist bullying, and whole societies can become unsafe, as in Milgram's (1963) experiments.

The core principle of humanism is that students will work productively and act thoughtfully, when their needs are met by what we are asking them to do and how we are asking them to do it. This is based on Maslow's hierarchy of needs (see Chapter 6). Humanists aim to create a caring school community, where students feel cared for and are encouraged to care about each other. In a safe environment, students will be more likely to take risks, knowing that they will not be humiliated or punished for mistakes, and so will learn more. A core component of this community is for teachers to relate to students with acceptance, respect, empathy, humanity, and as a real person, not hiding behind their role or what they see as their authority. Teachers can adapt the classroom to facilitate learning and co-operation, either by enriching it through a variety of activities and teaching methods or by impoverishing or restricting it, to help easily distracted students concentrate. Good feedback is important, as are meetings for airing issues. Compulsory homework is seen as a source of coercion and irrelevance.

Stanley **Milgram**, a psychologist at Yale University, wanted to look at the conflict between personal conscience and obedience to authority. He examined justifications for genocide offered by those at the Second World War Nuremberg war criminal trials who said they were just following orders. The experiment involved pairs of men, one a participant and one part of the experiment (unknown to the participants). One of the participants in each pair was the 'teacher', and the other was the 'learner'. The learner was attached to electrodes and asked questions about word pairs. For each mistake, the 'teacher' administered an electric shock. The 'learners' deliberately gave incorrect answers, and the 'teachers' continued to give electric shocks, 65 per cent continuing to the highest level, even though they had been told this was painful for the participants, because the researcher (an actor), who was understood by the teachers to be an authority figure, told them to (see www.youtube.com/watch?v=xOYLCy5PVgM; accessed March 2014).

One of the aims of humanism is to find a solution not a culprit. Communication is important in resolving problems. Humanism is not permissive, but has rigorous standards for personal conduct – for example, guidelines around basic courtesy, such as not harming another person. Working in collaboration is important. Although humanists do not support exercising power and control, they may impose time out – time out allows students to take some quiet or solitary time. They cannot force students to change behaviour, but they can insist that, when people cannot be sociable, they cannot be social.

Critics say that humanists do not do anything when behaviour problems erupt, although humanism does not do anything to students, but rather works with them to solve the problem. Critics also argue that humanism demands that teachers have sophisticated communication skills, whereas others say that communication is at the heart of all teaching, and so it is legitimate to expect teachers to master it.

Behaviour for learning

The philosophy underlying 'behaviour for learning' is that it concentrates on positive or desired behaviours, rather than negative, and works towards a clear purpose – effective learning. The behaviour for learning conceptual framework, which came from a systematic literature review (Powell and Tod 2004), is put forward as an alternative perspective on behaviour.

Using the term 'learning behaviour', suggest Ellis and Tod (2009), may reduce perceptions that 'promoting learning' and 'managing behaviour' are separate issues for teachers. Within the framework, learning behaviour is placed at the centre, to recognise that the promotion of learning behaviour is a shared aim and purpose of those people responsible for providing appropriate learning experiences for children. The 'triangle of influence' surrounding the learning behaviour signifies that the development of this behaviour is influenced by social, emotional and cognitive factors: the social

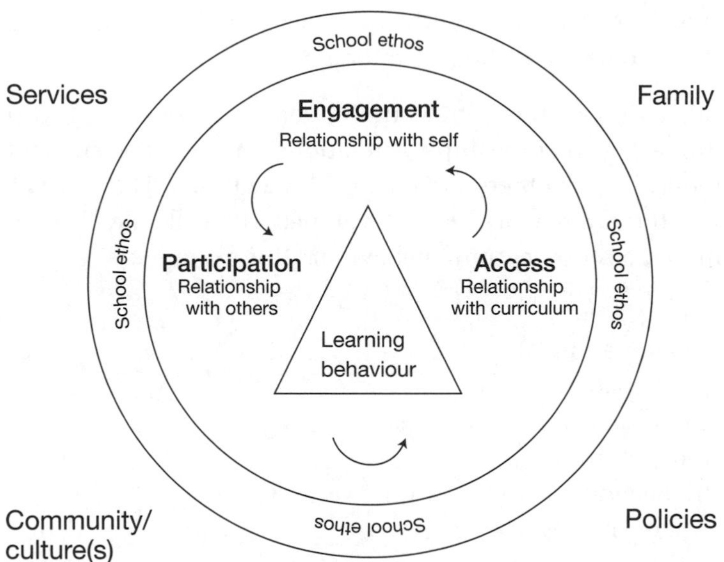

Figure 8.1 The behaviour for learning conceptual framework

Note: Adapted from Powell and Tod 2004

context in which the learner is placed (social), the feelings and interpretations of the learner (emotional) and the curriculum or task (cognitive). The rest of the diagram illustrates the processes that underpin learning and the relationships and context within which they occur. 'The overall purpose of the behaviour for learning conceptual framework is to encourage teachers to focus on what learning behaviour they need to develop in order to replace or reduce the problematic behaviour the pupil currently exhibits' (Ellis and Tod 2009, p. 53). The idea underpinning the framework is that there are particular behaviours necessary for learning, and that we should not assume that pupils enter school or a different phase of their education with these behaviours already learned – it is necessary for teachers to think about how they create opportunities to develop learning behaviour.

If we think about our own learning in school, suggest Ellis and Tod (2009, p. 54), factors that influenced behaviour probably included:

- how interested and capable you were in the subject;
- how well you got on with your teacher and peers in your class;
- how you were feeling emotionally.

For this reason, the behaviour for learning framework focuses on three key relationships – relationship with the curriculum, relationship with others and relationship with self. The review from which the framework was developed (Powell and Tod 2004) identified a set of learning behaviours, for example:

- engagement
- collaboration
- participation
- communication
- motivation
- independent activity
- responsiveness
- self-regard
- self-esteem
- responsibility.

The underpinning principles behind the model are:

- Learning behaviour(s) transcends curriculum areas, age and stages of development and arguably should be of lifelong relevance to the learner. As such their identification and development focus on the needs of the individual, which may be different to those prescribed by policy makers.
- The learning behaviour is the focus for development and should be used to evaluate the effectiveness of ongoing teaching and interventions.
- Learning behaviours recognise the social, emotional and cognitive components of development and are underpinned by a set of relationships – the relationship with self, the relationship with others, and the relationship with the curriculum and/or task.

(Ellis and Tod 2009, p. 67)

In undertaking their research, Ellis and Tod (2009) found that, when teachers were asked about behaviour in the classroom, they were more able to think about the behaviours they did not want than the behaviours they wanted to promote – the language of behaviour management focuses on unwanted behaviour. Research commissioned from the University of Birmingham by the QCA looked at the criteria used by local authorities throughout England for measuring pupils' emotional and behavioural development and produced a table of positive behaviours (see Table 8.1). These behaviours are further developed in the QCA document.

The DfES document *Behaviour in the Classroom: A course for newly qualified teachers* (Department for Education and Skills 2004) treats learning behaviour and behaviour for learning similarly and suggests:

- 'Learning behaviours' is a positive description. It tells the children what you do want them to do and why this will help them to learn rather than focusing on what you do not want.
- It puts value on behaving in ways which enable and maximise learning.

Table 8.1 Criteria for measuring emotional and behavioural development

Learning behaviour	Conduct behaviour	Emotional behaviour
1 Is attentive and has an interest in schoolwork	1 Behaves respectfully towards staff	1 Has empathy
2 Has good learning organisation	2 Shows respect to other pupils	2 Is socially aware
3 Is an effective communicator	3 Only interrupts and seeks attention appropriately	3 Is happy
4 Works efficiently in a group	4 Is physically peaceable	4 Is confident
5 Seeks help where necessary	5 Respects property	5 Is emotionally stable and shows good self-control

Source: QCA 2001, in Ellis and Tod 2009

- Depending on the child, effective learning behaviours can range from high-level listening or collaborative learning skills to remaining on your seat for two minutes.
- The concept is one which is relevant to all children.

(Department for Education and Skills 2004, p. 96)

In looking at how to promote learning behaviours, Ellis and Tod make a distinction between 'skill' and 'disposition':

> Put crudely, when you have learned a skill, you are able to do something you couldn't do before. But you may not spontaneously make use of that ability when it is relevant in the future, if you do not realise its relevance; or if you still need a degree of support or encouragement that is not available. In common parlance, it is not much use being able if you are not also ready and willing.
>
> (Claxton 2006, p. 6)

Put briefly, this means that, when teachers are thinking about learning behaviours, they also need to consider aspects such as skill and disposition. For example, if a child continually interrupts the teacher in class, is this because they do not know how to behave differently (skill), or because this behaviour fits with their view of themselves – they cannot do the work so they will interrupt others (disposition)? Ellis and Tod (2009, p. 81) also give the example of a teacher trying to improve a pupil's capability in phonics through intensive practice, but, in doing so, adversely affecting the pupil's disposition towards reading for pleasure.

The idea of behaviour for learning in focusing on behaviours you do want, rather than behaviours you do not, goes beyond this, as it is necessary also to think about a purpose – in this instance, learning. Thinking about the relationships in the behaviour for learning framework – with self, with others, with the curriculum – teachers would still do many of the same things in classrooms, but thinking differently; for example:

> - More attention would be given to the reciprocal nature of the process. We would be more aware of what the pupil brings to the process, accepting that this may or may not fit with what we had in mind. Whatever the behavioural manifestation, it is useful data about the ongoing nature of the relationship.
> - Strategy choice would be based on its likely impact on sustaining and improving the pupil's contribution to the relationship.
> - We would acknowledge that there are a few pupils who exhibit a *cluster* of learning behaviours that have pervasive effects on their behaviour in the classroom. For these pupils we would directly target one of the three relationships as a focus for action.
>
> (Ellis and Tod 2009, p. 92)

Further reading

Behaviour for Learning: Proactive approaches to behaviour management
Simon Ellis and Janet Tod, 2009, Routledge
Located in research, this gives teachers a conceptual framework for understanding behaviour management strategies.

Behaviour in Schools: Theory and practice for teachers
Louise Porter, 2006 (2nd edn), Open University Press
This book explains in detail the theories behind behaviour and gives teachers practical advice, drawn from research and experience, on how to manage their classroom.

The Art of Peaceful Teaching in the Primary School: Improving behaviour and preserving motivation
Michelle McGrath, 2000, David Fulton
A very accessible book, practical rather than theoretical, with some useful examples and practical advice for teachers.

References

Bate, C. and Moss, J. (1997) Towards a behaviour curriculum, *Educational Psychology in Practice*, 13(3): 176–80.

Claxton, G. (2006) *Expanding the Capacity to Learn: A new end for education?* Keynote address at the British Educational Research Association annual conference, 6 September, University of Warwick. Available at: www.tloltd.co.uk/downloads/BERA-Keynote-Update-Feb10.pdf (accessed 14 August 2014).

Department for Children, Schools and Families (2009) *Learning Behaviour: Lessons learned, a review of behaviour standards and practices in our schools*, Nottingham, UK: DCSF.

Department for Education and Science (1989) *Discipline in Schools (The Elton Report)*, London: HMSO.

Department for Education and Skills (2004) *Behaviour in the Classroom: A course for newly qualified teachers.* Course notes. Nottingham, UK: DfES.

Department for Education and Skills (2005) *Learning Behaviour: The report of the Practitioners' Group on School Behaviour and Discipline (The Steer Report)*, London: DfES.

Didau, D. (2012) Children are at school to learn, not to behave, *The Guardian Teacher Network*, 13 February. Available at: www.theguardian.com/teacher-network/2012/feb/13/learning-behaviour-teaching (accessed 14 August 2014)

Ellis, S. and Tod, J. (2009) *Behaviour for Learning: Proactive approaches to behaviour management*, Oxford, UK: David Fulton.

Maag, J. W. (2001) Rewarded by punishment: Reflections on the disuse of positive reinforcement in schools, *Exceptional Children*, 67(2): 173–86.

Milgram, S. (1963) Behavioral study of obedience, *Journal of Abnormal and Social Psychology*, 67: 371–8.

Ofsted (2005) *Managing Challenging Behaviour*, London: Ofsted.

O'Leary, K. D. (1972) Behaviour modification in the classroom: A rejoinder to Winett and Winkler, *Journal of Applied Behaviour Analysis*, 5(4): 505–11.

Porter, L. (2006) *Behaviour in Schools: Theory and practice for teachers* (2nd edn), Maidenhead, UK: Open University Press/McGraw Hill.

Powell, S. and Tod, J. (2004) A systematic review of how theories explain learning behaviour in school contexts, in *Research Evidence in Education Library*, London: EPPI-Centre, Social Science Research Unit, Institute of Education, University of London.

Qualifications and Curriculum Authority (QCA) (2001) *Supporting School Improvement: Emotional and behavioural development*, Sudbury, UK: QCA.

Taylor, M. (2008) Violence on the increase in schools, teachers warn. *The Guardian*, 17 March. Available at: www.theguardian.com/education/2008/mar/17/schools.uk (accessed March 2014).

Wheldall, K. and Merrett, F. (1984) *Positive Teaching: The behavioural approach*, London: Allen & Unwin.

9 Assessment for learning

The process of seeking and interpreting evidence for use by learners and their teachers to decide where the learners are in their learning, where they need to go and how best to get there

(Assessment Reform Group)

If you think for a moment about the question 'What is assessment?', you may come up with a range of activities – from a teacher putting ticks and crosses against the 'sums' in a 7-year-old's exercise book, walking around the classroom commenting on practical work or setting an end of unit test, to pupils sitting GCSE and A-level examinations. All of these, and more, are assessment. When the National Curriculum was introduced in 1988, it had a major impact on children's assessment. It significantly increased the amount of formal assessment in schools, with testing or teacher assessment happening at the ages of 7, 11 and 14 (SATs) and 16 (GCSEs). By the early 1990s, it was clear that the curriculum had become assessment driven, and the national tests were very expensive. Teacher assessment has, therefore, become more prominent, to reduce costs.

What is assessment for?

Assessment is about measurement, and it can be used for several purposes:

- formatively, to give feedback to support pupils' future learning (assessment *for* learning);
- diagnostically, to identify the cause of any problems with learning;
- summatively, to provide information about students' achievements at particular points, usually the end of a school year or a module (assessment *of* learning);
- to provide certification and qualifications;
- for evaluation.

Broadfoot (1999, p. 64) suggests that assessment has political ramifications: 'Assessment procedures are the vehicle whereby the dominant rationality of the corporate capitalist societies typical of the contemporary Western world is translated into the structures and processes of schooling'.

Since the introduction of the National Curriculum, according to Jones and Tanner (2006), the emphasis of assessment has been on audiences outside the classroom, on accountability and management, and not on improving the effectiveness of learning and teaching. Here, they are referring to, for example, the debate around the publication of SATs results and school league tables. They group the aims of assessment under three broad headings – managerial, communicative and pedagogical.

Managerial aims for assessment include:

- demonstrating or testing the effectiveness of government policies;
- holding schools and LAs accountable for students' progress;
- holding teachers accountable for the progress of their classes;
- motivating teachers through payment by results schemes such as the threshold;
- selecting students to benefit from a limited resource, for example, university education;
- controlling the curriculum by emphasising particular forms of knowledge, such as key skills.

Communicative aims for assessment include:

- providing information to parents about their children's progress against nationally agreed standards;
- providing information to other teachers, educational institutions or employers about individual students' knowledge and skills;
- producing league tables of schools to inform parental choice;
- informing teachers and students which parts of the curriculum are considered valuable enough to examine.

Pedagogical aims for assessment include:

- evaluating the success of your own teaching;
- analysing students' learning and identifying misconceptions;
- supporting the teaching process by providing feedback to inform future planning;
- supporting the teaching process by identifying precisely what individuals and groups of students need to know to improve, in order to inform the planning of future teaching;
- giving students an appreciation of their achievements and encouraging success;
- motivating students and holding them accountable;
- supporting the learning process by helping students to identify areas of weakness or misunderstanding and suggesting strategies for development;
- encouraging students to develop skills of self-assessment;
- providing students with the information they require to become self-regulating learners.

(Jones and Tanner 2006, p. 2)

Over recent years, the consistent message from Ofsted has been that the quality of assessment is lagging behind other aspects of teaching. The commentary to the 2007–8 Annual Report (Ofsted 2008a, p. 8) states that, 'assessment is a key component of good teaching and learning, but also a vital management tool to highlight progress or the lack of it and to help evaluate the impact of support mechanisms'. The Report goes on to say that, in secondary schools, 'The best teaching challenges and encourages pupils, making regular use of assessment to match activities to their needs and abilities' (p. 28), but:

> The use of assessment to track pupils' progress, plan work and manage approaches to whole-class discussion continues to be a common weakness. Efforts to improve it have been concentrated mainly on English and mathematics. In these and other subjects, however, ongoing assessment is often underused so that pupils do not know the strengths and weaknesses of their work and the steps needed to improve their attainment. A survey of the impact of the 'assessment for learning' strand of the National Strategies found that it was good or outstanding in only a minority of schools, with a generally lower impact in secondary than in primary schools . . . Across the curriculum, in the minority of schools in the survey where inspectors saw good practice in assessment, teachers had understood and applied carefully the key principles of assessment for learning. In the majority of schools, however, assessment remained an area of relative weakness.
>
> (Ofsted 2008a, p. 29)

Assessment for learning can be defined as: 'The process of seeking and interpreting evidence for use by learners and their teachers to identify where the learners are in their learning, where they need to go and how best to get there' (Gardner 2006, p. 2).

Although assessment for learning is supported strongly by the QCA, its use remains limited: 'Systematic, rigorous and productive attention to the strengths and weaknesses of students' work remains the exception rather than the rule . . . In all subjects, feedback to students which helps them to improve is still too variable' (Ofsted 2004, p. 6).

Underlying theories of learning

Assessment cannot be considered in isolation, an idea we will return to later. Arguably the best forms of assessment are aligned with an underlying theory of learning, although, 'learning theorists themselves rarely make statements about how learning outcomes within their models should be assessed' (James 2006, p. 47).

Jones and Tanner (2006) argue that assessment can never be a precise science, because what children can achieve depends on more than their ability – social and emotional factors affect learning, as well as the context in which learning takes place. It is not the case that children can only learn when the task before them is at the right level for their background, knowledge and experience. Whole-class teaching can take place because children can learn when a task comes within range of their current knowledge – into the learning zone (Newman *et al.* 1989). The learning zone is based on Vygotsky's ZPD:

> The zone of proximal development . . . is the distance between the actual developmental level as determined by independent problem solving and the level of potential development as determined through problem solving under adult guidance or in collaboration with more capable peers.
>
> (Vygotsky 1978, p. 86)

As a lesson proceeds, effective teachers make continual assessments to keep the class in the learning zone. These assessments would not be recorded – they should be out of date by the end of the lesson. In the learning zone, children can only operate with some form of support – which might come from the teacher, another student or a resource such as a book or computer (see Table 9.1). One of the most common forms of support provided by teachers comes from questioning – skilled questioning can generate assessment information for teachers to use to guide the teaching and learning process, or to evaluate the extent to which students have understood the issue, or to engage and motivate students by encouraging them to participate in an explanation. Supporting learning through questioning is sometimes referred to as Socratic dialogue, after the Greek philosopher Socrates. More recently, the support that a learner can draw from structured questioning has been described as 'scaffolding' – experienced teachers can structure their questioning in such a way that they lead the class through a problem or argument, with most or all of the class engaged and taking part. Bruner suggests the teacher may be acting as 'a vicarious form of consciousness' (1985, pp. 24–5), taking most of the strategic decisions and guiding progress in order to reduce the cognitive load on the student. However, if too much of the hard work is done by the teacher, and the student is just left with simple

Table 9.1 The learning zone

Out of range	Activities are too hard, work goes over their heads	Off-task behaviour, poor discipline	No learning
The learning zone or ZPD	Activities can only be completed with help	Working noise, teacher kept busy	Maximum learning
Current level	Activities involve familiar and secure knowledge	Silent working, teacher is not needed	No learning or very little learning

Source: Tanner and Jones 2000, p. 80

recall questions to answer, the potential for real learning is curtailed. The trick, according to Jones and Tanner (2006, p. 9), is to provide just enough support to allow students to progress through their own efforts.

Tanner and Jones (2006) suggest that the scaffolding metaphor is attractive in many ways. On a building site, scaffolding guides the shape of the emerging structure, enabling people to work at higher levels before the structure is complete and being removed when the building is secure. Although scaffolding for building knowledge is intended to work in the same way, students are not inanimate bricks and mortar. The task is more complicated, because students have a range of personalities, opinions and backgrounds, and will each create their own structures according to their own free will, irrespective of the teacher's intentions (Askew *et al.* 1995).

Scaffolding on a building necessarily has to be fixed and rigid, and perhaps that is where the metaphor ends, because, in a classroom, scaffolding that is dynamic and responsive to the opinions and beliefs of students is more effective (Tanner and Jones 2006). For there to be effective learning, students must engage with the teaching in a meaningful way, not just passively absorbing information but actively taking part in the process. This interactive teaching and learning provide numerous opportunities for formative assessment.

Table 9.2 Learning interaction

	Nature of the interaction	Control
Lecture	No interactivity or only internal interactivity	High degree of teacher control
Low-level/ funnelling questioning	Rigid scaffolding and surface interactivity	High degree of teacher control
Probing questioning	Looser scaffolding and deeper interactivity	High degree of teacher control
Focusing or uptake questioning	Dynamic scaffolding and deep interactivity	High degree of teacher control
Collective reflection	Reflective scaffolding and full interaction	High degree of pupil control

Tanner *et al.* (2005) show interactivity in whole-class teaching on a continuum, according to the nature of the teacher–student control, the nature of the interaction and the character of the scaffolding (see Table 9.2).

Links with theory

Behaviourists see learning as a permanent change in behaviour and emphasise measurable changes and outcomes. Learning is seen as a conditioning process, a response to a stimulus. The stimulus is seen as the source of learning – it acts upon the individual, evoking the response or increasing the chance of a response. If there is no reinforcement, the behaviour is less likely to occur: learning is seen in terms of the strength of the stimulus–response connection. Skinner (1968), the founder of operant conditioning, is considered by some to have had the greatest impact on education and learning. The behaviourist approach to learning takes the view that complex tasks are best broken down into smaller tasks. So, teachers should:

- create environments in which students can respond effectively to stimuli;
- be clear about what are appropriate responses;
- reward appropriate responses to shape behaviour;
- model good behaviour.

Historically, assessment has changed from being something that happened after learning has taken place – a test given at the end of a lesson, perhaps, to see what pupils have understood and remembered. This works on the idea of pupils as empty vessels, with teachers pouring in knowledge. It also emphasises the division between academic or technical knowledge (*knowing that*) and practical or vocational knowledge (*knowing how*) – practical knowledge can be difficult to teach and is harder to assess through 'pencil and paper' tests. The emphasis on *knowing that* reflects a debate that has persisted in education for many years – which is more important and more valued: academic or practical knowledge? Now, we focus on *assessment for learning*, so that assessment and learning are inextricably linked.

Formative assessment sits most comfortably with the constructivist theories of Piaget, Bruner and Vygotsky. The constructivist model assumes that some things are learned quickly and easily, whereas others take time and effort. New understanding is placed in the context of what we knew before, and sometimes we have to change the foundations of what we previously knew, to make way for new concepts and ideas. Scaffolding is the way teachers can support students' learning as they construct new knowledge. We teachers can only do this – devise effective learning activities – if we use good assessment to tell us about the next steps for students.

Assessment for learning

Assessment for learning is increasingly used to refer to the ways in which teachers and pupils can gain a clear understanding of what learning has taken place and how pupils' future learning can best progress. It is an important strand of personalised learning.

Gardner (2006) identifies ten principles that underpin assessment for learning. Assessment for learning:

- is part of effective planning;
- focuses on how students learn;
- is central to classroom practice;
- is a key professional skill;
- is sensitive and constructive;
- fosters motivation;
- promotes understanding of goals and criteria;
- helps learners know how to improve;
- develops the capacity for self-assessment;
- recognises all educational achievement.

Assessment does not stand alone, but should be embedded in preparation, planning, teaching and learning. Assessment should be a two-way process, showing that the teacher has a clear understanding of the student's needs, and that the student is clear about the purpose of the assessment and how results can be used to improve attainment. Marking should tell students what they have achieved in their work and what they need to do to improve. It should be motivational, supporting students' efforts and pointing out the strengths as well as any weaknesses in their work. It might also be disciplinary, when a teacher wants to give feedback on a student's lack of engagement with a task. Teachers can spend a great deal of time marking, and so it is important to make sure this is not time wasted – if the marking merely acknowledges that the student has completed a task, and if the student gains little helpful information from the marks, there is little point. It is not necessary to mark every piece of work in the same way or to the same depth.

In a review of 250 pieces of literature on formative assessment, Black and Wiliam (1998) found that frequent feedback through assessment can 'yield substantial learning gains' (p. 7). They suggest that, during the two years spent studying for a GCSE, a student could improve their performance by one or two grades, if formative assessment methods were used regularly.

According to Gardner (2006), assessment for learning comprises the same 'time-honoured' practices as formative assessment – it is what good teachers do.

The process of formative assessment is as important as the product (the grades or marks), if not more. Formative assessment is central to learning and helps students understand what they do well and what they need to improve, how to work on any problems, and what might be realistic targets.

Our view of intelligence influences our view of assessment. If we think that ability is fixed at birth, then teachers are just preparing students for assessments and results that are largely predetermined. If we believe that teachers can support students and scaffold their learning, then formative assessment can make a difference.

- **Summative assessment** is used to monitor educational outcomes, often for purposes of external accountability. Summative assessment comes at the end of a learning process and measures whether information has been retained.
- **Formative assessment** is either formal or informal assessment used by teachers during the learning process. It usually involves qualitative feedback, rather than scores, that focuses on the detail of content and performance. According to Black and Wiliam (1998), it includes, 'all those activities undertaken by teachers, and/or by students, which provide information to be used as feedback to modify the teaching and learning activities in which they are engaged.'

High stakes and low stakes

If you think about, for example, having to achieve the right grades at A level to take up a university place, it is clear why some assessment is described as 'high stakes'. This term normally relates to public and external exams. Sometimes, a great deal depends on them – being able to continue to the next level of education, the choice of courses and/or institutions available, future employment

– hence, high stakes. These issues do not just affect individual students, but also schools and departments, as examination results are published in league tables, and so there are accusations of teachers 'teaching to the test' to help students get through their exams. This can mean that teachers concentrate on cramming or rote learning to get across the responses to likely examination questions, which can mean that students' involvement in, and enjoyment of, their learning is reduced. Lessons usually include less class discussion and fewer activities such as games, and so the teacher may feel they have delivered the curriculum, but students are less satisfied.

Assessment for learning is low-stakes assessment – small, day-to-day assessment that is a matter for the student, teacher and parents (although the assessment may build up into a bigger picture). This is designed to support students' learning and could include question and answer sessions, watching students as they work, self-assessment and setting targets.

The Ofsted report *Assessment for Learning: The impact of National Strategy support* (2008b, p. 5) says:

> Where assessment for learning had had less impact, the teachers had not understood how the approaches were supposed to improve pupils' achievement. In particular, they used key aspects of assessment for learning, such as identifying and explaining objectives, questioning, reviewing pupils' progress and providing feedback without enough precision and skill. As a result, pupils did not understand enough about what they needed to do to improve and how they would achieve their targets. Teachers did not review learning effectively during lessons; opportunities for pupils to assess their own work or that of their peers were infrequent and not always effective. Procedures in these schools for monitoring performance and evaluating progress did not lead to sustained training and support from senior staff or local authorities to ensure that key approaches were embedded effectively. In the secondary schools visited, despite the more regular monitoring of students' progress, work planned for them was rarely matched closely enough to their understanding and to what they had learnt before.

- **Norm-referenced assessment** involves the student's performance being compared with the norm for the class, cohort or age group. Norm referencing is used when people are being compared with each other – when candidates are interviewed for a job, for example, or the top of the class – or when only a fixed number or percentage can pass or enter. High-stakes external examinations are usually norm referenced. Often grades are determined on the results of the whole population, so that, rather than saying that a mark above 60 per cent will result in an A grade, grades may be determined on percentage of population, and so the top 10 per cent will receive an A grade, the next 10 per cent a B grade, and so on. For tests with a large population, the distribution of marks usually produces a normal curve, hence, norm referenced.
- **Criterion-referenced assessment** is where the student's attainment is compared with specific criteria – being able to count to 20, or conjugate a French verb, or a driving test. Students' performance is not compared with that of other students in the assessment.
- **Ipsative assessment** is when a student's attainment is compared with their previous best performance.

Instruments of assessment also have to be *valid and reliable*. Validity means whether the task or question actually measures what it is intended to measure. Reliability means designing a test that is consistent and would produce the same results if repeated with a different group of students.

So, to raise standards, teachers should:

- explain clearly to pupils what they are to learn, by what criteria they will be assessed and how they will know when they have been successful so that they are increasingly involved and responsible for their learning outcomes

- develop their skills in targeting questions to challenge pupils' understanding, prompting them to explain and justify their answers individually, in small groups and in whole class dialogue
- employ a range of strategies to assess pupils' progress in lessons and use the information gained to give feedback to pupils and plan further work.

(Ofsted 2008b, p. 7)

The National Curriculum and assessment

A new primary national curriculum is being implemented in September 2014 (Department for Education 2014). As part of this implementation, it has been decided to remove level descriptors from the National Curriculum, because it was agreed that levels had become too abstract, did not give parents meaningful information about how their child was performing, and did not give pupils information about how to improve. It was stated that levels had detracted from real feedback, and schools found it difficult to apply them consistently – the criteria were said to be ambiguous and to require teachers to decide how to weight a huge array of factors. Apart from the tests at KS2 and GCSEs at KS4, schools will decide how they assess pupils' progress.

The following are the attainment target-level descriptions for English (reading), as an example:

- *Level 1*: Pupils recognise familiar words in simple texts. They use their knowledge of letters and sound–symbol relationships in order to read words and to establish meaning when reading aloud. In these activities, they sometimes require support. They express their response to poems, stories and non-fiction by identifying aspects they like.
- *Level 2*: Pupils' reading of simple texts shows understanding and is generally accurate. They express opinions about major events or ideas in stories, poems and non-fiction. They use more than one strategy, such as phonic, graphic, syntactic and contextual, in reading unfamiliar words and establishing meaning.

- *Level 3*: Pupils read a range of texts fluently and accurately. They read independently, using strategies appropriately to establish meaning. In responding to fiction and non-fiction, they show understanding of the main points and express preferences. They use their knowledge of the alphabet to locate books and find information.
- *Level 4*: In responding to a range of texts, pupils show understanding of significant ideas, themes, events and characters, beginning to use inference and deduction. They refer to the text when explaining their views. They locate and use ideas and information.
- *Level 5*: Pupils show understanding of a range of texts, selecting essential points and using inference and deduction where appropriate. In their responses, they identify key features, themes and characters and select sentences, phrases and relevant information to support their views. They retrieve and collate information from a range of sources.
- *Level 6*: In reading and discussing a range of texts, pupils identify different layers of meaning and comment on their significance and effect. They give personal responses to literary texts, referring to aspects of language, structure and themes in justifying their views. They summarise a range of information from different sources.
- *Level 7*: Pupils show understanding of the ways in which meaning and information are conveyed in a range of texts. They articulate personal and critical responses to poems, plays and novels, showing awareness of their thematic, structural and linguistic features. They select and synthesise a range of information from a variety of sources.
- *Level 8*: Pupils' response is shown in their appreciation of, and comment on, a range of texts, and they evaluate how authors achieve their effects through the use of linguistic, structural and presentational devices. They select and analyse information and ideas, and comment on how these are conveyed in different texts.
- *Exceptional performance*: Pupils confidently sustain their responses to a demanding range of texts, developing their ideas

and referring in detail to aspects of language, structure and presentation. They make apt and careful comparison between texts, including consideration of audience, purpose and form. They identify and analyse argument, opinion and alternative interpretations, making cross-references where appropriate.

Further reading

The Assessment Reform Group was set up to research and challenge all aspects of assessment, including assessment for learning. Now dissolved, its archived reports and publications (with other useful information on assessment) can be found at: www.nuffieldfoundation.org/assessment-reform-group (accessed 14 August 2014).

Assessment and Learning
John Gardner (ed.), 2006, Sage
Written by authors from the Assessment Reform Group, a useful and informative guide to using assessment to support learning.

Assessment for Learning and Teaching in Primary Schools
Mary Briggs, Angela Woodfield, Peter Swatton and Cynthia Martin, 2008, Learning Matters
A useful, practical guide, but relates to the 2007 standards for QTS.

Inside the Black Box: Raising standards through classroom assessment
Paul Black and Dylan Wiliam, 1990, GL Assessment Limited, available at http://weaeducation.typepad.co.uk/files/blackbox-1.pdf (accessed March 2014)
Perhaps the definitive guide to assessment. A paper rather than a book (21 pages).

References

Askew, M., Bliss, J. and Macrae, S. (1995) Scaffolding in mathematics, science and technology, in P. Murphy, M. Selinger, J. Bourne and M. Brigs (eds) *Subject Learning in the Primary Curriculum*, London: Routledge/Open University Press.

Black, P. and Wiliam, D. (1998) Assessment and classroom learning, *Assessment in Education: Principles, Policy and Practice*, 5(1): 7–74.

Broadfoot, P. (1999) Assessment and the emergence of modern society, in B. Moon and P. Murphy (eds) *Curriculum in Context*, London: Paul Chapman/Open University.

Bruner, J. S. (1985) Vygotsky: A historical and conceptual perspective, in J. V. Wertsch (ed.) *Culture, Communication and Cognition: Vygotskian perspectives*, Cambidge, UK: Cambridge University Press.

Department for Education (2014) *National Curriculum and Assessment from September 2014: Information for schools.* Available at: www.gov.uk/government/uploads/system/uploads/attachment_data/file/286428/National_curriculum_and_assessment_from_September_2014_fact_sheet_updated_28_Jan.pdf (accessed March 2014).

Gardner, J. (ed.) (2006) *Assessment and Learning*, London: Sage.

James, M. (2006) Assessment, teaching and theories of learning, in J. Gardner (ed.) *Assessment and Learning*, London, Sage.

Jones, S. and Tanner, H. (2006) *Assessment: A practical guide for secondary teachers* (2nd edn), London: Continuum.

Newman, D., Griffin, P. and Cole, M. (1989) *The Construction Zone: Working for cognitive change in school*, Cambridge, UK: Cambridge University Press.

Ofsted (2004) *The Key Stage 3 Strategy: Evaluation of the third year*, London: TSO.

Ofsted (2008a) *The Annual Report of Her Majesty's Chief Inspector of Education, Children's Services and Skills 2007/8*, London: TSO.

Ofsted (2008b) *Assessment for Learning: The impact of National Strategy support*, London: Ofsted.

Skinner, B. F. (1968) *The Technology of Teaching*, New York: Appleton-Century Crofts.

Tanner, H. and Jones, S. (2000) *Becoming a Successful Teacher of Mathematics*, London: RoutledgeFalmer.

Tanner, H. and Jones, S. (2006) *Assessment: A practical guide for secondary teachers*, London: Bloomsbury.

Tanner, H., Jones, S., Kennewell, S. and Beauchamp, G. (2005) Interactive whole class teaching and interactive whiteboards, in *The Proceedings of the Mathematics Education Research Group of Australasia* (MERGA28), Melbourne.

Vygotsky, L. S. (1978) *Mind in Society: The development of higher psychological processes*, edited by M. Cole, V. John-Steiner, S. Scribner and E. Souberman, Cambridge, MA: Harvard University Press.

10 Research

If we knew what it was we were doing, it would not be called research, would it?

(Albert Einstein)

As you are a teacher, research will be a part of your life in two ways. Conducting your own research is an important part of gaining qualified teacher status (QTS) and then of your work as a teacher, as you improve your practice by reflecting on and evaluating it. You will also want to keep up to date with developments and try different ways of 'what works' (or what might work) by looking at others' research. 'Research' can sometimes be thought of as something that experts do, but it is just structured, planned and deliberate enquiry. According to the Oxford English Dictionary, research is 'the systematic investigation into and study of materials and sources in order to establish facts and reach new conclusions'. Teachers should be constantly reflecting on what is happening in their classroom, assessing children's learning and getting feedback from them, and so, in a way, they are always researching, except that this is not necessarily structured or planned. According to Koshy (2005, p. 1), 'ultimately the quality of educational experiences provided for children will depend on the ability of the teacher to stand back, question and reflect on his or her practice, and continually strive to make the necessary changes'.

Although the connection between educational research and teachers' professional learning and development is widely recognised, the precise nature of the relationship is not yet fully understood (Whitty *et al.* 2012). A report from the British Educational Research Association (BERA) (2014, p. 6) notes that what is striking about educational provision in both Finland and Singapore, which frequently come out 'on top',

> is the extent to which teachers' engagement with research and enquiry-oriented practice is embedded throughout the education system. Nevertheless, it is important to stress that a causal connection between specific features of the training programme (including the research components) and the success of the education system can only be inferred rather than directly proven.

The current Teachers' Standards (Department for Education 2013) do not contain any explicit references to the need for teachers to engage in or with research, but do mention the use of research-based knowledge and research-related activities, such as critical reflection and collaborative enquiry. For example, teachers must 'reflect systematically on the effectiveness of lessons and approaches to teaching'.

A press release announcing the Educational Endowment Foundation (EEF) launch of a £1.5 million fund to improve use of research in schools (2014) reads:

> The Government wants teachers to be able to use research to inform their practice and raise standards in schools, believing that the use of robust evidence will help improve the quality of teaching and support a school-led system.
>
> Minister of State for Schools David Laws said: 'It is absolutely vital that teachers are supported with the latest research into what works in the classroom. I am delighted to announce this substantial investment which will help ensure that research impacts on the frontline as effectively as possible – and will ultimately improve outcomes for children.'
>
> Sir Peter Lampl, Chairman of the Education Endowment Foundation and the Sutton Trust, said: 'Internationally, the top performing systems apply the results of research to drive up teaching quality and outcomes. We're delighted to receive this new funding, which will be used to evaluate the best ways

to translate research findings into better outcomes in this country.'

Dr Kevan Collins, Chief Executive of the EEF, said: 'We know that it can take decades before new research has an impact on outcomes in the classroom. This funding round is about ensuring that high-quality research gets into the hands of teachers, to inform their practice and support their decision making.'

The first part of this chapter looks at research as evidence, and the second looks at undertaking your own action research project.

Finding evidence

Good teachers should read, reflect on and use research findings in their teaching. That does not mean having to find the time to read everything written, or blindly following each new idea, but you should keep up to date with new thinking in the subject area or age range you teach, and in teaching generally. You should be able to evaluate what you read or hear about and decide whether you want to use it or investigate it further. It is helpful to keep a reading journal, whether this is a notebook or a software package such as EndNote, for keeping a record of what you have read and your thoughts on it. There are several sources of information:

- *Newspapers*: for example, *The Guardian* has an education page on Tuesdays and useful web-based resources and, of course, there is the *Times Education Supplement.*
- *Practitioner journals*: these are usually focused on a particular age range or subject, with articles for teachers written by teachers and researchers; they usually include ideas for teaching activities and, as they are often published monthly, will have current issues of interest.
- *Academic journals*: written with the academic community in mind, usually by university researchers, these tend to be heavier reading; they are usually available online, through university libraries, and are useful if you are interested in a particular topic or want to read the key thinkers in your area or subject.

- *Books on education*: these may not be as up to date as practitioner journals, may be on a particular topic or on education generally and can be theoretical or have very practical advice and tips for teachers; there are so many, it can be difficult to know what to read – what colleagues have found useful is a good guide; sites such as Amazon will also say which are the best-selling texts.
- *The Internet*: a hugely important source of evidence and research papers, but, unless you search carefully, you can waste a lot of time sifting through a bewildering amount of information; it can sometimes be difficult to know about the origin and validity of papers and information on the Internet – some sites that can be trusted are listed under Further reading, including the Department for Education and the National Foundation for Education Research.

Types of research

There are many different approaches to research, each of which is situated within a theoretical perspective. At one end of the theoretical continuum is a *positivist* approach, which suggests that the world can be measured through empirical, scientific observation. A positivist approach is seen as objective and measurable and generally involves testing a hypothesis, using an experimental group and a control group. Research results are presented as facts and truths, and the research is unlikely to provide an explanation. At the other end of the continuum is the *interpretivist* stance, which argues that the world is interpreted by those within it. So, it is acknowledged that there is no single objective reality, and different versions of events are inevitable. The research process is central, and theory develops from data after the research has begun, not from an initial hypothesis. Empirical research is probably the most common form of published research, where a researcher formulates a research question and then uses various research methods – surveys, interviews, experiments, observation – to try and answer the question.

The research debate

There has been a lot of debate over the past 20 years or so about the usefulness and relevance of some educational research. In 2006, Whitty noted that the relationship between research, policy and practice in education had been a particular issue in the UK in the 1990s, although it had been an issue in other countries, such as the US and Australia, too. Tooley (1998) suggested that Hargreaves sparked off the debate in 1996 by criticising educational research for being poor value for money, remote from practice and often of indifferent quality. One of Hargreaves' criticisms was that there was very little replication in educational research, even though contextual and cultural variations are important. Woodhead, then Chief Inspector of Schools, wrote in the foreword to Tooley (1998) that:

> Ofsted inspection evidence confirms what common sense suggests: the better the teaching pupils receive, the more they will learn.
>
> To a significant extent teachers' effectiveness depends, of course, upon their intellectual command of the subject discipline(s) they teach and ultimately their personality. The training they receive as student teachers and teachers in service can, however, have a profound influence on their beliefs about the nature of the educational enterprise and the appropriateness and effectiveness of different teaching methods. The findings of educational research are important because for better or for worse they shape these influences and, in doing so, help to define the intellectual context within which all involved in education work.

On one hand, there have been claims that research is unscientific and not useful for classroom teachers and, on the other, claims from academic researchers that policymakers ignore sound evidence. More recently, though, there has been a move towards evidence-based practice in education, although Hammersley (2001) suggested that the term evidence-based practice is itself contentious: because it is very difficult to argue that practice should not be based on evidence, opposition to it can only be irrational, although critics then deny that practice can be based on evidence. One reaction to this has been to use the term evidence-informed, rather than evidence-based, practice.

Hammersley suggests the central claim of the evidence-based policy movement is that research can make an important contribution to policy and practice, and so evidence is interpreted in a narrow way. In their book about evidence-based policy and practice in the public services, Davies *et al.* comment, 'the presumption in this book is that evidence takes the form of "research", broadly defined. That is, evidence comprises the results of "systematic investigation towards increasing the sum of knowledge"' (Davies *et al.* 2000, p. 3).

Although, within medicine, there has been emphasis on practitioners using available research evidence through initiatives such as the Cochrane Collaboration, which produce and disseminate systematic research reviews, in education there has been more emphasis on the absence of good-quality research that could underpin evidence-based practice.

The assumption that research is systematic and rigorous and produces objective evidence contrasts with the idea that evidence from professional experience is unsystematic and lacking in rigour. Hammersley (2001) suggests that, 'sometimes the contrast is presented in a form that can only be described as caricature, as with Cox's reference to teachers often relying on "tradition, prejudice, dogma and ideology" (quoted in Hargreaves 1996 pp. 7–8)', but Nutley *et al.* argue, 'There is no such thing as "the" evidence: evidence is a contested domain and in a constant state of becoming' (2003 p. 133). In the social sciences, theory is always underdetermined by the facts (Sayer 1992).

One of the issues around educational research is the pressure on university researchers to publish four articles in academic journals in order to be entered for the Research Assessment Exercise (as it was in 2008) or Research Excellence Framework (2014), which, in brief, is the assessment exercise designed to judge the quality of research and allocate funding to universities. It is argued by some that this pressure to publish can lead academics to work only on small-scale projects. As Bassey (1993) suggested, in general, researchers working in isolation cannot generate the research data necessary to make a significant impact on the practice of education, and can be engaged in trivia. Others, for example Deem (1996), have objected to this, on the basis that, 'Lone does not necessarily equal "trivial" and insignificant research results are not unknown in team-based studies' (p. 150). The issue here, however, is not just the pressure to publish, but also the cost of large-scale research projects, particularly in the current economic climate, when educational research funding has been significantly cut. The Department for Education, for example, cut its research funding by more than half, from £28 million in 2010–11 to £13 million in 2011–12 (Scienceogram UK 2013) (although see the section on the EEF, below).

One of the issues that affect educational research is that education itself is such a political matter. When Minister for Education David Blunkett argued, in 2000, that, 'we need social scientists to help determine what worked and why, and what types of policy initiative are likely to be most effective' (cited in Evans and Benefield 2001, p. 527), some researchers took this to mean that they were required to provide evidence to support government policy (Whitty 2006).

Whitty (2006) gives the example of evidence on class sizes used during the 1997 general election:

> Evidence on the effects of class size is notoriously contentious and difficult to interpret, and the controversies continue to this day (see Blatchford *et al.* 2004). Even so, New Labour's commitment in the 1997 to cut class sizes at Key Stage 1 traded quite consciously on research findings accepted by most researchers and most teachers – evidence that, if smaller classes have an unambiguously positive impact anywhere, it is most marked in the very early years of schooling and in the most socially disadvantaged areas. So, the manifesto commitment to cut class sizes at Key Stage 1 to below 30 using monies that had formerly been used to send able children to private schools looked like a socially progressive policy based on robust research findings. Yet, as a policy it was probably driven as much by the findings of election opinion polling as those of education research, given that most classes over 30 were in

> marginal suburban constituencies, not in inner-city areas where classes were already below that level. Some even more robust findings on the beneficial effects of cutting infant class size to 15 in disadvantaged areas did not influence the policy at all, presumably because it would have been extremely expensive, but possibly also because additional votes in these inner-city constituencies would not swing the election.
>
> (Whitty 2002)

In research terms, education is sometimes linked with medicine: for example, the systematic literature reviews in education followed the lead of the Cochrane Collaboration in synthesising evidence. From 2000, the DfES funded a 5-year programme of systematic reviews of educational research, supported by the Evidence for Policy and Practice Information and Co-ordinating (EPPI) Centre at the Institute of Education. Whitty (2006) suggests that New Labour has used research selectively and is apparently unconcerned about the quality of research, as long as it serves its political purposes. The 2001 White Paper *Schools: Achieving success* (Department for Education and Skills 2001) states, 'There are those who have said that specialist schools will create a two-tier system. They won't' (p. 40), but, according to Whitty (2006):

> In making its case on specialist schools the White Paper unashamedly used research carried out for the Specialist Schools Trust, which at the time had not been submitted to peer review and was regarded as flawed by key researchers in the field . . . This particular example is even more striking given that, at the very same time, the Department of Health was publicly rejecting some potentially damaging research on the measles, mumps and rubella vaccine and autism on the grounds that it could not be taken seriously because it had not been subjected to scientific peer review.

Another example, from Clegg (2005), describes how early feminists in the women's health movement:

> delivered a radical critique of medical practices, especially those concerning the management of child birth, by pointing out that

> despite the veneer of scientificity, medical practitioners had no evidence that routine interventions (e.g. routine episiotomy, shaving, etc.) increased positive health outcomes for women or babies (Our Bodies Ourselves, 2003). Evidence, including that from quantitative studies, as well as the qualitative work that gave voice to women as agents, was used to challenge the scientificity of medicine and expose its practices. One of the ironies was that much medical practice denying a voice to women and other marginalised groups was not based on data from RCTs [randomised controlled trials], or indeed from anywhere else. Rather, assumed patriarchal authority was used to bolster routine and often abusive interventions.

There is not space here to look into these examples in more depth, but they do illustrate the fact that the quality of the research or the strength of the evidence may not always be what is seen as important.

In some fields, particularly science and medicine, **randomised controlled trials** (RCTs) are regarded as the 'gold standard' for research. Participants are randomly assigned to an experimental group, which is involved in the intervention or whatever is the focus of the experiment, or a control group, which does not receive any special treatment. Their use in social research is controversial – one argument is that we should not be subjecting people to an intervention if we do not know what the results are; another argument is that, if we think an intervention will have a positive effect, it is unethical to have a control group that does not benefit from it. The counter-argument is that – in this case – the children are no more disadvantaged than they were before, and the trial or study could improve their prospects. Other views include that they do not provide clear-cut findings and are inappropriate for understanding social phenomena.

When the government determined that young children should be taught to read using basic phonics, to write short sentences and use punctuation, it commissioned research by academics at the Institute of Education to look at the effectiveness of policies. The research showed teaching phonics, sentences and punctuation to young children had little effect on literacy skills later on: encouraging them to talk and communicate was more effective. The government suppressed the report, but it was released under a Freedom of Information Act request by the Liberal Democrats (Curtis 2008).

A more current example of the problematic use of research evidence is the academies programme. The programme has continued to expand, even though there have been various negative voices; for example, Smithers *et al.* (2005) said that we did not yet have the data against which to assess Tony Blair's claims that academies are working. Gorard (2005) showed that there were serious questions about the way in which the government had used performance data to justify continuing with the programme, concluding: 'To expand the [Academies] programme on the basis of what has happened so far is so far removed from the evidence-based policy making that is a mantra of government today that it is scarcely worth pointing out' (p. 376). In an interesting twist, Vernoit and Machin from the London School of Economics published research in 2010, just after the coalition government came to power, to show that the policy had been reasonably successful under the Labour government (see Machin 2012). They were:

> somewhat surprised to see it used extensively by supporters of the coalition's policy on academies: for example, by the Department for Education in a recent debate with the Local Schools Network, and again by Jonathan Hill, the under-secretary of state for schools, last month. This seems rather hard to justify, given that the new academy programme is different in a number of ways.
>
> (Machin 2012)

Most notable of the differences was that the schools that became academies under Labour were previously poorly performing schools, whereas schools that became academies under the coalition government were better than average schools, and, in the early days of the new government, outstanding schools were fast-tracked into academy status.

In January 2014, there were 3,613 academies in England. A report for the DfE in January 2014, looking at Ofsted reports for converter academies (those that had previously been mainstream schools), found that, on average, attainment is higher than in mainstream schools, reflecting their origin as predominantly higher-performing schools. At Key Stage 4, in 2013, 67.9 per cent of pupils in converter academies achieved five or more A*–C GCSEs (including equivalent qualifications), including English and mathematics – higher than the 58.8 per cent of pupils in local authority-maintained mainstream schools. In primary converter academies, in 2013, 81 per cent of pupils achieved level 4 or above in reading, writing and mathematics, and 25 per cent of pupils were above the expected level (achieving level 5 or above) in reading, writing and mathematics. In local authority-maintained mainstream schools, the proportions were 76 per cent and 21 per cent, respectively. Recognising the difficulties of comparison, the remainder of the report focuses on the difference between consecutive Ofsted inspections for individual schools, to take account of the fact that academy converters were high-performing schools, and so overall results cannot be directly compared.

Statistics can also be used to tell a particular story. In 2008, the Tory party publication *A Failed Generation* claimed the education gap between rich and poor had widened under Labour, but Schools Minister Jim Knight presented an alternative analysis of the achievement gap, which showed it had narrowed since 1997 (*The Guardian*, 8 August 2008). The report by the Cabinet Office Strategy Unit *Getting On, Getting Ahead* suggested initiatives introduced in the past 10 years – predominantly early years and primary – were beginning to pay off. Family background was now less important to the academic success of 15-year-olds than it had been for the same age group born in 1970, and Bangladeshi pupils had risen from being the lowest performers to above average. Tory shadow work and pensions secretary Chris Grayling dismissed the report: 'This has all the hallmarks of a government propaganda exercise. The reality in Britain today is that we have some of the lowest social mobility in the industrialised world'. Writing in *The Guardian*, John Crace argued that, 'the truth lies between the two'. Crace (2008) argued there had been significant improvements in raising attainment levels in some areas, especially for minority ethnic groups, but one section of the population had missed out on rising standards – the white middle class.

The EEF is an independent grant-making charity, 'dedicated to breaking the link between family income and educational achievement, ensuring that children from all backgrounds can fulfil their potential and make the most of their talents' (http://educationendowmentfoundation.org.uk; accessed March 2014). Founded by education charity the Sutton Trust, the EEF is funded by a £125 million grant from the DfE and, with investment and fund-raising income, intends to award as much as £200 million over the 15-year life of the Foundation.

The EEF aims to raise the attainment of disadvantaged children by:

- identifying and funding promising educational innovations that address the needs of disadvantaged children in primary and secondary schools in England;
- evaluating these innovations to extend and secure the evidence on what works and can be made to work on a larger scale;
- encouraging schools, governments, charities and others to apply evidence and adopt innovations found to be effective.

The EEF aims to make a lasting contribution to education in the UK by developing the evidence base of what works in education and to promote the use of evidence-based practice in schools. Where possible, the impact of projects or interventions on attainment is evaluated through the use of randomised controlled trials (RCTs). Evidence is shared by providing accessible information through the Sutton Trust–EEF Teaching and Learning Toolkit (http://educationendowmentfoundation.org.uk/toolkit; accessed March 2014), which summarises educational research from the UK and elsewhere and provides guidance for teachers and schools on how best to use their resources to improve the attainment of pupils.

The EEF website also has a very useful DIY evaluation guide, for teachers wishing to carry out small-scale evaluations in school, which you may find useful in undertaking your own research.

Undertaking research

What is action research?

According to McNiff and Whitehead (2006), action research began in the 1930s and 1940s with the work of John Collier, then acting as Commissioner for Indian Affairs, and Kurt Lewin. Lewin, a Jewish refugee from Nazi Germany who worked as a social psychologist in the US, thought that people would be more motivated about their work if they were involved in decision-making in the workplace. His ideas are still influential, and many researchers follow his ideas and organise their work as a cycle of steps:

observe → reflect → act → evaluate → modify

These can then turn into a series of cycles.

Action research was taken up in education in the 1950s, specifically by the teaching profession and particularly in the US. According to Miller (2002), this was in the context of the progressive education movement, where the emphasis was on education for the promotion of democratic practices that would enable all people to take a full and active part in political life, and so education was concerned with the production of thoughtful and responsible citizens (McNiff and Whitehead 2006). The popularity of action research declined in the US with the move towards space travel and the rise of technical, scientific research, but it became influential in Britain, notably through the work of Lawrence Stenhouse. Stenhouse moved away from the previous approach to education, where teachers studied the psychology, sociology, history and philosophy of education, seeing teachers as competent professionals who should be responsible for their own practice. He thought professional education should involve:

> the commitment to systematic questioning of one's own teaching as a basis for development;
> the commitment and the skills to study one's own teaching;
> the concern to question and to test theory in practice by the use of those skills.
>
> (Stenhouse 1975, p. 144)

Action research is often referred to as practitioner research (or practitioner-led or practitioner-based research) – it is about researching your own learning or practice. Action research can be undertaken by anyone, regardless of their position. It means learning through action and reflection and involves you, as the researcher, thinking or reflecting about what you are doing. Action research has always been linked with social change for social justice – Noffke (1997) says that the term 'action research' appeared in a 1961 speech by Martin Luther King. For some, action research is evangelical, a quest for personal and professional fulfilment (McNiff with Whitehead 2003), and, according to Cohen *et al.* (2007, p. 297), action research is 'a powerful tool for change and improvement at the local level', although for others it is at the level of problem-solving for teachers. It often has a very local focus and is concerned with effecting change in a particular situation or setting.

Action research sits within the qualitative, interpretivist perspective (Taylor *et al.* 2006). The key difference between action research and other forms of empirical research is that self-reflection is central. In other forms of research, the researcher 'does research' on other people; in action research, researchers undertake research involving themselves and others – practitioners are researchers. Action research is practical, cyclical, problem-solving and open ended.

Action research is research that focuses and impacts on practice. It recognises the importance of contexts for practice – locational, ideological, historical, managerial and social – and accords power to those who are operating in those contexts. So, it gives practitioners a 'voice', participation in decision-making and control over their environment and professional lives (Cohen *et al.* 2007, p. 29). Some might argue that, because of its day to day approach, action research is less rigorous than other forms of research, but many researchers would disagree – examples include Hopkins (2008, p. 47), who says that action research 'combines a substantive act with a research procedure; it is action disciplined by enquiry, a personal attempt at understanding while engaged in a process of improvement and reform', and Kemmis and McTaggart (1992, p. 10), who argue that 'to do action research is to plan, act, observe and reflect more carefully, more systematically, and more rigorously than one usually does in everyday life'.

According to Ebbutt (1985, quoted in Hopkins 2008), action research 'is about the systematic study of attempts to improve educational practice by groups of participants by means of their own practical actions and by means of their own reflection upon the effects of those actions'.

There is a growing body of research that suggests there is a 'performance gap' between behaviour and intention in the classroom; for example:

- there can be incongruence between a teacher's declared philosophy or beliefs about education and how they behave in the classroom;
- there can be incongruence between a teacher's declared goals and objectives and the way in which the lesson is actually taught; and
- there can be a discrepancy between a teacher's perceptions or account of a lesson and that of pupils or other observers in the classroom.

(Hopkins 2008, p. 64)

This gap can provide an important starting point for classroom research. Ebbutt (1985, quoted in Hopkins 2008) suggests six questions that demonstrate the gap between the curriculum in action and the curriculum as intention, which could be useful in refining your list of topics for research:

1. What did the pupils actually do?
2. What were they learning?
3. How worthwhile was it?
4. What did I do?
5. What did I learn?
6. What do I intend to do now?

This is an example of action research:

> Charlotte wanted to research the endings of her class music lessons: the 'final plenary' or summing up. With permission from her mentor, she audio-recorded the last ten minutes of three lessons. At the same time she read about the plenary and discovered that she only had a rough idea of its purpose; she hadn't realised that it is intended for the pupils to reflect on their own learning processes. Listening to her recordings she understood that her final plenaries were dominated by her – she spoke for over 80 per cent of the time and expected clear, 'correct' answers to her questions. This approach, she wrote, was 'contravening the purpose of the plenary!' She put in place an action plan for improving her final plenaries, recorded five more lessons and analysed the improvements in her teaching.
>
> (Sewell 2008, p. 63)

Getting started: the research question

The first thing you need to do is to define your research question or topic. Try not to begin with a problem, but take a more positive, reflective stance: What is happening now? What can I do about it? The most important thing is to decide on a topic that is interesting and relevant to you or your pupils, or something that you have to be involved in anyway as part of your work – then it will be easier to maintain your interest and enthusiasm.

Then think about what is manageable. Do not try to tackle an issue that you cannot do anything about. Only take on small-scale and relatively limited issues: particularly if this is your first experience of research, it is important to aim for success, which you could perhaps build on in the future. It is easy to underestimate the amount of time a project can take, and it can be very discouraging to find you have 'bitten off more than you can chew'.

As you determine your research question, ask yourself the following:

- What am I trying to find out?
- How will I go about this?

- How will my research support my/my pupils' learning?
- What kind of data do I need to gather?
- How will I ensure that any conclusions I come to are reasonable, fair and accurate?
- How will I change my ideas, concerns and practice in the light of my research?

Clough and Nutbrown (2007, pp. 33–4) have an interesting approach to looking at a research question:

> In our own work we have developed two simple tools that can be employed in the generation of research questions: the 'Russian doll' principle and the 'Goldilocks test'. Applying the Russian doll principle means breaking down the research question from the original statement to something which strips away the complication of layers and obscurities until the very essence – the heart – of the question can be expressed. This may well mean phrasing and rephrasing the question so that each time its focus becomes sharpened and more defined – just as a Russian doll is taken apart to reveal a tiny doll at the centre.
>
> The generated questions can then be subjected to the 'Goldilocks test' – a metaphor for thinking through the suitability of the research questions for a particular researcher in a particular setting at a particular time. So, we can ask: is this question 'too big', such that it cannot be tackled in this particular study at this time – perhaps it is a study which needs significant research funding or assistance which is not usually available to students doing research for an academic award? We can ask 'Is this too small?' – perhaps there is not enough substance to the question to warrant investigation. We can ask if the question is 'too hot' – perhaps an issue which is so sensitive that the timing is not right for investigation – or such that researching it at this point would be not only difficult but damaging in the particular social context. These questions will enable us finally to identify those questions which might be 'just right' for investigation at this time, by this researcher in this setting.

You might want to focus on a whole-school issue, rather than on your particular subject. Ensure that you can make connections between your classroom research work, teaching and learning and the school's development plan or aims. This may not be a direct relationship, but it is important to relate your research to whole-school initiatives. If you are working in a school with other trainees, you might find it useful to pair up and use each other as critical friends.

As examples of research topics, you might look at different methods of feedback and the impact they have on pupils' learning, including talking to pupils about what they find most useful. Or you could ask teachers taking pupils on a camping trip about the benefits and risks of such a venture, and compare what they see as the educational benefits with what pupils think they have learned.

Literature review

Your report will need to include a literature review that provides a context for your research – it may also help you to focus on your topic. Reading as much as you can about others' research might also give you ideas about how you might classify and present your own data. You should start to read around your topic and think about your literature review before you begin your research, but you may need to revisit it as you undertake your project. Writing up your review means appraising and evaluating the sources you have found so that you can assess their relevance and importance to your project. 'A review should provide the reader with a picture, albeit limited in a short project, of the state of knowledge and of major questions in the subject area being investigated' (Bell 1999, p. 93). Try to avoid what Haywood and Wragg called, 'the *uncritical* review, the furniture sale catalogue, in which everything merits a one paragraph entry . . . Bloggs (1975) found this, Smith (1976) found that, Jones (1977) found the other, Bloggs, Smith and Jones (1978) found happiness in heaven' (1978, p. 2).

Your literature review should show your knowledge of your topic or area of research, justify and support your arguments and make comparisons with other research. It should present a balanced view. The purpose is not to impress the reader with how much you have read or litter your writing with names and quotations. The literature review does not mean that you do not have to express your own thoughts, nor that you can misrepresent others' work.

Methodology

The next stage is to consider what information you will need and how you will collect it. The most likely methods for collecting your data will be observation, diaries, journals and field notes, documentary sources, questionnaires and interviews. The following gives only very brief details of these methods – any book on research methods will give more information. Whatever method(s) you choose, make sure you explain to participants the purpose of the research, that their participation is voluntary, issues of confidentiality and data handling.

Observation

'Observation is not simply a question of looking at something and then noting down the facts. Observation is a complex combination of sensation (sight, sound, touch, smell and even taste) and perception' (Gray 2004, p. 238). Observation is not just looking – it involves the systematic and close viewing of events or actions, and recording and analysing them. There is a real danger that we will 'see' what we want to see. Structured observation has predetermined categories for the observation, perhaps using an observation checklist. This has many advantages, including reliability and ease of analysis, but it may mean that interesting actions outside the predetermined categories are missed. Unstructured observation is more flexible. Participant observation comes from ethnographic methodology, or studying people in their natural settings. The researcher becomes part of the group and understands the situation by experiencing it, but the observer inevitably influences what is happening. The non-participant observer operates in a more detached way and tries to be objective and unbiased, but may find it harder to understand and interpret events.

Diaries, journals and field notes

These can be a very useful record of observations, significant events and your feelings about the research. To be useful, they must be as comprehensive as possible. As they are your notes, you will bring personal meaning to the account, and so they may be subjective. Notes of this kind are usually supported by other forms of data collection.

You will also find it useful to keep your own research journal, to keep records of everything you read and do and to make a note of thoughts as they occur to you.

Documentary sources

School-based action research is likely to include evidence from printed sources such as pupil records, school documents or examples of pupils' work.

Questionnaires

It takes thought to design a clear questionnaire. Another drawback to questionnaire surveys is that the response rate is often very low, although this is less likely to be the case with research located in the school where you are working. Think carefully about what information you are seeking before you design the questionnaire – open questions (usually beginning with words such as 'what', 'where', 'when', 'how') will give more detailed information but can be difficult to analyse, whereas closed questions will usually have predetermined responses ('yes', 'no', 'true', 'false'), as will multiple-choice questions. You could also use a Likert scale (where respondents rate a factor, perhaps from 1 to 5). When you have designed your questionnaire, ask yourself:

- Are the questions clear and concise?
- Is the language used appropriate for the respondents?
- Does the wording of the question lead to a particular answer?
- Have you used jargon, or stereotyping linked to gender, race or disability?

When your questionnaire is complete, always try it out on a pilot group of respondents or perhaps a group of fellow students, to make sure the questions are understood in the way you intended.

Interviews

Interviews are more flexible than questionnaires, as the interviewer has the opportunity to follow up ideas and probe answers. Interviews may be structured, semi-structured or unstructured – you may have a list of questions you want to ask, or just a list of prompts to explore. Think about whether you will take notes or tape-record the interviews (but remember that transcribing tapes can be very time consuming). Make sure that you have a quiet, comfortable room for the interview and, if tape-recording, that the equipment works and you have spare batteries. Put the interviewee at their ease and do not ask leading questions. If you are interviewing pupils, think about issues of power relationships and whether it would be better to interview them in a small group, rather than individually.

Ethics

As your action research project is located in an education setting, involving pupils/students and colleagues, you will need to think about the ethical considerations. If you are studying with a university, it will have clear ethical procedures that you must follow. This does not absolve you of responsibility, however, and you will still need to ensure that the research you do, as well as the way you behave, is responsible and ethical. Your report will need to show how you identified and managed ethical issues. If you are involving children in your research, you need to think particularly carefully about how you obtain their informed consent and whether you also need to inform their parents about your research and obtain their consent. The BERA's *Ethical Guidelines for Educational Research* can be found on its website (www.bera.ac.uk; accessed March 2014).

Analysing and presenting your data

This involves going through your data to order them, looking for trends, patterns and themes, and thinking about how you will present your data so they are clear to others. You will probably have a mix of qualitative and quantitative data. Various researchers have noted that there are no obvious ways for analysing qualitative data. Freeman (1998 in Taylor *et al.* 2006) says that action research is concerned with investigating what you feel you know already, but, in carrying out the investigation, you have to 'examine the sense of certainty, to expose, to scrutinise, to question, not because you are mistaken but to find out what is true and why' (p. 96). As part of this, he suggests that taking apart and reassembling the data are vital processes, and he identifies four activities necessary as part of the analysis:

- naming
- grouping
- finding relationships
- displaying.

Remember, when you analyse and write up your data, that they should 'tell a story', and also that you should give enough information for another researcher to be able to replicate your study.

Particularly if you are computer literate, you may want to include charts and diagrams in your report. This can be very positive – it breaks up the text and allows the reader to assess your findings quickly. Bear in mind, however, that using something like a pie chart may mean that you cannot show all the detail of your data.

Writing up

It is likely that you will have a large amount of information, from your literature review and your data collection, and so, as far as possible, you should draft your final report as you go along, to make the task easier, and then edit and revise when the report is complete. Table 10.1 shows what a usual report structure would be.

Although this is the typical structure, that does not mean you cannot individualise it. Before you write the summary and

Table 10.1 A typical report structure

Title page	Details of your name, the date and the title of your study (which should clearly indicate what the study is about)
Acknowledgements	You should acknowledge the help given to you in your research (but remember to preserve the anonymity of participants if you agreed to do this)
Abstract	A brief – typically 150 words – summary of what you set out to do, the methods you used and what you found
Aims and purpose of the study	A brief introduction to what you were setting out to do – your aims, objectives, research question – and any background necessary to place the study in its context. Mention any limitations of the study – perhaps the restricted time you had, or that the study was only concerned with one class in one school
Literature review	Review the literature around your research, to set the context and show what is already known, including any gaps
Methodology	Information on how the problem was investigated, why particular methods were used, ethical considerations, details of the procedure, how the sample was selected, and so on
Results	Tables and/or figures and/or text to describe what you found. Charts, graphs and other figures should illustrate the text – if they do not, omit them. Do not use them just to show off your computer skills. Text should not duplicate information in figures or tables, but should just highlight significant points. All tables and figures should be numbered, given a heading, and carefully checked for accuracy
Analysis and discussion	It is useful to begin this section with a re-statement of your research question and then a discussion of how your results affect existing knowledge of the subject and any implications for practice. If you set

Table 10.1 *continued*

	out to test a particular theory or hypothesis, and you have not come up with the results you expected, you have not 'failed', but, in this section, you should discuss possible reasons for your results and whether there is anything you would do differently if you repeated your study
Summary and conclusions	This section should briefly summarise the main conclusions, discussed above. Make sure you only include conclusions that can reasonably be drawn from your findings, not some opinion that is not supported by evidence. Describe any implications for practice and possibilities for future research
References	Your list of references, or bibliography, should include all those works (and only those) that have been referred to or cited in the report. You *must* acknowledge and provide a reference for all work you use that is not your own, or you could be accused of plagiarism, which will incur severe penalties
Appendices	It is usual to include any research instruments (questionnaires, interview schedules, etc.) as an appendix. If you have used abbreviations and acronyms in your report, you may want to include a glossary

conclusions, read through your report to note the key points. Bear in mind that some readers who are short of time might only read your abstract, introduction, summary and conclusions.

If your research has identified particular issues in school, think about how you write these up – being critical or apportioning blame will not be helpful.

It is often a good idea to take a break from writing, so that you can go back and look at your work with a fresh eye, but, if you do this, re-read everything that has gone before to ensure a smooth flow to your work and avoid repetition or missing something out.

Even the most gifted of writers do not produce a finished piece of work the first time, so allow plenty of time for checking through your draft(s) and making revisions. It is usually good advice to write the whole report and then go back to make revisions, rather than making too many revisions as you go along, which can send you off at a tangent. Sometimes, if you spend too long drafting and redrafting, you can reach a point where things make sense simply because you have read them so many times, because you are so familiar with the work, or where you have tried to make changes and it no longer works. If you have time, leave your draft for a few days and then come back to it, or ask a friend or partner to read through it. Just as you would critically read and evaluate someone else's work, so you should give yourself the best chance of getting good marks for your work, by doing the same and correcting any weaknesses or errors before you hand it in – it is surprising how many people do not.

References

Bassey, M. (1993) *Educational Research in the Universities and Colleges of the United Kingdom: Significant insights or trivial pursuits*? Paper presented to a conference on Evaluation, Social Science and Public Policy, Ottawa, Social Sciences and Humanities Research Council of Canada.

Bell, J. (1999) *Doing Your Research Project: A guide for first-time researchers in education and social science*, Buckingham, UK: Open University Press.

Blatchford, P., Bassett, P., Brown, P., Martin, C. and Russell, A. (2004) *The Effects of Class Size on Attainment and Classroom Processes in English Primary Schools (Years 4 to 6) 2000–2003*, Research Brief, London: DfES.

British Educational Research Association (2014) *The Role of Research in Teacher Education: Reviewing the evidence. Interim report of the BERA–RSA Inquiry*, London: BERA. Available at: www.bera.ac.uk/wp-content/uploads/2014/02/BERA-RSA-Interim-Report.pdf (accessed March 2014).

Clegg, S. (2005) Evidence-based practice in educational research: A critical realist critique of systematic review, *British Journal of Sociology of Education*, 26(3): 415–28.

Clough, P. and Nutbrown, C. (2007) *A Student's Guide to Methodology: Justifying inquiry* (2nd edn), London: Sage.

Cohen, L., Manion, L. and Morrison, K. (2007) *Research Methods in Education* (6th edn), London: RoutledgeFalmer.

Crace, J. (2008) Long division, *The Guardian*, 11 November.

Curtis, P. (2008) Education: Early years writing lessons 'do no good', *The Guardian*, 14 July.

Davies, H. T. O., Nutley, S. M., Smith, P. C. (eds) (2000) *What Works? Evidence-based policy and practice in the public services*, Bristol, UK: Policy Press.

Deem, R. (1996) The future of educational research in the context of the social sciences: A special case? *British Journal of Educational Studies*, 44(2): 143–58.

Department for Education (2013) *Teachers' Standards: Statutory guidance for school leaders, school staff and governing bodies*. Available at: www.gov.uk/government/uploads/system/uploads/attachment_data/file/283198/Teachers__Standards.pdf (accessed March 2014).

Department for Education and Skills (2001) White Paper *Schools: Achieving success*, London: TSO.

Educational Endowment Foundation (2014) Press release: EEF launches £1.5 million fund to improve use of research in schools, 16 January. Available at: http://educationendowmentfoundation.org.uk/news/eef-launches-1.5-million-fund-to-improve-use-of-research-in-schools (accessed March 2014).

Evans, J. and Benefield, P. (2001) Systematic reviews of educational research: Does the medical model fit? *British Educational Research Journal*, 27: 527–42.

Freeman, D. (1998) *Doing Teacher Research*, London: Heinle & Heinle.

Gorard, S. (2005) Academies as the 'future of schooling': is this an evidence-based policy? *Journal of Education Policy*, 20(3): 369–77.

Gray, D. (2004) *Doing Research in the Real World*, London: Sage.

Hammersley, M. (2001) *Some Questions About Evidence-based Practice in Education*. Paper presented at the symposium on 'Evidence-based practice in education' at the Annual Conference of the British Educational Research Association, University of Leeds, England, 13–15 September.

Hargreaves, D. (1996) *Teaching as A Research Based Profession: Possibilities and prospects*, London: Teacher Training Agency.

Haywood, P. and Wragg, E. C. (1978) *Evaluating the Literature*, University of Nottingham School of Education Rediguide 2, Oxford: TRC-Rediguides.

Hopkins, D. (2008) *A Teacher's Guide to Classroom Research* (4th edn), Berkshire, UK: Open University Press.

Kemmis, S. and McTaggart, R. (1992) *The Action Research Planner* (3rd edn), Geelong, Australia: Deakin University Press.

Koshy, V. (2005) *Action Research for Improving Practice: A practical guide*, London: Paul Chapman.

Machin, S. (2012) Academies: Old research is being wrongly used to validate them, *The Guardian*, 9 April.

McNiff, J. and Whitehead, J. (2003) *Action Research Principles and Practice* (2nd edn), London: RoutledgeFalmer.

McNiff, J. and Whitehead, J. (2006) *All You Need to Know About Action Research*, London: Sage.

Miller, R. (2002) *Free Schools, Free People: Education and democracy after the 1960s*, Albany, NY: SUNY Press.

Noffke, S. (1997) Themes and tensions in US action research: Towards historical analysis, in S. Hollingsworth (ed.) *International Action Research: A casebook for educational reform*, London: Falmer.

Our Bodies Ourselves (2003) Available at: www.ourbodiesourselves.org (accessed March 2014).

Sayer, A. (1992) *Method in Social Science: A realist approach*, London: Routledge.

Scienceogram UK (2013) *SET Statistics: Departmental cuts masked by budgeting*. Available at: http://scienceogram.org/blog/2013/09/set-statistics-government-departments-research/(accessed March 2014).

Sewell, K. (2008) *Doing your PGCE at M-Level: A guide for students*, London: Sage.

Smithers, R., Curtis, P. and Taylor, M. (2005) Academies claim boost for GCSEs, *The Guardian*, 26 August.

Stenhouse, L. (1975) *An Introduction to Curriculum Research and Development*, London: Heinemann.

Taylor, C., Wilkie, M. and Baser, J. (2006) *Doing Action Research: A guide for school support staff*, London: Paul Chapman.

Tooley, J. with Darby, D. (1998) *Educational Research: A critique*, London: Ofsted.

Whitty, G. (2002) *Making Sense of Education Policy: Studies in the sociology and politics of education*, London: Sage.

Whitty, G. (2006) Education(al) research and education policy making: Is conflict inevitable? *British Education Research Journal*, 32(2): 159–76.

Whitty, G., Donoghue, M., Christie, D., Kirk, G., Menter, I., McNamara, O., Moss, G., Oancea, A., Rogers, C. and Thomson, P. (2012) *Prospects for the Future of Educational Research*, London: BERA and UCET.

11 Critical reading and writing

Reading furnishes the mind only with materials of knowledge: it is thinking that makes what we read ours.

(John Locke)

What is critical reading and writing?

As a trainee teacher, you need to be able to read and write critically. This is not the sort of critical reading where someone reads an article in the tabloid press and says, 'This is absolute ******! How can they write this kind of **** rubbish!', which is unlikely to get you high marks in a presentation or written assignment!

Why are critical reading and writing important? At one level, because criticality is an important part of higher-level study and will be used in the assessment of your work. On another level, because, in training to be a teacher, you are entering an area that is clouded by debate and contentious issues – whether phonics should be used to teach reading, whether children with SEN should be included in mainstream schools, and whether all children should have to learn a modern foreign language are just some examples. Education is also a field where untrained people think they can voice an opinion in a way that they would not do with, say, medicine or engineering. So, as a teacher, you need to be able to look at education policies and pronouncements and make a reasoned assessment of their worth and the evidence on which they are based.

Critical reading and writing in an academic context are concerned with evidence and analysis, and not taking anything at face value.

Definitions

Critical thinking

Critical thinking, for a trainee teacher, means:

- finding out where the best evidence lies for the subject you are discussing;
- evaluating the strength of the evidence to support different arguments;
- coming to an interim conclusion about where the available evidence appears to lead;
- constructing a line of reasoning to guide your audience through the evidence and lead them towards your conclusions;
- selecting the best examples;
- providing evidence to illustrate your argument.

(Cottrell 2005, p. 9)

Analytical writing

Analytical writing is writing that looks at the evidence in a detailed and critical way. In particular, it weighs up the relative strengths and weaknesses of the evidence, pointing these out to the reader, so that it is clear how the writer has arrived at judgements and conclusions (Cottrell 2005, p. 168). Critical analysis looks at good and bad points, strengths and weaknesses. It is not enough to simply list good and bad points, or say that something is good, or that something does not work – you need to evaluate and provide evidence that helps you to say why something does or doesn't work.

According to Wallace and Wray (2006, p. 7):

> *The skill of critical reading* lies in assessing the extent to which authors have provided adequate justification for the claims they make. This assessment depends partly on what the authors

have communicated and partly on other relevant knowledge, experience and inference that you are able to bring into the frame.

The skill of self-critical writing lies in convincing your readers to accept your claims. You achieve this through the effective communication of adequate reasons and evidence for these claims.

So, how can you critically read a piece of academic writing? It is not difficult, but, like most things that are worth doing, it takes a bit of practice, and it may require you to change the way that you work. If you have been working in education for a number of years, for example, you are probably not used to having to explain or provide evidence for your opinions – you just know. Or you may wonder how you, as a trainee and beginning teacher, can question and challenge government policy, or the work of very experienced and respected practitioners and researchers. The answer is that you can, and you must – your work and views are just as valid as theirs, but they must be supported by evidence and analysis. Without really thinking about it, you are probably already used to thinking critically in other areas of your life.

Think about making a fairly big purchase – a laptop computer perhaps, or a new mobile phone. What do you do? First, you probably decide how much you can afford to spend. Next, you need to think about what you will use it for, or what you need it to do – are free texts more important to you than cheap calls? Then, you need to do your research. If you are buying a mobile phone, for example, will you just look at the company websites for O_2, Orange and Vodaphone, or will you try to find a website that does a comparison for you? How will you know that the information is valid and impartial? And what about the deals offered by the supermarkets – how does Tesco compare with O_2? What have your friends got – what is their experience? You gather information, make your decision and you buy.

To put it another way:

- You set out the question you need to answer (which mobile phone, which tariff?).

- You gather information (your needs, company websites, comparison sites, friends).
- You assess the validity of the evidence.
- You put together your reasons and arguments.
- You come to a conclusion.

And that, basically, is critical thinking.

Critical reading

Learning to be critical in your reading means looking beyond the words for the evidence, but also being open-minded and willing to be convinced. Keep a balance – remember that the authors of a paper do not know who their audience will be, or what experience or beliefs they have, and also that, particularly in journals, they are constrained by a maximum word length for their writing and so cannot include every detail. Published materials also vary considerably in their rigour and writing style – some papers may be badly written, where the author does not include sufficient details of how they designed and carried out their research or analysed their results.

This example is taken from Wallace and Wray (2006, p. 5). It is an extract from a fictional paper on a study in which some children were taught to read using the phonics method (sounding out words on the basis of the individual letters) and others were taught using the whole-word method (learning to recognise and pronounce complete words): 'In the reading test, the five children who were taught to read using phonics performed better overall than the five children taught using the whole-word method. This shows that the phonics method is a better choice for schools.'

You will probably have a number of questions about this, which might include:

- Is a study of only ten children sufficient to draw such a firm conclusion?
- What does 'performed better overall' mean? Did some children using the whole-word method perform better than the children using phonics? What implications does this have for the results?

- Were the differences between the two groups sufficiently great that we could be confident that they would occur again if the experiment was re-run with different subjects?
- How were the two teaching programmes administered? Can we be sure that there was no 'leakage' of whole-word teaching into the phonics teaching, and vice versa?
- What was the reading test actually testing? Might it have been unintentionally biased to favour the children taught using phonics?
- What care was taken to check how parental involvement at home might have influenced what and how the children learned to read?
- Were the children in the two groups matched for intelligence, age, gender and other factors?
- Is it reasonable to infer that what works in a small, experimental study will work well in all school environments?
- How does the author envisage phonics being used in schools? Would there still be a place for the whole-word method?

If you were reading the entire paper, the questions would probably be answered elsewhere in the text. But, if they are not, and you want to use this paper in your own writing, you will need to be critical and refer to the weaknesses your questions identify, as a balance to what you say about the author's claims. Using this example, you might write something along the lines of:

> Browning (2005) found that children taught to read using phonics did better in a reading test than children taught using the whole word method. However, the study was small, the test rather limited, and the subjects were not tightly matched either for age or gender. An examination of Browning's test scores reveals that, although the mean score of the phonics group was higher, two of the highest scorers in the test were whole word learners. Since this indicates that the whole word method is effective for some learners at least, Browning is perhaps too quick to propose that 'the phonics method is a better choice for schools' (p. 89).
>
> (example taken from Wallace and Wray 2006, p. 6)

Note that this paragraph is not saying that Browning is wrong, but is raising some questions that would need to be considered before the evidence was accepted.

Critical reading of others' work will often be in the context of producing your own written work. This will enable you to develop a sense of what is (or is not) a robust piece of research, which will be useful when planning your own research. You will begin to see where existing research has left a gap, which your research might fill and your writing style will change.

Critical reading is rarely about questioning the facts – unless you have carried out similar research, you would be unlikely to have a basis on which to do so – but is about assessing the case that has been made for evaluating and interpreting the facts in a particular way, whether there is evidence to support a claim, whether the facts could have been interpreted differently, and whether the conclusions could also apply to other situations.

It can be a new idea for students to think that 'the facts' can be interpreted in different ways, but there are many examples of this. Just think of the way that opposing political parties will put a different 'spin' on a new report, or the way different TV stations and newspapers will report a news story. When you are reading critically, you need to focus on:

- the evidence the author provides;
- whether the conclusion drawn follows logically from the author's arguments;
- the implications of the author's own values and assumptions;
- whether the author's claims are in line with those of other authors;
- whether the author's claims or predictions are in line with your own knowledge and evidence.

Particularly early on in your course or career, you will not know all there is to know on a topic, nor will you be expected to, but you do need to acquire the skills of critical reading and building up your own knowledge. There are far more books and papers than you will have time to read, however, and so you will need to be selective.

Different types of knowledge

The type of knowledge you are trying to gain from a book or paper can affect the way you read it. For example, you may be reading because the author has used a method of research that you are thinking about using in your own work, and so, then, you will need to read in a different way, or perhaps read different sections, than if you were reading for another purpose. It may also mean that you need to read it more than once.

There are four different **types of knowledge** that you will come across in your reading:

- *theoretical knowledge*: concerned with a theory about something, a system of related concepts; can be a personal reflection or closely linked to finding evidence;
- *research knowledge*: the conducting and outcomes of a systematic investigation;
- *practice knowledge*: ideas for good practice from professionals and practitioners, based on personal experience or evaluating others' practice;
- *policy*: policymakers describe a vision for improved practice and the means for achieving the vision.

Critically evaluating a piece of writing

The following is a list of questions you might ask (based on Cottrell 2005, p. 190):

1 Is the writer's own position on the issues clear?
2 Are there reasons for the writer's own point of view?
3 Is the writer's conclusion clear and based on the evidence?
4 Are reasons presented in a logical order, as a line of reasoning?
5 Is the argument well structured and easy to follow?
6 Are reasons clearly linked to one another, and to the conclusion?
7 Is all the text relevant to the argument?

8 Do the main reasons and key points stand out clearly to the reader?
9 Does the writer make good use of other people's research as supporting evidence to strengthen the argument?
10 Does the writer make a reasoned evaluation of other people's views, especially those that contradict his or her own point of view?
11 Does the writer provide references in the text when introducing other people's ideas?
12 Does the writer provide a list of references at the end of the work?
13 Has the writer successfully removed any non-essential descriptive writing?
14 Does the writing contain any inconsistencies?
15 Are the writer's own beliefs or self-interests unfairly distorting the argument?

Writing a critical summary

If you are writing a critical summary of a research article or report, the structure of your work should be along the lines shown in Table 11.1. The indicative word limits are based on a piece of writing of about 500 words – if you are writing a longer piece, you would increase the word limits accordingly.

How to decide what to read

You will not be able to read all that has been written on a particular topic, and so you will need to be selective. You also need to make sure that you have covered the main texts or authors in a particular field, which can be difficult if it is new to you. The following are some suggestions for finding relevant literature:

- Begin with the recommended reading list for the module or subject area, if you have one.
- Note whether your tutor or mentor has mentioned a particular author and look at his/her work.
- Use the library to search electronic databases and journals.
- Look in specialist journals.

Table 11.1 Critical summary structure

Section/ Content	**Questions to answer**	**No. of words**
Title		
Introduction		
Introducing the text	Why am I reading this? Why is this text worth mentioning?	50–100
Main text		
Reporting the content	What are the authors trying to do in writing this? What are they saying that is relevant to what I want to find out?	100–200
Evaluating the content	How convincing is what the authors are saying?	100–200
Conclusion		
Drawing your conclusions	What use can I make of this?	100–150

- Search abstracts databases, using author names or keywords.
- When you have a key text, search the library catalogue or library shelves using its subject code or catalogue number.
- Look at the bibliographies for papers and books on the topic and note the authors cited most frequently.
- Check Google Scholar for details of citation frequency (http://scholar.google.com; accessed March 2014) and to search for work on a particular topic.

Critical writing

Critical reading and writing are inextricably linked – what you write, others will read! This is a profile of a typical academic who might assess your writing, to give you some pointers on what you need to consider (based on Poulson and Wallace 2004, p. 8; Wallace and Wray 2006, p. 41):

- *Age*: Old enough to have read plenty of other work, so that they will have a measure by which to judge yours.
- *Lifestyle*: Busy – appreciates writing with a logical structure, clear focus and fluent writing style that communicates efficiently.
- *Attitudes*: Fair and respectful – concerned solely with the quality of your writing. Sceptical – will not accept your arguments unless you can prove your case. Open minded – ready to be convinced.
- *Favourite subject*: The area of study – knowledgeable about the area in general but not about detailed issues or about your professional experience, so welcomes a brief description, but only insofar as it is relevant to your argument.
- *Likes*: Books – so knows the literature well and expects you to have read the literature you write about and to report it accurately. Reading high-quality writing: carefully constructed, well argued, balanced, meticulous on detail and reflective.
- *Pet hates*: Waffle – ill-structured writing whose focus is diffuse and that leads nowhere. Avoidable errors, whether typographical, punctuation or grammatical, that careful proofreading could have picked up. Overgeneralisation – wild claims that go far beyond any backing they may have. Poor referencing – failure to acknowledge authors, inaccurate or incomplete reference lists. Plagiarism.
- *Believes*: Conclusions must be warranted by evidence from research, literature or experience if they are to be convincing. Everything in a written account should be relevant to the focus and the conclusions.
- *Most likely to say*: 'Address the question or task set in your assignment.' 'Keys to writing success are a logical structure and a clear focus.' 'Take the criteria for assessment into account when planning your written work.' 'Your literature review should be critical, not just descriptive.'

Table 11.2 illustrates how critical reading and critical writing are linked.

You need to make sure that your work has a logical structure, that you begin with a brief introduction and develop the arguments that support your conclusion. In your writing, there are various

Table 11.2 Elements of critical reading and self-critical writing

Element of critical reading	**Element of self-critical writing**
When I read an academic text, I:	*When I write an academic text, I:*
Try to work out what the authors are aiming to achieve	State clearly what I am trying to achieve
Try to work out the structure of the argument	Create a logical structure for my account, to help me develop my argument and to help the reader follow it
Try to identify the main claims made	Clearly state my main claims
Adopt a sceptical stance towards the author's claims, checking that they are supported by appropriate evidence	Support my claims with appropriate evidence, so that a critical reader will be convinced
Assess the backing for any generalisations made	Avoid making sweeping generalisations
Check how the authors define their key terms and whether they are consistent in using them	Define the key terms employed in my account and use the terms consistently
Consider what underlying values may be guiding the authors and influencing their claims	Make explicit the values guiding what I write
Keep an open mind, am willing to be convinced	Assume that my readers can be convinced, provided I can adequately support my claims
Look out for instances of irrelevant or distracting material, and for the absence of necessary material	Sustain focus throughout my account, avoid irrelevancies and digressions and include everything that is relevant
Identify any literature sources to which the authors refer, that I may need to follow up	Ensure that my referencing in the text and the reference list are complete and accurate, so that my readers are in a position to check my sources

Table 11.3 Words to structure arguments

Introducing the argument:	First, initially, to begin, at the outset
Developing the argument:	
– Reinforcing with similar reasons	Similarly, equally, likewise, also, again, correspondingly
– Reinforcing with different reasons or evidence	Also, in addition, besides, as well as, not only . . . but also, either
– Stronger reinforcement	Furthermore, moreover, indeed, what is more
– Introducing alternative arguments	Alternatively, a different perspective might be, it could be argued that
– Rebutting alternative arguments	However, on the other hand, nonetheless, in spite of this, despite this, at the same time, even though
– Contrasting	By contrast, although, on the one hand . . . on the other hand
Concluding:	
– Expressing results and conclusions	Therefore, this suggests that, this indicates, as a result, as a consequence, we can infer from this, because of this
– Conclusions	Therefore, in conclusion, thus we can see

words you can use to structure your argument – introducing the argument, moving it along, summing it up. Table 11.3 has some suggestions.

These 'signal' or 'signposting' words are useful when you are reading other people's work too and can help you pick out the different arguments and conclusions.

Academic writing of the kind you will be doing avoids absolutes and uses more tentative words, because you will not be in a position to make definitive statements. Table 11.4 has examples.

Table 11.4 Tentative vocabulary

Avoid	Try
All, every	Most, many, some
Always	Usually, generally, often, in most cases, so far
Never	In few cases, rarely, it is unlikely that
Proves	The evidence suggests, indicates, points to, it would appear that, it could be argued that

Values

Critical reading and writing mean being objective and making accurate judgements, based on reasoning: reasoning involves analysing evidence and drawing conclusions from it. The way in which we view other people's work or analyse the evidence can be affected by our own assumptions, prejudices, beliefs and values. In order to become more skilled at critical reading and writing, you may need to become more self-aware, to think about your motivation, beliefs, expertise and gaps in your knowledge. You should be able to:

- have reasons for what you believe and do, and be aware of what these are;
- critically evaluate your own beliefs and actions;
- be able to present to others the reasons for your beliefs and actions.

(Cottrell 2005, p. 3)

If you are not able to be objective but take a particular stance in a piece of work, this should be stated, and you will need to be able to present evidence to support your views.

Evaluating your writing for critical thinking

You can use the self-evaluation tool in Table 11.5 to check through your assignments.

Table 11.5 Self-evaluation tool

Self-evaluation	Yes/no	Action
I am clear on my position on this subject and the reasons for my point of view		Write your position down as a statement in one or two sentences. If you cannot do so, this suggests that your position isn't yet clear in your own mind. If possible, check whether your point of view is clear to a friend or colleague who knows little about the subject
My conclusions and/or recommendations are clear, based on the evidence, and written in tentative language where appropriate		Write your conclusions first. Read these aloud; check that they make sense. Imagine someone tells you that your conclusion is wrong. What reasons would you give to defend it? Have you included all these reasons in your writing?
The material included is the most relevant to the subject		Double-check that your line of reasoning meets the task requirements, such as meeting the project brief or answering the questions set for an essay. Does it match the statement you wrote about your position?
All sections of the assignment or report are relevant to the exact specifications of the task		Read through each section or paragraph in turn, checking how the information contributes to your line of reasoning, leading to your conclusion or recommendations. Check that each meets the project brief, or is necessary to answer the set question
I have analysed the structure of my argument. Reasons are presented in the best order and lead clearly towards the conclusion		If not, write the reasons out in brief and consider how each is linked to the conclusion. Check whether the argument 'hops' from one point to another. Cluster similar reasons together and indicate how each contributes to the main argument or conclusion
The argument stands out clearly from other information. I have selected the best examples		Check you have not presented so much detail that the main argument is lost. An analysis of a few examples or details is much better than a superficial approach to lots of material. Select carefully to meet the task requirement

continued

Table 11.5 *continued*

Self-evaluation	Yes/no	Action
My reasons are clearly linked to one another and to the conclusion(s)		Check that each paragraph opens with a clear link to what has gone before or signals a change in the direction of your argument, using 'signal words'
My main reasons and key points stand out clearly to the reader		Take a marker pen and highlight the sentence that sums up the main point or reason covered in each paragraph. If you find this difficult, it is likely that your reader will find it hard to identify your points. If large sections of a paragraph are highlighted, then it is probable that you haven't summarised its main point sufficiently
My facts are accurate		Do not rely on opinion or memory. Check that your sources are reputable and up to date. Investigate whether anything published more recently gives different information. Check that you have reported the facts accurately, and without distortion
I have included reference to relevant theories		Find out the schools of thought or theories related to the subject. Make a critical evaluation of these to identify where they support or conflict with your argument
I make use of other people's research as supporting evidence to strengthen my argument		Check what has been written or produced on this subject by other people. Include references to relevant items that best support your point of view
I have cited the source of information for evidence and theories to which I refer		Write out the details of the references in brief within the text, and in full at the end of the writing
I include a reasoned evaluation of views that do not support my own argument		Find out what has been written that contradicts your point of view, and consider any other potential objections that could be raised. Evaluate these as part of your line of reasoning. Make it clear why your reasons are more convincing than opposing points of view

Table 11.5 *continued*

Self-evaluation	Yes/no	Action
		Identify any flaws, gaps or inconsistencies in the counter-arguments
My writing is mainly analytical and contains only brief, essential descriptive writing		Check whether all sections of descriptive writing and background information are essential to understanding your reasoning or are part of the conventions of the type of report you are writing. Keep descriptions very brief, look for ways of summarising them and link them clearly to your main argument. Beware of wordy introductions
I have checked my argument for inconsistencies		Check whether any of the reasons or evidence you have used could be interpreted as contradicting what you have written elsewhere in the piece of writing
I have given clear indications of levels of probability or uncertainty		Check that your writing indicates your judgement of how likely it is that the conclusion is accurate and irrefutable. If there is a chance that research findings could be interpreted differently by someone else, use appropriate language to indicate a level of uncertainty or ambiguity
My current beliefs are not unfairly distorting my argument		If any section of your assignment covers a subject where you have strong beliefs or interests, be especially careful that you have checked that the evidence supports your reasoning. It is important that your arguments come across in a calm and reasoned way that will convince your reader. Check several times, and be careful not to include emotive language or poorly substantiated opinions
I have covered all the required aspects of the assignment		Check the assignment's details carefully. Tick aspects already completed, so it is clear what else you must do

Note: Taken from Cottrell 2005, p. 196

Further reading

Learning and Teaching at M Level
Hazel Bryan, Chris Carpenter and Simon Hoult, 2010, Sage
A guide through the various stages of Masters level training.

Why Action Research?
Mary Brydon-Miller, Greenwood Davydd and Maguire Patricia, 2003, *Action Research*, 1(9), available at: http://arj.sagepub.com/cgi/content/abstract/1/1/9 (accessed March 2014)
An interesting introduction to action research, with some personal stories from researchers.

Critical Thinking Skills: Developing effective analysis and argument
Sheila Cottrell, 2011(2nd edn), Palgrave
A useful guide from a writer of many books on study skills.

Critical Reading and Writing for Postgraduates
Mike Wallace and Alison Wray, 2006, Sage
A very clearly written and useful book for postgraduates.

Doing Your PGCE at M-Level: A guide for students
Keira Sewell, 2008, Sage
A fairly short, easy-to-read guide to all aspects of the PGCE.

Action Research for Professional Development: Concise advice for new action researchers
Jean McNiff, 2002 (3rd edn), Hyde Publications, available at: www.jeanmcniff.com/booklet1.html (accessed March 2014)
Arguably the best guide to action research and helpfully published in full online.

A Teacher's Guide to Classroom Research
David Hopkins, 2008 (4th edn), Open University Press
An excellent discussion of classroom research, including models and disadvantages of action research.

Real World Research
Colin Robson, 2011 (3rd edn), John Wiley
Over 600 pages that will tell you all you need to know about researching settings where you work. Contains a lot of information for education students and is aimed at those without a social science background; a practical, helpful book.

Doing Action Research: A guide for school support staff
Claire Taylor, Min Wilkie and Judith Baser, 2006, Paul Chapman
A short, easy-to-read book with some useful tips, but aimed at school support staff and so not Masters level.

Doing Your Research Project: A guide for first-time researchers in education, health and social science
Judith Bell, 2005 (4th edn), Open University Press
Described as a worldwide best seller, a very good general guide for beginning researchers.

Research Methods in Education
Louis Cohen, Lawrence Manion and Keith Morrison, 2007 (6th edn), Routledge
Arguably the seminal text on education research methods.

References

Cottrell, S. (2005) *Critical Thinking Skills: Developing effective analysis and argument*, Basingstoke, UK: Palgrave.

Poulson, L. and Wallace, M. (eds) (2004) *Learning to Read Critically in Teaching and Learning*, London: Sage.

Wallace, M. and Wray, A. (2006) *Critical Reading and Writing for Postgraduates*, London: Sage.

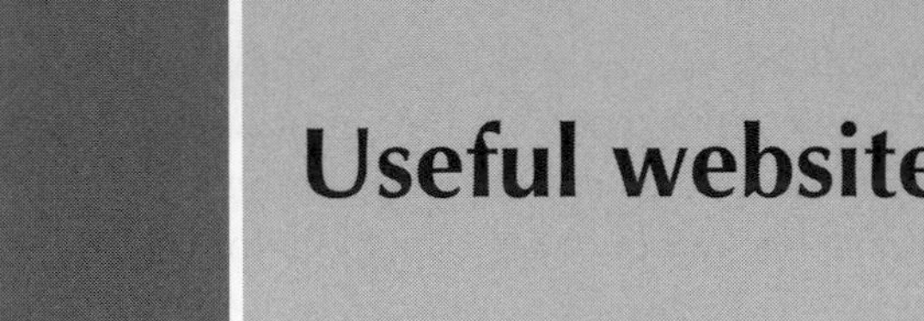

Useful websites

Assessment Reform Group: although its work has now finished, publications can still be downloaded: www.aaia.org.uk/afl/assessment-reform-group (accessed March 2014).

Association for the Study of Primary Education (ASPE): works to advance primary education through research and professional collaboration; publishes the journal *Education 3–13*: www.aspe-uk.eu (accessed March 2014).

British Educational Research Association: supports educational research: www.bera.ac.uk (accessed March 2014).

Department for Education: provides statistics and performance tables, publications and reports and online information: www.education.gov.uk (accessed March 2014).

Education in England: a brief history – a history website, with useful links to important legislation and reports: www.educationengland.org.uk/history (accessed March 2014).

Joseph Rowntree Foundation: a social policy and development charity that funds research into poverty and inequality: www.jrf.org.uk (accessed March 2014).

National Association for Primary Education (NAPE): works to support teachers and others involved in primary education; publishes a number of journals, including *Primary First*: www.nape.org.uk (accessed March 2014).

National Association for Special Educational Needs (NASEN): a charity that publishes journals and other publications and provides resources for teachers: www.nasen.org.uk (accessed March 2014).

National Foundation for Education Research: undertakes research and dissemination activities nationally and internationally: www.nfer.ac.uk (accessed March 2014).

Ofsted: has links to reports on individual schools and institutions and publishes a number of reports: www.ofsted.gov.uk (accessed March 2014).

YouTube can also be a very useful resource. See, for example, the animation of Sir Ken Robinson talking about education: www.youtube.com/watch?v=zDZFcDGpL4U (accessed March 2014), or Piaget's conservation task: www.youtube.com/watch?v=YtLEWVu815o (accessed March 2014).

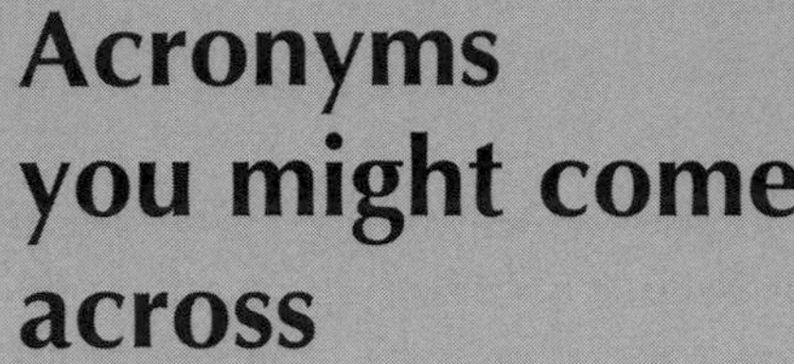

Acronyms you might come across

AfL	assessment for learning
APP	assessing pupils' progress
AQA	qualification awarding body, also known as the Assessment and Qualifications Alliance
ATL	Association of Teachers and Lecturers
AWPU	age-related pupil unit, measure used to distribute funding to schools
BME	black and minority ethnic
BSS	local authority-run body to provide training and services to schools to tackle behaviour issues
BTEC	Business and Technology Education Council, vocational qualification-awarding body
C&G	City and Guilds
CAF	common assessment framework, used to assess student needs and how they might be met
CAMHS	Child and Adolescent Mental Health Services
CP	child protection
CPD	continuing professional development, including on-the-job training
CRB	Criminal Records Bureau, now the DBS
CSIE	Centre for Studies on Inclusive Education
D&T or DT	design and technology
DBS	Disclosure and Barring Service (previously the CRB)
DCPO	designated child protection officer, also known as the designated child safeguarding officer
DDA	Disability Discrimination Act

DfE	Department for Education
EAB	Examinations Appeals Board
EAL	English as an additional language
EBac	English Baccalaureate
EBD	emotional and behavioural difficulty
EEF	Education Endowment Foundation
EFL	English as a foreign language
EP	educational psychologist (ed. psych.)
ESOL	English for speakers of other languages
ESW	education social worker
EWO	education welfare officer
EYCS	Early Years and Childcare Service
EYFSP	early years foundation stage profile
FSM	free school meals
FTE	full-time equivalent
G&T	gifted and talented
GCSE	General Certificate of Secondary Education
H&S	health and safety
HMCI	Her Majesty's Chief Inspector (of schools)
HMI	Her Majesty's Inspector(ate)
HOD	head of department
HSE	Health and Safety Executive
IB	International Baccalaureate
IEP	individual education plan
INSET	in-service education and training
ITT	initial teacher training
IYSS	Integrated Youth Support Service, provides services for young people
KS	key stage
LA	local authority (used to be local education authority, or LEA)
LAC	looked-after children, or children in care
LAP	local achievement partnership, collaboration between schools and local authorities
LSW	learning support workers, usually support children with special needs
MFL	modern foreign languages
MLD	moderate learning difficulty

NAHT	National Association of Head Teachers
NAPE	National Association for Primary Education
NASUWT	National Association of Schoolmasters and Union of Women Teachers
NC	National Curriculum
NCTL	National College for Teaching and Leadership, amalgamation of the former National College for School Leadership and the Teaching Agency
NEET	school leavers who are not in education, employment or training
NFER	National Foundation for Education Research
NoR	number on roll – number of pupils in a school
NQT	newly qualified teacher
NUT	National Union of Teachers
OECD	Organisation for Economic Co-operation and Development
OFQUAL	Office of Qualifications and Examinations Regulation
Ofsted	Office for Standards in Education
PAN	planned admission number
PGCE	postgraduate (or professional graduate) certificate in education
PISA	Programme for International Student Assessment
PPA	preparation, planning and assessment. The Workload Agreement for England and Wales guarantees teachers in maintained schools 10 per cent of timetabled teaching to be set aside during the school day as PPA time
PRP	performance-related pay
PRU	pupil referral unit
PSHE	personal, social and health education
PTA	parent teacher association
PTR	pupil–teacher ratio
QTS	qualified teacher status
RARPA	recognising and rewarding progress and achievement
SATs	standard assessment tasks (or standardised achievement tests or standard assessment tests)

SDP	school development plan
SEAL	social and emotional aspects of learning
SEBD	social, emotional and behavioural difficulties
SEF	self-evaluation form for schools, issued by Ofsted
SEN	special educational needs
SENCo	special educational needs co-ordinator
SEND	special educational needs and disabilities
SLD	severe learning disability
SLT	senior leadership team
SRE	sex and relationship education
STEM	science, technology, engineering and maths
TA	teaching assistant
TEFL	teaching English as a foreign language
ULN	unique learner number
VA	voluntary aided
VC	voluntary controlled

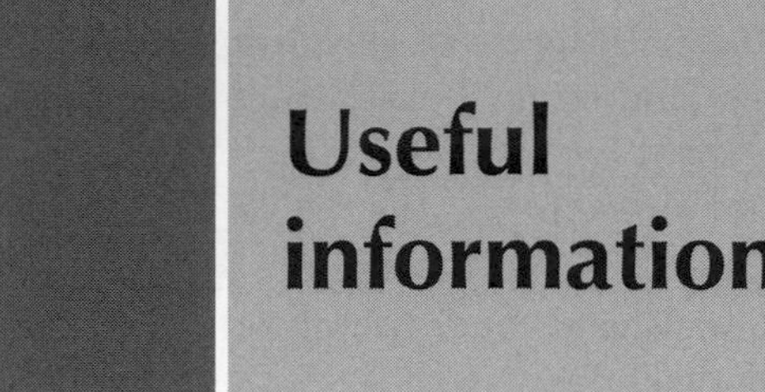

Useful information

Timeline: key reports and legislation in England since 1940

1943 The Norwood Report *Curriculum and Examinations in Secondary Schools* backed the tripartite system recommended by the Spens Report (1938)

1944 The McNair Report *The Supply, Recruitment and Training of Teachers and Youth Leaders* recommended the rationalisation of teacher training provision and a 3-year course

1944 The Education Act 1944 (the Butler Act) set out the tripartite structure of post-war education

1947 School leaving age raised to 15

1951 General Certificate of Education (GCE) examinations introduced

1958 The White Paper *Secondary Education for All: A new drive*

1959 The Crowther Report *15–18* recommended raising the school leaving age to 16 and the provision of further education for 15–18-year-olds

1960 The Beloe Report *Secondary School Examinations Other than the GCE* led to the introduction of the Certificate of Secondary Education (CSE) in 1965

1960 Teacher training courses extended from 2 to 3 years

1962 The Education Act 1962 placed a legal obligation on parents to ensure that children received a suitable education at school or otherwise and made LEAs responsible for ensuring that pupils attended school

1963 The Newsom Report *Half our Future* considered the education of 13–16-year-olds of average or less than average ability

1963 *Higher Education*, the report of the Robbins Committee, recommended a massive expansion of higher education

1963 The Children and Young Persons Act extended LEAs' responsibilities for the welfare of young children

1964 The Ministry of Education was renamed the Department of Education and Science, and the Minister became the Secretary of State

1964 Education Act 1964 (the Boyle Act) allowed the creation of middle schools

1965 The Certificate of Secondary Education (CSE) introduced in England and Wales

1966 Polytechnics established

1967 The Plowden Report *Children and their Primary Schools* promoted child-centred education

1968 *Fight for Education: A Black Paper*, edited by C. B. Cox and A. E. Dyson

1969 *Black Paper Two: The Crisis in Education*, edited by Cox and Dyson

1970 Conservative government Circular 10/70 withdrawing Labour's Circular 10/65 – LEAs were no longer compelled to implement comprehensive schooling. (Later withdrawn by Circular 4/74)

1970 *Black Paper Three: Goodbye Mr Short*, edited by Cox and Dyson

1971 Education (Milk) Act 1971 limited the provision of free milk in schools and led to the saying 'Thatcher, Thatcher, milk snatcher'

1972 The James Report *Teacher Education and Training*

1973 School leaving age raised to 16

1973 Circular 7/73 halved the number of places for student teachers

1974 Circular 4/74 confirmed the Labour government's intention to go ahead with comprehensivisation

1974 The William Tyndale affair – problems at a London primary school gave ammunition to the writers of the *Black Papers* and paved the way for Callaghan's Ruskin Speech in 1976

1975 Sex Discrimination Act

1975 *Black Paper 1975: The Fight for Education*, edited by Cox and Dyson

1976 Race Relations Act

1976 Jim Callaghan's Ruskin College speech began 'the great debate' about education

1976 Neville Bennett's paper *Teaching Styles and Pupil Progress* attacked progressive education

1977 The Taylor Report *A New Partnership for Our Schools* recommended major changes in the management of schools, implemented in the 1980 Act

1978 The Warnock Report *Special Educational Needs*

1978 The Waddell Report *School Examinations* recommended a single exam at age 16 to replace O Levels and CSEs – the first GCSE exams were taken in 1988

1979 The Education Act 1979 repealed Labour's 1976 Act and allowed LEAs to retain selective secondary schools

1980 The Education Act 1980 gave parents greater power over governing bodies and admissions, removed LEAs' obligation to provide school milk and meals, and began the assisted-places scheme (financial provision for children to go to independent schools)

1981 The Rampton Report *West Indian Children in Our Schools* was the interim report of the inquiry into the education of children from minority ethnic groups (the final report was Swann 1985)

1981 The Education Act 1981, based on the Warnock Report, gave parents new rights in relation to special educational needs

1984 The Council for the Accreditation of Teacher Education (CATE) was established to set standards for initial teacher training courses

1984 Green Paper *Parental Influence at School* proposed more parent power

1985 Swann Report *Education for All*: the final report of the Committee of Inquiry into the Education of Children from Minority Ethnic Groups

1986 GCSEs replaced O-level and CSE examinations

1986 National Council for Vocational Qualifications (NCVQ) established

1987 *The National Curriculum 5–16*: consultation document in which the government set out plans for the introduction of a national curriculum

1988 The Black Report *National Curriculum Task Group on Assessment and Testing* set out the structure of tests and school league tables

1988 Education Reform Act 1988 was a major Act establishing the National Curriculum, testing, local management of schools

1991 The Parents' Charter gave parents the right to information about schools and their performance

1991 Polytechnics granted university status

1992 Education (Schools) Act 1992: new arrangements for the inspection of schools, the creation of Ofsted

1992 Discussion paper *Curriculum Organisation and Classroom Practice in Primary Schools: A discussion paper* (known as the Three Wise Men Report) commissioned by Kenneth Clarke

1992 The Department of Education and Science became the Department for Education (DfE)

1993 The Education Act 1993 changed the funding of grant-maintained schools, laid down rules for pupil exclusions and failing schools, defined special educational needs

1993 The independent National Commission on Education published *Learning to Succeed: A radical look at education today and a strategy for the future*

1994 The Dearing Review *The National Curriculum and its Assessment: Final Report* – Lord Dearing was called in to sort out the complicated National Curriculum and assessment arrangements

1994 The *Code of Practice on the Identification and Assessment of Special Educational Needs* came into force

1995 The Department for Education became the Department for Education and Employment (DfEE)

1996 Education Act 1966 consolidated all Education Acts since 1944

1996 *Nursery Education and Grant Maintained Schools Act* introduced the voucher scheme for nursery education, later withdrawn by Labour

1997 Dearing Report: a review of higher education

1997 The Kennedy Report reviewed under-participation in further education

1997 The White Paper *Excellence in Schools* formed the basis of the 1988 School Standards and Framework Act

1997 *The Implementation of the National Literacy Strategy*: report of a working party established by David Blunkett

1997 Green Paper *Excellence for All Children: Meeting Special Educational Needs* set out a 5-year plan

1998 Labour's first Green Paper on the teaching profession, *Teachers: Meeting the challenge of change*

1998 School Standards and Framework Act limited infant class sizes, established Education Action Zones, encouraged selection by specialisation

1998 The Crick Report *Education for Democracy and the Teaching of Democracy in Schools* recommended that citizenship education should be a statutory entitlement in the curriculum

1998 The first twelve Education Action Zones were established

1999 *The National Curriculum: Handbook for primary teachers in England* gave information and advice from the DfEE and QCA

1999 National Numeracy Strategy launched

2000 David Blunkett announced the intention to create a network of academies

2001 The DfEE became the Department for Education and Skills (DfES)

2001 Green Paper *Schools: Building on success*: New Labour's rewriting of the history of comprehensive schools

2002 Education Act implementing the proposals in the 2001 White Paper *Schools: Achieving success*

2003 The first three city academies opened

2003 *Workforce Remodelling*: government initiative to reduce teachers' workload by employing more classroom assistants

2003 Green Paper *Every Child Matters*

2004 Higher Education Act allowed universities to charge top-up fees

2004 Children Act based on *Every Child Matters*

2006 Equality Act 2006 established the Commission for Equality and Human Rights

2006 *Primary National Strategy*: primary framework for literacy and mathematics

2006 Cambridge Primary Review launched

2006 *2020 Vision*: report of the Teaching and Learning in 2020 Review Group

2007	Ofsted became the Office for Standards in Education, Children's Services and Skills
2007	*Teaching 2020*: paper setting out the government's vision for schooling in the future
2007	General Teaching Council called for all national school tests for 7-, 11- and 14-year-olds to be scrapped
2007	Green Paper *Raising Expectations: Staying in education and training post-16* argued that all young people should stay in education or training until age 18
2007	Ajegbo Report *Diversity and Citizenship*
2007	The DfES split into two – the Department for Children, Schools and Families (DCSF) and the Department of Innovation, Universities and Skills (DIUS)
2007	*Faith in the System*: faith schools agreed to promote social cohesion
2007	*The Children's Plan*: plan for all future government policy relating to children, families and schools
2008	Special Educational Needs (Information) Act 2008 amended the 1996 Education Act in relation to the provision and publication of information about children with special educational needs
2008	Education and Skills Act 2008 raised the school leaving age to 18 and effectively abolished Key Stage 3 SATs
2008	*Testing and Assessment*: report by the House of Commons Children, Schools and Families Committee
2008	Conservatives' free schools policy announced by Michael Gove
2008	*Interim Report of the Independent Review of the Primary Curriculum*
2009	Cambridge Primary Review *Towards a New Primary Curriculum* (interim reports) *Past and Present* and *The Future*
2009	*National Curriculum* report by the House of Commons Children, Schools and Families Committee
2009	*Final Report of the Independent Review of the Primary Curriculum*
2009	Steer Report *Learning Behaviour: Lessons learned* (follow-up to 2005 report *Learning Behaviour*)
2009	DIUS abolished – responsibilities transferred to new Department of Business, Innovation and Skills (BIS)
2009	11 plus abolished in Northern Ireland, but grammar schools vow to set their own tests

2009 White Paper *Your Child, Your Schools, Your Future* proposals including the removal of central government prescription of teaching methods and reduction in the use of private consultants to improve schools

2010 The DCSF became the Department for Education (DfE)

2010 Cambridge Primary Review final report *Children, Their World, Their Education*

2010 Child Poverty Act 2010 – targets and provisions

2010 Children, Schools and Families Act 2010 – reduced (owing to impending election) version of the 2009 White Paper

2010 Equality Act 2010 replaced nine major Acts of Parliament and many regulations that had been introduced over several decades

2010 A quarter of primary schools boycotted the SATs tests

2010 Academies Act 2010 provided for huge expansion of academies

2010 Government proposed cuts of up to £3.5 billion in the schools budget

2010 IRPC primary curriculum proposals scrapped

2010 Building Schools for the Future scrapped

2010 White Paper *The Importance of Teaching* covering teaching, leadership, behaviour, new schools, etc.

2011 Education Act 2011 – increased schools' powers relating to pupil behaviour and exclusions, further reduced the role of local authorities, further expansion of academies

2011 Tickell Report *The Early Years: Foundations for life, health and learning* made recommendations relating to the Early Years Foundation Stage

2011 Bew Report *Independent Review of Key Stage 2: Testing, assessment and accountability* recommended published test results should be more comprehensive and seen as part of a bigger picture

2011 *The Framework for the National Curriculum* report by the Expert Panel for the National Curriculum review

2011 All-Party Parliamentary Group for Education *Report of the Inquiry into Overcoming the Barriers to Literacy*

2011 Report by the House of Commons Education Committee *Behaviour and Discipline in Schools*

2011 Green Paper *Support and Aspiration: A new approach to special educational needs and disability*

2011	Discussion document and implementation plan from the DfE *Training Our Next Generation of Outstanding Teachers*
2012	*Equality Act 2010: Advice for school leaders, staff, governors and local authorities*: non-statutory advice from the DfE
2012	Report by the House of Commons Education Committee *Great Teachers: Attracting, training and retaining the best*
2012	White Paper *Reform of Provision for Children and Young People with Special Educational Needs*
2012	Henley Report *Cultural Education in England*
2012	*Statutory Framework for the EYFS* setting out the standards for learning, development and care for children from 0 to 5
2013	*EYFS Profile Handbook* published by the Standards and Testing Agency

Political parties in government and Education Ministers since 1944

Title/ Name	Party	Date of appointment
Minister of Education		
R. A. Butler	Conservative	3 August 1944
Richard Law	Conservative	25 May 1945
Ellen Wilkinson	Labour	3 August 1945
George Tomlinson	Labour	10 February 1947
Florence Horsbrugh	Conservative	2 November 1951
David Eccles	Conservative	18 October 1954
The Viscount Hailsham	Conservative	13 January 1957
Geoffrey Lloyd	Conservative	17 September 1957
David Eccles	Conservative	14 October 1959
Sir Edward Boyle	Conservative	13 July 1962
Secretary of State for Education and Science		
Quintin Hogg (formerly Viscount Hailsham)	Conservative	1 April 1964
Michael Stewart	Labour	18 October 1964
Anthony Crosland	Labour	22 January 1965
Patrick Gordon Walker	Labour	29 August 1967
Edward Short	Labour	6 April 1968
Margaret Thatcher	Conservative	20 June 1970
Reginald Prentice	Labour	5 March 1974
Fred Mulloy	Labour	10 June 1975
Shirley Williams	Labour	10 September 1976
Mark Carlisle	Conservative	5 May 1979
Sir Keith Joseph	Conservative	14 September 1981
Kenneth Baker	Conservative	21 May 1986
John MacGregor	Conservative	24 July 1989
Kenneth Clarke	Conservative	2 November 1990
Secretary of State for Education		
John Patten	Conservative	10 April 1992
Gillian Shephard	Conservative	20 July 1994

Title/ Name	Party	Date of appointment
Secretary of State for Education and Employment		
Gillian Shephard	Conservative	5 July 1995
David Blunkett	Labour	2 May 1997
Secretary of State for Education and Skills		
Estelle Morris	Labour	8 May 2001
Charles Clarke	Labour	24 October 2002
Ruth Kelly	Labour	15 December 2004
Alan Johnson	Labour	5 May 2006
Secretary of State for Children, Schools and Families		
Ed Balls	Labour	28 June 2007
Secretary of State for Education, responsible for education up to age 19 in the UK		
Michael Gove	Conservative (coalition)	11 May 2010
Nicky Morgan	Conservative (coalition)	15 July 2014

School year groups

Primary school	Foundation stage	Nursery and reception	
	Key Stage 1	Years 1 and 2	Age 5–7
	Key Stage 2	Years 3–6	Age 7–11
Secondary school			
	Key Stage 3	Years 7–9	Age 11–14
	Key Stage 4	Years 10 and 11	Age 14–16
	Key Stage 5 (6th form)	Years 12 and 13	Age 16–18

Structure of the National Curriculum

	KS1	KS2	KS3	KS4
Age	5–7	7–11	11–14	14–16
Year groups	1–2	3–6	7–9	10–11
Core subjects				
– English	✓	✓	✓	✓
– Mathematics	✓	✓	✓	✓
– Science	✓	✓	✓	✓
Foundation subjects				
– Art And Design	✓	✓	✓	
– Citizenship			✓	✓
– Computing	✓	✓	✓	✓
– Design and technology	✓	✓	✓	
– Languages*		✓	✓	
– Geography	✓	✓	✓	
– History	✓	✓	✓	
– Music	✓	✓	✓	
– Physical Education	✓	✓	✓	✓

Notes: *At KS2, the subject title is 'foreign language'; at KS3, it is 'modern foreign language'. All schools are required to teach religious education at all key stages. Secondary schools must provide sex and relationship education

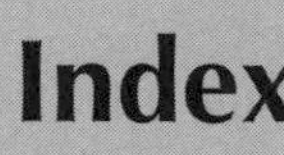

Index